POLITICIANS AND ETHICS

Other Books in the Current Controversies Series:

POLITICIANS AND ETHICS

DISCARD

David Bender, *Publisher*
Bruno Leone, *Executive Editor*

Scott Barbour, *Managing Editor*
Brenda Stalcup, *Senior Editor*

Charles P. Cozic, *Book Editor*

CURRENT CONTROVERSIES

Photo credit: AP/Wide World Photos

Library of Congress Cataloging-in-Publication Data

Politicians and ethics / Charles P. Cozic, book editor.
        p. cm. — (Current controversies)
    Includes bibliographical references and index.
    ISBN 1-56510-406-4 (pbk. : alk. paper). — ISBN 1-56510-407-2
(lib. bdg. : alk. paper)
    1. Political corruption—United States. 2. Political ethics—United
States. I. Cozic, Charles P., 1957-   . II. Series.
JK2249.P66   1996
172'.2—dc20   96-11848
                                                                        CIP

© 1996 by Greenhaven Press, Inc., PO Box 289009, San Diego, CA 92198-9009
Printed in the U.S.A.

Contents

No: Unethical Behavior Is Not a Serious Problem

Chapter 2: Is the Legislator-Lobbyist Relationship Improper?

Yes: The Legislator-Lobbyist Relationship Is Improper

No: The Legislator-Lobbyist Relationship Is Not Improper

Chapter 3: Is Scrutiny of Politicians' Character and Conduct Warranted?

Chapter 4: Should Legal Measures Address Ethics in Politics?

No: Legal Measures Should Not Address Ethics

Foreword

By definition, controversies are "discussions of questions in which opposing opinions clash" (Webster's Twentieth Century Dictionary Unabridged). Few would deny that controversies are a pervasive part of the human condition and exist on virtually every level of human enterprise. Controversies transpire between individuals and among groups, within nations and between nations. Controversies supply the grist necessary for progress by providing challenges and challengers to the status quo. They also create atmospheres where strife and warfare can flourish. A world without controversies would be a peaceful world; but it also would be, by and large, static and prosaic.

The Series' Purpose

The purpose of the Current Controversies series is to explore many of the social, political, and economic controversies dominating the national and international scenes today. Titles selected for inclusion in the series are highly focused and specific. For example, from the larger category of criminal justice, Current Controversies deals with specific topics such as police brutality, gun control, white collar crime, and others. The debates in Current Controversies also are presented in a useful, timeless fashion. Articles and book excerpts included in each title are selected if they contribute valuable, long-range ideas to the overall debate. And wherever possible, current information is enhanced with historical documents and other relevant materials. Thus, while individual titles are current in focus, every effort is made to ensure that they will not become quickly outdated. Books in the Current Controversies series will remain important resources for librarians, teachers, and students for many years.

In addition to keeping the titles focused and specific, great care is taken in the editorial format of each book in the series. Book introductions and chapter prefaces are offered to provide background material for readers. Chapters are organized around several key questions that are answered with diverse opinions representing all points on the political spectrum. Materials in each chapter include opinions in which authors clearly disagree as well as alternative opinions in which authors may agree on a broader issue but disagree on the possible solutions. In this way, the content of each volume in Current Controversies mirrors the mosaic of opinions encountered in society. Readers will quickly realize that there are many viable answers to these complex issues. By questioning each author's conclusions, students and casual readers can begin to develop the critical thinking skills so important to evaluating opinionated material.

Current Controversies is also ideal for controlled research. Each anthology in the series is composed of primary sources taken from a wide gamut of informational categories including periodicals, newspapers, books, United States and foreign government documents, and the publications of private and public organizations. Readers will find factual support for reports, debates, and research papers covering all areas of important issues. In addition, an annotated table of contents, an index, a book and periodical bibliography, and a list of organizations to contact are included in each book to expedite further research.

Perhaps more than ever before in history, people are confronted with diverse and contradictory information. During the Persian Gulf War, for example, the public was not only treated to minute-to-minute coverage of the war, it was also inundated with critiques of the coverage and countless analyses of the factors motivating U.S. involvement. Being able to sort through the plethora of opinions accompanying today's major issues, and to draw one's own conclusions, can be a complicated and frustrating struggle. It is the editors' hope that Current Controversies will help readers with this struggle.

Introduction

Political clout in Washington, D.C., frequently depends on money. Seeking to promote their own agenda, interests such as political action committees (PACs), corporate and union representatives, and wealthy individuals use the lure of money—legally and illegally—to win access to key decisionmakers and gain their support on issues.

Campaign contributions are the most common way that money is used to influence politics. Each year, congressmembers receive hundreds of millions of dollars in campaign contributions. Regulated by federal law, these contributions can be considered illegal depending on the amount contributed, the source of the contribution, and how the money is spent.

Money is crucial to congressmembers who are seeking reelection. As of 1995, the average House of Representatives candidate spent approximately $440,000, while the average Senate race cost $4.4 million. According to senators and representatives, raising campaign contributions from constituents and other sources is a never-ending process that is necessary to pay for expensive campaigns and to gain advantage over opponents. In the words of Common Cause president Ann McBride, "A senator must raise, from the day when he or she arrives in the Senate, $15,000 a week . . . for the entire term."

Congressmembers' practice of soliciting campaign contributions has raised the question of whether money compromises politicians' ethics. Several observers argue that contributions can influence the way some members vote in Congress. According to former Virginia representative Leslie Byrne, "There are some colleagues that I've worked with whom I think it does compromise. They feel like they have to ameliorate or change their position or be careful of certain votes for fear of losing certain contributions." Others equate the acceptance of contributions with bribery. As former California governor and presidential candidate Jerry Brown said in a 1995 interview, "To get the money, you must commit common-law bribery. Campaign contributions are meant to influence public officials in their public capacity. That is bribery, per se."

Other experts disagree that contributions "buy" legislators' votes. Many politicians and lobbyists argue that although contributing money can help donors gain access to legislators, a contribution does not guarantee a vote in the contributor's favor. Herbert Alexander, a lobbying and PAC researcher, writes, "Access should not be confused with buying votes." Retired New York representative

Hamilton Fish Jr. states, "I look at a contribution as a 'thank you' for a position I took, not as expecting that I would take a position in the future. I always thought of it as a reward, not a bribe." Law professor Bradley A. Smith adds, "Those who have studied voting patterns on a systematic basis are almost unanimous in finding that campaign contributions affect very few votes in the legislature."

Regardless of whether they believe that contributions influence votes, many congressmembers and others agree that the acceptance of large amounts of money gives the appearance that politicians are beholden to contributors. In the words of former Florida representative Jim Bacchus, "It leads people to believe that we are working for someone other than for them; either that we are working for ourselves, or for some selfish special interests." But political scientist Gary Jacobson defends the extent of campaign contributions as a form of free speech that allows contributors to express their opinions on various issues to congressmembers. Congressmembers in turn, he maintains, use the contributions to finance their efforts to communicate their political views to the electorate. He argues, "The amount of information that voters have and [their] turnout directly relate to the amount of money spent."

Some senators and representatives, such as former Senate majority leader George Mitchell and former House minority leader Robert Michel, have cited the role of money in politics and a reluctance among congressmembers to reform the system as reasons for leaving Congress. Other legislators contend that receiving generous contributions is a legal campaign practice that is vital for a candidate's electoral success. The impact of money in Congress is among the issues considered in *Politicians and Ethics: Current Controversies*, in which authors examine the ethics of politicians' values and behavior.

Chapter 1

Is Unethical Behavior in Politics a Serious Problem?

Chapter Preface

In recent years, reports of congressmembers and government officials accused of bribery, fraud, sexual misconduct, and other unlawful or unethical behavior have provoked increased public disdain for politicians and cries of "Throw the bums out." According to *U.S. News & World Report* editor in chief Mortimer B. Zuckerman, "A popular national sport has developed: blaming politicians for everything, from lying and cheating to bouncing [House of Representatives bank] checks."

Many voting Americans and others, for example, rebuke senators and representatives for exploiting their positions for personal profit. They criticize privileged "insiders" for enjoying official perquisites—such as automatic raises, guaranteed pensions, and government-paid travel—that are unavailable to most Americans, as well as for accepting private gifts and spending campaign funds for personal use. According to *New American* writer William P. Hoar, "Congress has used ridiculous perks, scandalous conduct, and outright arrogance to promote its own well-being while sacrificing the very livelihood of American citizens."

Some observers argue that congressmembers have heeded the public's criticism. For example, in 1995 U.S. representatives passed a rule banning all private gifts, while senators prohibited themselves from accepting private gifts valued at more than fifty dollars. According to Senator Bob Dole, a gift ban "is fine with this senator, and I doubt many senators partake in that in any event."

However, other critics maintain that such measures will not prevent unethical behavior. North Carolina representative Tim Valentine contends, "It all goes back to the type of person that is elected. If it's a type of person who is looking to get around the rules . . . [or] is looking for a way to misbehave, he or she will find it."

Congressmembers, like regular citizens, may be tempted to act self-servingly. But as elected representatives, they are held to a higher degree of accountability by a public that demands forthrightness from them. The authors in this chapter debate the extent of unethical behavior in politics.

Unethical Behavior in Politics Demands Attention

by Peter deLeon

About the author: *Peter deLeon is a professor of public administration at the University of Colorado in Denver.*

Numerous authors, political observers, and just plain folk have commented on the presence of corruption in American politics, usually with some admixture of Puritan outrage and world-weary cynicism. Alexis de Tocqueville to Walter Lippmann, Sinclair Lewis to Bob Woodward, Ida Tarbell to Mike Royko, Thomas Nast to Herblock—the list would be endless. Certainly one would not have to look too far for culpable individuals throughout American history and politics, but somehow, we would like to think that political manners and mores "back then"—when politics were hurley-burley, the press less attentive (or less intrusive, depending upon your perspective), and public servants not trained in "good government"—were much more susceptible to wrongdoing than is currently the case.

In New York and Arizona

But this is patently not the case. Corruption often seems omnipresent in contemporary American political systems. No level of government appears particularly sacrosanct. In 1987, New York City had a scandal of such a magnitude regarding the purchase of hand-held computers to write parking tickets that Donald Manes, a former borough president of Queens, committed suicide rather than face charges; subsequently, less than six months later, it was discovered that over $3 million in pocket change was stolen from parking meters by the meter collection company, almost 10 percent of the revenue from the city's 56,000 parking meters. Rural southern law enforcement officers, FBI agents, and even a member of the Justice Department's Organized Crime Strike Force have succumbed to corruption from the millions of dollars culled from illegal drug money. In 1988, Ex-Governor Evan Mecham of Arizona was impeached; a few years later, state legislators were revealed to have accepted bribes from an ersatz gambler cum undercover police officer and then complained of the subterfuge. As if this were not enough for one state, both Arizona U.S. senators were reprimanded for violating Senate rules to keep Charles Keating's crumbling S&L [Savings and Loan] afloat and [a subsequent] governor was sued by the government for his role in Arizona's S&L debacle. James Fesler and Donald Kettl relate how "in an FBI 'sting' operation, 105 out of 106 offers of bribes to suspected municipal officials in the State of New York were accepted; the 106th was rejected as too small."

Federal Corruption

One might think that these cases are all local government incidents, where politics is more personal and less visible, hence more susceptible to corrupt dealings. Unfortunately, the highly illuminated halls of the federal government are also prone to corruption. An embarrassingly large number of Republican administration appointees under President Ronald Reagan (up to and including Attorney General Edwin Meese) were forced to resign for conflict-of-interest reasons. *Time* magazine counted "more than 100 members of the Reagan Administration [who] had ethical or legal charges leveled against them. That number is without precedent." Amazingly, the *Wall Street Journal*, never thought to be a Democratic

> *"Unfortunately, the highly illuminated halls of the federal government are also prone to corruption."*

apologist, went so far as to report how some scholars link Republican administrations with corruption, a trend "explained by the philosophical bent of those who tend to work for Republican presidents—a bent that often leads them afoul of the guidelines of government work."

Nor should one claim that corruption is strictly a public sector phenomenon. The continuing exposés of Wall Street financial institutions, such as Burnham Drexel Lambert and Solomon Brothers, the irrepressible greed of many bank executives that precipitated the disastrous Savings and Loan crisis, and the Pentagon procurement indictments regarding the misuse of inside information for ill-gained profits and falsifying test information would disabuse any such naive notion that the private sector has any particular concern for the well-being of the public sector beyond its anticipated profit margin.

Not So Pervasive

This dour litany is not to suggest that corruption runs rampant or even commonplace in either the private or public sectors, or that scoundrels and scalawags rule the various power roosts. We should not leap to the conclusion that corruption is as pervasive as *Miami Vice* or the *Godfather* trilogy would have us believe, or be swayed by *Time* magazine's emotion as it bemoaned the "scandal-scarred spring of 1987" in which close to one hundred major and minor federal government officials were accused of violating the public trust: "Lamentation is in the air, and clay feet litter the ground. A relentless procession of forlorn faces assaults the nation's moral equanimity." Even major government scandals, such as Watergate, influence peddling at HUD [Department of Housing and Urban Development], or the S&L embarrassments, should not shake the knowledge that government personnel are, by and large, dependably responsible, honest, and well-intended.

Future Developments

Still, the presence of corruption cannot be blithely ignored or treated as a minor social malaise. A 1988 Associated Press survey "found deep skepticism of federal government integrity. In the most critical finding, an overwhelming 70 percent said they thought taking illegal payoffs for favors was widespread. Fully half the respondents called government dishonest overall." If these findings are representative, and I have scant reason to think otherwise, this sentiment can lead to many things, none of them salutary. For instance, the perception of a corrupt bureaucracy could convince legislatures to enact a series of increasingly restrictive measures that would be counterproductive, that is, they would only serve to increase the likelihood of corruption rather than its intended decrease. A scandal "witch hunt" mentality—what [author and scholar] Suzanne Garment calls a "Culture of Mistrust in American Politics"—could develop that would greatly exaggerate minor peccadilloes and cause severe anguish to all those involved, including the political system that is putatively being defended. Or citizens will lose faith in their government at the very time when government is being asked to involve itself in an increasing number of activities. Finally, and most ominously, "corruption in high places, or the mere *appearance* of wrongdoing, cannot only reduce popular trust in leaders and institutions; it may also let citizens off the hook for their own misdeeds. They may ask why they must be better than others are," with the inevitable answer dangerously threatening to rend the social fabric.

> *"Government personnel are, by and large, dependably responsible, honest, and well-intended."*

Unethical Behavior Characterizes Washington, D.C.

by Jon Meacham

About the author: *Jon Meacham is an editor for* Washington Monthly *magazine.*

> *Increasingly, there is a sense in Washington that the Arkansas political culture does not work in the White House. . . . Little Rock culture was rooted in an informal way of doing business, in which behind-the-scenes relationships played at least as large a role as the evident formal structure of power.*
>
> —Maureen Dowd, in the *New York Times*, on the day
> [associate U.S. attorney general] Webster Hubbell resigned

Washington is simply shocked—*shocked*—at the loose morals the upstart crowd from the South has brought to the capital. On "Inside Washington," National Public Radio's Nina Totenberg sighed in 1994, "Everybody scratches everybody's back in Little Rock. It's a tiny little community. It's not the same."

Rapping Little Rock

Not the same as Washington? The rap against Little Rock is that everybody seems so cozy—politicians, lawyers, and businessmen grow up together, go to school together, marry each other, and then move in the same circles. On "Washington Week in Review," *Newsweek*'s Howard Fineman said, "Arkansas is the kind of big and basically poor state where maybe 200 people run the whole show. They have the money. They've got the power. They're on a first-name basis with each other. Most of them work in downtown Little Rock within about a mile of each other. They all go to the Little Rock Country Club and the bar at the Capital Hilton . . . and the line between public money and private business is very fuzzy." The *New York Times* editorialized, "[T]he genius of the

Excerpted from Jon Meacham, "Is Little Rock Corrupting Washington? C'mon," *Washington Monthly,* May 1994. Reprinted with permission from the *Washington Monthly.* Copyright by The Washington Monthly Company, 1611 Connecticut Ave. NW, Washington, DC 20009; (202) 462-0128.

Federal system does not reside in importing to Washington the faults and idiosyncrasies of the state capitals."

But the enormous irony in assuming Little Rock is corrupting the national capital is this: If the Arkansans ever needed a how-to guide on operating in an ethical twilight, they would look to Washington, not Baton Rouge or Atlanta. Washington has long been home to apparent conflicts of interest, lawyer overbilling, sweetheart deals, and scheming political spouses. "There are three things in life," Edward Bennett Williams, the consummate Washington lawyer, used to say. "Money, power, and public relations."

That is Washington's creed. So even though Whitewater [an Arkansas real estate and savings and loan affair that prompted congressional investigation] will inevitably fall off the radar screen (there are already signs of that happening) Washington's patronizing disdain for Southern clubbiness—and the appearance of possible conflicts in two-career marriages—is laughable coming from pundits like Fineman, whose wife, Amy Nathan, practices with Akin Gump, a well-connected, socially important law firm that has a very permeable wall between lawyering and lobbying. Its leading lights include veteran fixers Vernon Jordan and Robert Strauss, and, until 1993, Ruth Harkin, the wife of Senator Tom Harkin. CBS White House correspondent Rita Braver is married to Robert Barnett, a Washington lawyer who has done personal work for the Clintons. Congressman John Dingell of Michigan watches out for the interests of the Detroit automakers, most recently derailing legislation that would have required more energy-efficient vehicles, and is married to a General Motors executive. Sounds a lot like what the press is calling "incestuous" in Little Rock, doesn't it?

> *"The back-scratching arts the Clintons are accused of importing from down South have been practiced here with unmatched skill for years."*

Take a hard look at what the Washington media say about the Clintonites and you cannot escape the not-so-subtle disparaging message—a cultural dismissiveness that says, *Oh, what else can you expect from a crowd of hillbillies?* Of course, this does not excuse the Clintonites for things they may have done wrong in Arkansas or in Washington. Nor are all Washingtonians who are connected to other Washingtonians crude influence peddlers. Many coincidences of blood, marriage, and career are just that—coincidences. But journalists are forgetting—or, worse, simply not noting—that the back-scratching arts the Clintons are accused of importing from down South have been practiced here with unmatched skill for years. This makes the press' condescension both ahistorical and hypocritical—and the more Washingtonians get away with assuming the capital's ethical murkiness is due to the Arkansas invasion, the less they have to examine their own sins.

• *Washington assumption: Before the Clintons arrived from Dogpatch, official Washington was a sophisticated, ethical nirvana.*

In the *Wall Street Journal*, Paul Gigot wrote in 1994, "Far from shedding the Arkansas political culture, the Clintons have brought it with them, complete with cronies, a mind-set for cutting ethical corners, and the arrogance that often comes from governing a one-party state."

But a case study in how Washington insiders conducted themselves long before the Arkansans showed up—and in how the press is cowed largely into silence by Beltway satraps, Democrat or Republican—unfolded when George Bush named his old friend James Baker secretary of State in 1988. Nobody in the eighties was more inside-Washington than Baker, so if Washington insiderdom is automatically held in higher ethical regard than Southern mores, we are in real trouble.

Consider this sequence of events, as reconstructed by the *Washington Post*'s Walter Pincus in 1989: When Baker became Ronald Reagan's chief of staff in 1981, he owned $3.5 million worth of stock in Texas Commerce Bancshares Inc., which rose in value to $4.2 million by 1985, the year he switched jobs with Donald Regan to become secretary of the Treasury. The stock was held in a "qualified blind trust," which meant Baker knew what he owned, though not the current size of the asset. He recused himself from Texas Commerce's direct affairs, but nevertheless was dramatically involved—as a Treasury secretary would be—in general banking matters, including testifying in favor of legislation that made interstate banking mergers easier.

In May 1987, Chemical Bank of New York took over Texas Commerce under those new laws in what was, at the time, an unprecedented banking merger. The deal had to be approved by the Federal Reserve Board, and parts of it had to pass muster by two federal officers who had been appointed by then-secretary of the Treasury James Baker: the comptroller of the currency, Robert L. Clarke, a Houston friend and political ally of Baker's, and FDIC [Federal Deposit Insurance Corporation] chairman William Seidman, with whom Baker had served in the Gerald Ford administration. Both approved.

> *"It was a sexy story: the ethics czar with an ethical problem of his own."*

Baker's Holdings

Meanwhile, Baker continued to be active in Third World debt issues while he was a knowing stockholder in Chemical, the third-largest U.S. lender to those countries, with $4.5 billion in outstanding loans. For example, in a 1987 meeting with the Brazilian finance minister, who was at the time urging Third World debtors to default, Baker strongly urged the opposite course—which obviously advanced the interests of debt-holders, especially Chemical. Yet during the Reagan administration, no reporter ever pointed out Baker's ownership of the bank stock, and he never mentioned it in his confirmation hearings for the job at either State or Treasury, although the subject of Third World debt came up at both.

According to people familiar with the situation, after the '88 election, Baker sent an intermediary to ask Boyden Gray, whom Bush had put in charge of ethics decisions for the transition, whether Baker could continue to hold the bank stock. (In 1988, a new Justice Department ruling required such a waiver for any holding that might pose an appearance of a conflict of interest, effectively changing the rules under which Baker had been playing in the Reagan administration.) Gray indicated that he would not waive the rule and would probably ask Baker to sell the stock.

> *"[James] Baker had mastered the art of stroking the Washington press corps in his days in the Reagan administration."*

The Press Catches On

At that point, Baker, a master political infighter, swung into action. Baker's camp apparently tipped off the *New York Times'* William Safire to the fact that Gray, while serving as counselor to Vice President Bush, had been paid as much as $50,000 a year to serve as chairman of his family's $500 million communications company. As a vice presidential aide, what Gray did was legal, but would have been barred if Gray had worked for the *president*. (The Bakerites were probably gambling that the distinction would be buried, still embarrassing Gray and shutting him up about Baker's holdings.) Nevertheless, it was a sexy story: the ethics czar with an ethical problem of his own. The *Times* was reportedly planning a Sunday story by investigative reporter Jeff Gerth, then a Monday morning column by Safire. But in February, on the Friday before the *Times* published, Pincus and Bob Woodward of the *Post* got wind of the competition's plans and called Gray, who cooperated in a preemptive story—one that was softer than the *Times'* would have been and which focused on the fact that Gray, as White House counsel, was reluctant to put his assets in a blind trust— that ran in the *Post* on Saturday. That forced the *Times'* hand. They ran their Gray piece in the late Saturday editions (which are not distributed nationally), and Safire wrote a snarling column the next week chiding Gray for media manipulation. The point remains, however, that *Baker,* not Gray, was the real culprit. Note that all this happened in Washington, not in Little Rock, and that at the beginning of the Bush administration, two intimates of the new president were calling each other out for apparent conflicts that existed while they were both high-ranking officers in the federal government.

Later that week in February 1989, Pincus wrote the first Baker/ChemBank stock story. It had all the elements of a major scandal: money (the holdings); cronyism (the appointments of Clarke and Seidman); the appearance of using public office for private gain (the meetings attended while Baker knew he still had a stake in ChemBank).

Congress' reaction? Claiborne Pell, the chairman of the Senate Foreign Relations Committee, wrote Baker an almost sheepish letter asking about the stock. Baker answered by fax, saying, "I will recuse myself from participation, on a case by case basis, in any particular matter in which, in my judgment, it is desirable for me to do so." In other words, the same rules he had been operating under in the eighties. (Baker did sell the stock a few days later.)

The press' reaction? Hardly a blip. There was no *Nightline* investigation, little jawing on the Sunday morning shows, no calls for a special prosecutor. The major reason for this was that Baker had mastered the art of stroking the Washington press corps in his days in the Reagan administration. As an invaluable source of leaks, Baker built up an enormous reservoir of good will; in fact, Baker spent several hours a week with reporters, an investment that paid off when the worm turned. For example, Margaret Carlson's *Time* story focused, amazingly, not on Baker's conflict but on Gray's non-problem: "Last week Bush got a whiff of trouble in what he had promised would be a squeaky clean administration. It came from none other than his chief ethics officer, C. Boyden Gray. . . ." Carlson passed over Baker in a single clause.

The Media: Soft on Baker

When *Newsweek* finally got to the bank stock story almost five weeks after Pincus broke it, it too was entirely spun in Baker's favor. Headlined "Off on the Wrong Foot," the piece, from top to bottom, criticized *Gray* for his "naivete" and "lousy political instincts" for taking on Baker. Not a word of disapproval about Baker's vast potential conflict of interest as a federal official, which was the real, substantive sin at issue.

On ABC's *This Week with David Brinkley*, there were only two mentions during Baker's season of scandal. The first was in a question from Cokie Roberts to John Sununu ("How ethical is this administration?") around the time John Tower was having problems with his nomination to become secretary of Defense. Sununu ducked it, and Roberts failed to follow up. The other was by Sam Donaldson, who asked Baker a who's-up-who's-down question about Gray, who had also criticized Baker's agreement to clear Central American policy with Congress:

> *"[Hillary Clinton's] machinations aren't on par with what happens in Washington—a point the press has consistently failed to make."*

> Donaldson: C. Boyden Gray, a few weeks ago, embarrassed you publicly by calling attention to your bank stock. You sold it at that point. Now, he is complaining that you have made a [foreign policy] deal that is wrong. Is there room for both of you in this administration?

> Baker: Nice try, Sam.

There the matter dropped, and the show bantered on. Baker the insider was unscathed; the culture had taken care of its own.

Comfortable Deals

• *Washington assumption: Hillary [Clinton's] greed led her to take advantage of her husband's position in a tiny capital where it was business-as-usual for people with interests before the state to help politicians with their personal finances.*

"Hillary was exceedingly ambitious for herself and her husband, and was the main family breadwinner for years," argued a *Newsweek* cover story in March 1994. "Reared in a thrifty home, married to a spouse with a casual attitude about money, she developed a perhaps excessive concern for her family's finances. . . . The question now is whether any of those pressures led her to cross ethical lines in various legal and business deals—and whether she used her husband's role as governor of Arkansas to help her to do so."

A major source of press outrage has been Mrs. Clinton's seventies'

> *"California friends bought the Reagans a retirement house in Bel Air. And remember Nancy Reagan's habit of keeping gifts?"*

commodities speculation which, with the advice of a lawyer for Tyson Industries, turned, as a *USA Today* headline trumpeted, "$1,000 into $99,537." At the time, Bill Clinton was the incumbent attorney general and ahead in the polls in his first campaign for governor.

The *Times* wrote, "Their behavior may not have been illegal, but it was reckless and politically unattractive." But while Mrs. Clinton may indeed be guilty of middle-class, yuppie greed, her machinations aren't on par with what happens in Washington—a point the press has consistently failed to make. Many political families indulge in comfortable deals. When Bush, for example, was planning his first run for president in 1978, his friend (and later secretary of Commerce) Robert Mosbacher cut Bush and a third friend, Baker, into a lucrative deal involving a barge company called Hollywood Marine Inc. According to a 1988 story by Pincus and Woodward, Bush and Baker each put up $50,000 (a much lower average investment than others in the enterprise) and, by 1992, Hollywood had netted Bush $240,000, making it one of his most profitable personal ventures. Mosbacher later said that inviting Bush and Baker into the deal in the late seventies was "not a big favor, but a favor" because the barge deal turned out to be "a very, very good investment."

Friends and Cronies

It might not have been as good, however, if Bush had not become vice president when he did. Cut to 1981. Hollywood Marine manufactures "single hull" barges; the Coast Guard proposes a rule requiring a second hull to protect against oil spills. Bush, head of Reagan's Task Force on Regulatory Relief, kills the rule after Hollywood and others lobby against it. Yet save for a single report in the summer of 1992, nobody picked up on Bush's possible conflict of interest. In addition, Bush collected $387,000 in directors' fees in the late seventies from four corporate boards (one of which was Purolator Inc., whose chairman, Nicholas Brady, became Bush's Treasury secretary). But the clear connections between Bush's private wealth and the friends he named to high office have never been the target of cultural or pejorative comment; the terminology is "friends and relatives," not "cronies" and "back-scratching." This is largely because Bush and his friends, especially Baker, are Washington creatures, and what they did—while no different from what Mrs. Clinton did with cattle futures and her sundry mutual funds—struck journalists as ordinary establishment business dealings. Had these deals been made on the golf course in Little Rock, instead of Burning Tree or Kennebunkport, you can bet the cultural tone would have been different.

Nor have other presidents passed up chances to accept expensive gifts or to get rich quick. California friends bought the Reagans a retirement house in Bel Air. And remember Nancy Reagan's habit of keeping gifts of designer dresses, jewelry, perfumes, handbags, and watches? After an early flirtation with criticizing Mrs. Reagan, the Washington press was charmed and conned by her boffo turn at a Gridiron Club dinner as "Secondhand Rose," a spoof of her own expensive tastes. But just because the First Lady could joke about it does not mean the story should have gone away. Nevertheless, thanks to press secretary Sheila Tate's p.r. instincts, away it went.

It goes on and on. LBJ [Lyndon Baines Johnson] became a millionaire only after he went to the modestly salaried Senate. Even Dwight D. Eisenhower had exceedingly generous rich friends such as Robert Woodruff, the chairman of Coca-Cola, and George Allen, a Washington millionaire, and a circle including two cattlemen, two oilmen, two distillers, two golf champions, two realtors, and three bank presidents. According to Stephen E. Ambrose, the leading Eisenhower scholar, "the gang" made Ike a member at Augusta National, built him a cottage there, and installed a stocked bass pond for fishing. They also advised him on his other investments, including purchasing the Gettysburg farm, refurbishing its colonial farmhouse, and equipping it with livestock. Allen even bought up all the surrounding land to make sure the Eisenhowers wouldn't be bothered by potential neighbors or development.

"The children of Washington's powerful are as well-skilled in the art of using family connections as their mothers."

Families Benefit Themselves

And while Mrs. Clinton has been cast in the Whitewater drama as Lady Macbeth obsessing over the family checkbook, it is old hat in Washington for the wives of prominent men to worry about money. In the fifties and sixties, for example, the former New Dealer and Washington lawyer Abe Fortas' wife, Carolyn Agger, herself a lawyer, urged her husband, at the time the guiding force of his firm and an informal advisor to LBJ, to stay out of government in order to represent lucrative clients such as Western Union and Sun Oil. Together, Fortas and Agger made about $300,000 in those years, or close to a million dollars a year in 1994 terms. According to Fortas biographer Bruce Allen Murphy, they spent it fast: They had a house in Georgetown, a vacation house in Westport, Connecticut, a Rolls Royce, and Agger spent vast sums on jewelry, art, and 150 pairs of shoes. In 1965, when Johnson pressured Fortas onto the Supreme Court (salary: $39,500, or a tenth what they had been making together), Agger was furious.

> *"Middle-of-the-road reporters . . . are so deeply embedded in the folkways of their city that they are inclined to overlook its shortcomings."*

"It's the goddamnedest thing," Agger said to Johnson aide Douglass Cater and his wife at a White House reception. "We can't afford it. Now I'll have to make all the money in the family and support him."

Under this kind of extreme domestic pressure, it is easy to understand why Fortas cast around for a few extra dollars after he went on the Court. He found a cash cushion in a $20,000-a-year consulting fee from Louis Wolfson, a Florida business-man who was under investigation by the SEC [Securities and Exchange Commission] for alleged stock improprieties. In setting the terms for the fee—ostensibly to compensate him for occasional advice to Wolfson's philanthropic foundation and companies—Fortas arranged for Agger to receive the $20,000 each year after his death. In exchange, Fortas had to attend a single annual meeting. (And of course, it was possible that one of Wolfson's cases would end up affected by a decision of the Court.) Murphy reports that two weeks to the day after the first check was sent, Fortas was writing the White House to boost two of Wolfson's companies—both of which were under federal investigation at the time. It was a quiet deal, and became public only when Johnson tried to make Fortas chief justice in 1968. Fortas, finding himself facing impeachment rather than promotion, resigned.

Although Chelsea Clinton hasn't been accused of cronyism yet, the children of Washington's powerful are as well-skilled in the art of using family connections as their mothers. In the eighties, Jamie Whitten, Jr., representing the barge industry, lobbied for the Tennessee-Tombigbee Waterway before his father's House Appropriations Committee. In 1990, the *Wall Street Journal* described how lobbyist Clifford Gibbons, son of the ranking Democrat on the House Ways and Means Committee, brokered campaign contributions and access between his clients and his father. The Scripps Howard news service identified a dozen such congressional children who were lobbying in Washington, including Laurie Michel, the daughter of House Republican Leader Bob Michel, who represents a French drug company, and N. Hunter Johnston, son of Senate Energy and Commerce Committee chairman Bennett Johnston, who lobbies for General Atomics Corp. . . .

Intimacy and the Status Quo

• *Washington assumption: In a small Southern state, everybody knows every-body else—politicians, lawyers, lobbyists, journalists—and that intimacy leads to a go-along, get-along atmosphere.*

As Arkansan after Arkansan has died, resigned, or been demoted—Vincent Foster, Jr.; Webb Hubbell; William Kennedy—an I-told-you-so sense has emerged among the Washington media. "They're running out of cronies, and that's a good thing," Eleanor Clift opined on [*The McLaughlin Group*]. Gwen Ifill, of the *Times*, said, "in the world that is Arkansas politics and in the legal world, a lot of that intersected." The implication is that cronyism is an exotic dish just recently imported to the capital.

But consider Thomas Hale "Tommy" Boggs, Jr., of Patton, Boggs & Blow, ar-guably the most influential lawyer-lobbyist in Washington and the access his 1,500 active clients could get through his kith and kin. When Boggs' father, Hale, was in Congress (1947 to 1973), a client could buy some access to the powerful gentleman from Louisiana and the later House Majority leader. And Tommy's mother, Lindy, served in the House herself from 1973 to 1991, meaning she might be reachable, too. Tommy's sister is Cokie Roberts, of National Public Ra-dio and ABC News, so there are two major media outlets right there; Roberts is married to Steven V. Roberts, formerly of the *New York Times* and now of *U.S. News & World Report*, thus affording Boggs' clients a subtle connection to major print organizations as well. And Boggs' other brother-in-law is a Princeton politi-cal scientist, offering a conduit to a major Ivy League university. That's all here, in Washington, not off in Dixie.

> "[Robert Kerr] once proclaimed, 'I represent myself first, the state of Oklahoma second, and the people of the United States third.'"

When Ellen Proxmire gave a surprise birthday party for her husband, then the chairman of the Senate Banking Committee, did she give it at their house? Nope—at Tommy Boggs'. So while it's virtually impossible to demonstrate quid pro quos, the net cultural effect is a capital atmosphere of intimacy and shared interests in main-taining the status quo. It's no wonder, then, that middle-of-the-road reporters—the Robertses are just two examples—are so deeply embedded in the folkways of their city that they are inclined to overlook its shortcomings.

Morton Kondracke, of *The McLaughlin Group*, is another journalist whose immersion in the political culture is so complete that it is hard to separate him from the people he is supposed to cover. For example, when yet another veteran Washingtonian, Lloyd Bentsen, was in the Senate, he tried to found a fund-raising breakfast where supporters could pony up $10,000 apiece for eggs and a chat with the then-chairman of the Senate Finance Committee. Kondracke at-tacked Bentsen's idea in a column. But when asked about his own fees to speak to lobbying groups, Kondracke refused to disclose his finances, harrumphing that it would be "an exercise in voyeurism and an invasion of privacy."

But how can journalists who make at least $5,000 a pop to yap before trade groups be expected to challenge the capital culture that has treated them so well? George Will commands about $20,000 for his appearances (Will's current wife, by the way, Mari Maseng Will, is a former Bush staffer whose p.r. firm represents the Japanese Automobile Manufacturers

> *"Most of what BCCI's lawyers, lobbyists, and political advisors did was within the standard bounds of legal practice in Washington."*

Association). And Pat Buchanan made nearly $1 million speaking and writing the year before he ran for president [in 1992].

So the overwhelming cultural urge is not to queer a good deal by calling for what mainstream Washington would view as whacked-out, naive reforms, like a single payer health system. Joe Cosby, a Washington agent who handles journalist bookings, says lecture invitations require that the reporter "be on television" and "be conservative." This is a world, in other words, for people who won't rock the boat too much, and conservatives are world-class non-boat-rockers. . . .

The BCCI Scandal

When [attorney] Clark Clifford was indicted in 1991 for allegedly fronting for the drug-profiteering and money-laundering BCCI [Bank of Credit and Commerce International, now defunct], the *Washington Post*'s Haynes Johnson remarked on PBS, "One of the great monuments of our times, Mr. Clark Clifford, who is an icon among virtually everyone who lives here, has had his own problems and is now fighting to repatriate his reputation at the age of 84. And this alone is a stunning story in this capital city." That he was an "icon" here tells us much about what Washington values. And it tells us how poorly the press perceives Washington's systemic faults.

BCCI, you see, was not Clifford's first ethical slip-up. In 1970, after Clifford had been LBJ's last secretary of Defense, he served on the board of the National Bank of Washington. The bank was then controlled by the United Mine Workers and its president, Tony Boyle, who was widely suspected of—and eventually convicted of—having arranged the murder of his predecessor, Jock Yablonski. At the time, the *Washington Monthly* revealed that the miners' pension fund was deposited in a non-interest-bearing account, with the result that the money benefited the bankers and the union executives instead of black-lung victims and their widows and orphans. As a lawyer, Clifford had to know the trustees' fiduciary responsibility to the miners was to ensure their pension fund was invested to their maximum benefit, not for the benefit of the bank that was paying Clifford to serve as its respectable front-man.

You could argue that 1970 predates Watergate and the rise of a more investigative, informed press. Fine—but look at the eighties, when BCCI got away with murder. In fact, BCCI's help in Washington makes Little Rock look like a kindergarten pageant: It included Clifford; a former senator (John Culver, Democrat of Iowa); three former federal prosecutors; two former Federal Reserve attorneys; and one high-level Senate staffer who was also a former assistant secretary of Defense. What's scariest about the 10 years the bank eluded U.S. investigators and reporters by lying and suppressing evidence is that Congress found in 1991 that "Most of what BCCI's lawyers, lobbyists, and political advisors did was within the standard bounds of legal practice in Washington."

All in a day's work, in other words. The fawning accorded Clifford for his six years in government (five with Harry S. Truman and one, 1968, with Johnson), compared to more than 50 in private practice was never more evident than on CNN's *Larry King Live*, where Clifford was flacking his memoirs at the height of the scandal. After hearing Clifford out on BCCI without question, King came back after commercial:

> King: Clark Clifford is our guest. The book is *Counsel to the President.* He has counseled many. We should also say, on that banking thing we were discussing, these are only allegations we are dealing with here. Nothing has been charged or proven. These are all based on newspaper stories and magazine stories. Nothing has been charged and the government has, to my knowledge, not said anything. Right?
>
> Clifford: Correct.
>
> King: OK. Back to the presidents.

Ron Brown's Deals

Is this world fading, as men like Clifford grow old? Not in the least, and the next Clark Clifford is no Southerner but a consummate Washingtonian born and raised in New York: Ron Brown. When Brown, a lawyer/lobbyist with Patton, Boggs & Blow and former Democratic chairman, was nominated to be Bill Clinton's secretary of Commerce, he sailed through a three-hour confirmation hearing. Senator Fritz Hollings defended Brown's representation of the repressive Haitian Duvalier regime with this morally dubious point: "Let the record show that before I got to the Senate, I used to represent murderers." Even Republican Senator Trent Lott tossed softballs, telling Brown, "I have to say that there's no doubt in my mind you're qualified by experience and background to do this job." Lott quickly ran down Brown's laundry list of influence-peddling, concluding:

> Lott: How do you respond to the fact that all of this background and these things perhaps send the wrong message as we begin with this new administration?
>
> Brown: Well, I would disagree, Senator, that it sends the wrong message. I think it sends the right message. I think it sends a message that I am someone who is a good advocate, who gets things done.

In 1993, the country had two vivid reminders of the kinds of things Brown used to get done for clients. First, his friends tried to pay for an inaugural party for Brown by attracting corporate sponsors at $10,000 each—corporations Brown would be dealing with officially at Commerce. (They ended up canceling the bash.) And later that year, a Vietnamese businessman claimed that Brown had been paid $700,000 after Clinton's election to help lift the trade embargo against Vietnam. Although Justice eventually cleared Brown of any indictable crime, he did have three meetings with a Vietnamese representative that his spokesman at first denied. Brown, like BCCI, shrewdly hired a lawyer who knew the inside ropes: Reid Weingarten, a former Justice Department white-collar crime prosecutor who successfully put away John Jenrette in Abscam [a 1980 FBI sting operation by agents posing as representatives of an Arab businessman], among others. Jenrette, you may recall, was the congressman who seduced his wife, Rita (who later became a *Playboy* model) on the Capitol steps. Yet there was little press comment on the Brown charges, or on the lobbying culture that could lead to Brown's straightfacedly defending one of the meetings with the Vietnamese—which occurred in the Commerce Department— as a "social visit."

> *"Laying blame elsewhere deflects attention from Washington, the country's real center of ethical sloppiness."*

The Clintons may end up lucky; the minutiae of Whitewater will probably join Spiro Agnew trivia in the political junkyard. [Agnew resigned as Richard Nixon's vice president in 1973 while under investigation for committing graft as a Maryland governor.] But the larger question is why the press is content to caricature the South so broadly. For one, it's easy for reporters who grew up with *The Andy Griffith Show*, dimly remember reading *All the King's Men* in school, or who have seen *Blaze*, the wonderful Paul Newman movie about Earl Long and his stripper girlfriend. So there is a ready store of conventional wisdom about the South to juice up copy or talk-show comments. The second reason is the one that's more troubling. Laying blame elsewhere deflects attention from Washington, the country's real center of ethical sloppiness in which the press is thoroughly mired; not on the take, perhaps, but marinated in a culture that discourages seeing how business is truly done. Dumping on Little Rock— "that could never happen *here*"—is at best a distraction. And at worst it's protective coloration for the people who schmooze along the Potomac for bigger money and higher stakes.

Campaign Contributions Have Corrupted the Political Process

by Edmund G. Brown Jr.

About the author: *Edmund G. (Jerry) Brown Jr. served as governor of California from 1975 to 1983 and was a presidential candidate in 1992. Brown hosts a radio talk show in Berkeley, California.*

In May 1993, President Bill Clinton unveiled his plan to change corrupt campaign practices. The President calls his proposal the "most comprehensive reform of the political system in the history of this country." I call this a scam. If every line of the President's legislation were adopted tomorrow, the same corruption in Washington would continue—at conveniently reduced prices. The checks that buy the votes would still be signed by those who sign them now. Corporate executives and the wealthy would still call the tune.

Brown's Fundraising

I grew up in politics. My father rose from San Francisco district attorney to state attorney general to governor of California. He beat Richard Nixon, lost to Ronald Reagan, and missed just one Democratic National Convention in 50 years. I have been present at hundreds and hundreds of fundraising events. Maybe thousands. I have lost count, but I know I have raised roughly $20 million since the early seventies.

Contributions of $10,000 and even $100,000 are not unfamiliar to me. I have spent days on end cajoling all manner of rich and powerful people out of money to mount multimillion-dollar campaigns for the U.S. Senate, the California governorship, and the presidency. More recently, as chairman of the Democratic Party of California, I collected more millions. In 1989, for example, I organized a dinner honoring Mario Cuomo at the Beverly Hilton Hotel in Los Angeles and raised $750,000. In 1990, I put on another dinner with Lloyd Bentsen at the Fairmount

Hotel in San Francisco and collected $550,000. I know what I am talking about. This is about corruption, not a mere "money chase."

I know that our entire campaign system rests on the twin pillars of $1,000 donations, bundled and multiplied 10, 20 or even 100 times, and the massively repetitive TV ads and expensive mailings these $1,000 donations buy. House Speaker Thomas Foley [1989–1995] said that it is a "tremendous distortion of reality" to say that Congress is getting more corrupt. That depends on what you call corruption.

The corruption I speak of is not legally defined as a felony—at least not yet— but rather is the current method of paying for American elections. You take money from the richest and best connected 1 percent to get elected and then pretend that this does not affect your judgment.

Jess Unruh, the famous speaker of the California State Assembly in the sixties, coined the phrase, "money is the mother's milk of politics." He said that you had no business in politics unless "you could take their money, eat their food, drink their booze, f— their women and then vote against them." That's what I call either naive or skillfully self-deceptive.

As you might expect, Speaker Foley also defends political action committees (PACs), calling them "one of the most effective ways for people to make smaller contributions." Who is he kidding? PAC donations are managed and guided by the same elite who write the $1,000 checks, i.e., corporate vice presidents in charge of "government relations." The only difference between PACs and individual high rollers is that PACs are permitted to

> *"The corruption I speak of is not legally defined as a felony—at least not yet."*

ante up $5,000. Of course, there are labor and liberal PACs, but these mainly act as a foil to the better-financed corporate and trade association PACs. Worse, the operatives of the so-called progressive PACs often take on the Beltway [Washington, D.C.] perspective of their corporate counterparts. Jeffrey H. Birnbaum of the *Wall Street Journal* describes it this way: ". . . lawmakers and lobbyists moving together in a largely closed and isolated system, discussing decisions that affect millions of other Americans."

For the Democratic leadership, the temptation is denial, to believe that they are good but practical men able to govern for all while relying on money from the few. For all the incumbents, Republican and Democrat, the tendency is to fight every effort to reduce the role of the wealthy. Enjoying as they do $135,000-a-year salaries, the best health care, and innumerable perks, these men and women are insulated from the real world most of their constituents face. And it all begins with those fundraising dinners.

Clinton's Proposals

President Clinton's campaign "reform" proposals do nothing to stop this subversion of democracy. True, the cost of running some campaigns would go down under his plan, but the same type of people would remain in charge by writing large checks beyond the reach of most Americans. Only those candidates who attract the favor of the powerful will be able to amass large campaign war chests to run successfully. For the House, Clinton proposes business as usual with the same $5,000 PAC and $1,000 individual donations. The voluntary $600,000 spending limit is above the 1992 average of $557,000 spent by incumbents and way above the $169,000 spent by challengers. And even this so-called spending limit—which applies to those candidates who accept public funds—is deceptive. Candidates who win their primary by less than 20 percent can spend an additional $150,000 in the general election; fundraising costs up to $75,000 are also exempt from the limit. All this is indexed to inflation as well, which puts the "cap" at roughly $900,000 in 1996.

> *"House incumbents had a 5-to-1 financial advantage over challengers in 1992; senators had a 3-to-1 edge."*

And the public financing provisions of the plan are so limited that they do not remove the need to raise large sums to win office. For House races, candidates may receive up to $200,000 in media vouchers to purchase radio, television, and print ads and postage only after they have first raised $75,000—not a trivial sum for those without affluent supporters. Taken as a whole, Clinton's plan leaves intact a system dependent on the same narrow sources of money.

For the Senate, expenditure limits are set between $1.2 million and $5.5 million, depending on the state's voting age population, but this "cap" does not include up to $2.75 million for primary election campaigning or cost of living adjustments. The Senate, which has already passed its version, bans PAC contributions but allows candidates to keep collecting the coveted $1,000 checks from individuals. Under pressure, the Democratic leadership, instead of fighting, quickly capitulated to the Republicans and stripped publicly funded media and mail vouchers from the bill.

Why is the Congress so incapable of changing the status quo? I suggest you look at the March 4, 1993, Federal Election Commission report on the 1992 election. It shows that congressional campaign spending jumped 52 percent—from $446 million in 1990 to $678 million in 1992. That's more than a million dollars for each of the 535 members of Congress. House incumbents had a 5-to-1 financial advantage over challengers in 1992; senators had a 3-to-1 edge. And of the Top 40 House recipients of PAC money in 1992, each and every one were incumbents, and 37 were Democrats. Congressmen Richard Gephardt, Vic Fazio, Dan Rostenkowski, David Bonior, and John Dingell—certainly among the House's most influential leaders—ranked one through five, raising a total of over $5 million from PACs. In the Senate, 25 of the Top 40 PAC recipients were Democrats.

We also learn that as a group House Democratic incumbents received more than 50 percent of their $126 million in campaign checks from PACs. No wonder they resist banning PACs. Is this the party of Franklin Roosevelt and Harry Truman, of the "common man," of the hard-pressed wage earner, of those who suffer despair in our cities?

Hostility to Change

To understand how deep the hostility to change is, consider what happened to President Clinton's plan as it went through the process. Before the plan was even announced, the incumbents served notice that they would accept no drastic changes. Clinton bowed to their wishes, abandoning his modest campaign commitment to limit PAC contributions to $1,000. He also went along with postponing the law's effective date from 1994 to 1996. Then, without bothering to hold hearings in which citizens could meaningfully participate, the Senate took up the weakened bill and desultory debate ensued. Senator Paul Wellstone offered an amendment to limit contributions to $100. Just 13 senators voted yes. More amendments. More discussion. There was little public notice or media attention. Then public financing was stripped away. But the $1,000 gift remained sacrosanct and the status quo—what Kevin Phillips calls "greedlock"—held firm. Like an insidious pathogen, the ingrained practice of money politics attacks and then kills every attempt at genuine reform.

> *"The congressional incumbents will not clean up a system that insures them a flow of money to smother their opponents."*

The great constitutional principle of "one person, one vote" has been betrayed and in its place we find a rogue system where the pursuit of "one dollar, one vote" takes over. And the obvious way for the public to learn about this—informed press coverage—is infrequent and thin. Reporters thrive on political combat and in the matter of campaign reform, there is more consensus than conflict among the incumbents. Their debate lacks intensity, and that discourages coverage. The *New York Times* and the *Washington Post* ritually editorialize about the need for campaign reform but dutifully embrace the empty packages the leadership puts together. Is anyone listening? Does anyone care?

What we have here is sham and pretense. The congressional incumbents will not clean up a system that insures them a flow of money to smother their opponents. As the electoral process now functions, it is the exception rather than the rule for citizens to have equal access and exposure to candidates. In this antidemocratic system, the objective of any prudent candidate must be to amass enough money to deter potential opposition, or failing that, to ensure that the quantity of their campaign messages overwhelms the opposition. For this plutocratic endeavor, money from the top 1 percent is almost always a *sine qua non*.

This money-driven system corrodes intelligent debate and rewards those candidates who win disproportionate access to the voters' minds through paid media repetition. It is not what you stand for but whether you can buy five or ten times more media or mail than your opponents. It is this evil that the President and Congress must address if there is to be honest reform.

• To radically reduce the influence of corporate and high-income donors, the $1,000 donation must be cut to $100 and PAC contributions outlawed. When I was running for president in 1992, I asked hundreds of audiences across the country to raise their hands if they had *never* given *$1,000* to a politician. Virtually all hands would go up, accompanied by laughter or disbelief. One thousand dollar donations are the prerogative of the few. A $100 limit, which is within reach of most Americans, together with the following reforms, will make the system democratic—in practice as well as in theory.

> *"Greedlock cannot be overcome by half measures."*

• Full public matching funds must be given for each $100 donation after a reasonable threshold has been attained. Such a system operates in presidential nominating campaigns and Democrats and Republicans alike gladly avail themselves of this form of public support.

• Significant amounts of free TV and radio broadcast time featuring the candidates addressing the viewers must be made available. Candidates would qualify by collecting a reasonable number of petition signatures. It is simply impossible for most people to ever see or hear a political candidate except through the mass media. Without exaggeration, the mail and public airwaves are the functional equivalent today of the public square of old. That is why their political use must be democratized.

Ending the Sound Bite

Only a plutocracy sanctions the rationing of political debate based on the ability to pay. I believe every broadcast outlet must devote at least one hour a day in a campaign's last month to debates or forums in exchange for the licenses we the people grant them. During this period, the stations would present the debates during the same primetime hour every night, free of film clips and gimmicks. Meanwhile, privately paid candidate advertising would be outlawed, breaking politics free of the 30- or 60-second commercial in which manufactured images dominate political debate. Incumbents and challengers alike could no longer use uplifting music and family dogs to sell a candidate like a Jeep Wagoneer. This would also end the dependency on quick, distorting sound-bite attacks. If the courts hold this unconstitutional, then an alternative rule should mandate that each time one candidate or party buys time, the opposition will be granted free, equivalent exposure.

• The postage for at least two district-wide mailings must be made available free to all candidates in both the primary and general elections. In House races where TV is not practical more mailings should be authorized.

• Once the costs of media advertising are out of the equation, it makes sense to set low limits on spending to reflect the average experience of challengers, not the incumbents. With free TV and postage, this becomes feasible.

• Drastically limit the incumbent's franking privilege during election years. Even in non-election years, franking should be substantially cut, stopping the flow of newsletters members of Congress mail out only to propagandize the voters.

I know that nothing less will alter the profoundly disordered state of American politics. Greedlock cannot be overcome by half measures. The first step is to expose the empty reforms [put] before the Congress. Unless reporters, activist groups, and fed-up citizens do this now, while Congress debates the issue, the charade will continue.

Political Muckraking Is Thriving

by Ruth Shalit

About the author: *Ruth Shalit is an associate editor for the* New Republic, *a biweekly magazine.*

John Galetta liked his job as a staff assistant in President George Bush's Office of National Service. "I was in charge of picking the daily Point of Light," he says. "It was fun. I was the one who got the program up and running." But after the November 1992 elections, Galetta decided it was time to try a different tack. "I wanted to hang up my own shingle," he says. So he founded TTCI Inc.—a for-profit, full-service opposition research boutique. The former Republican do-gooder now works around the clock exhuming dirt and scandal on people running for office. He pores over divorce records, shareholder suits and uniform commercial code filings. "Everyone politely despises negative campaigning," he says. "But personally, I don't see anything wrong with holding candidates accountable."

Digging for Dirt

Neither does Bernadine Healey, a 1994 Republican candidate for the Ohio Senate seat vacated by Democrat Howard Metzenbaum. In September 1993 she hired Galetta to trawl for clandestine data on Mike DeWine, her opponent in the Republican primary. The former National Institutes of Health director wasn't alone. A month later Mary Boyle, a Democratic contender for the Ohio seat, hired Shawn Garvey of the San Francisco–based Smart Campaigns Inc. to supervise her dirt-digging efforts. "My grandfather was a labor organizer," explains Garvey. "I was a young Socialist. Ten days that shook the world, all that kind of stuff." But after working for three Kennedys (Ted, Joe, Kathleen), he too made the jump to the dark side. "Times have changed," he says. "It's getting ugly out there." Garvey's company, started in 1992, is one of scores of opposition research firms now sprinkled across the country like a thousand points of spite.

With television politics and campaigns hinging more and more on the personal peccadilloes of candidates, the need for fresh dirt has spawned a cottage industry of professional life-ruiners. What used to be the handiwork of scrofulous teenagers hacking away in the basement of party headquarters is now performed by top-dollar "consultants" in Italian suits. "We're identifying good people, training them, counting on them," says Mike Plante of the Charleston, West Virginia–based Cunningham, Plante & Associates. "You try to pay them well and keep them. We're talking about getting folks up into the $50,000 range, if they stay around. I think the market will bear that. For

> *"The need for fresh dirt has spawned a cottage industry of professional life-ruiners."*

many of them, this is the first step to becoming political consultants."

He might be right. According to *Campaigns and Elections* magazine, opposition research is now the fastest-growing discipline among campaign professionals. In 1990 the magazine began listing opposition research firms as a separate category in its annual index of political vendors. Since then, the field has tripled in size (The 1994 index listed seventy-five oppo firms). "When I started in consulting, there were only one or two people who did this professionally," says Democratic political consultant Robert Squier. "Now I can't imagine any race—state assembly, state party chair, big-city mayoral contests—run without outside research consultants." And the campaigns are willing to pay top dollar. The preliminary results of a survey by *Campaigns and Elections* Editor Ronald Faucheux indicated that office-holders would dole out $16 million for opposition research during the 1994 election cycle alone.

Boasting nine full-time staffers and three stringers, Garvey's firm will take a cleaver to some fifty candidates. "I can fax you our proposal," he says. "It outlines our ideology of research. We have five tiers." Beginning with "the really nasty stuff, the cheap shots"— traffic tickets, liens outstanding, cellular phone receipts—"we just keep going up the ladder."

Expensive and Meticulous Probes

Richard Biltmeyer, research director for the National Republican Senatorial Committee, runs his own firm, RDB Associates, on the side. He too has a vision. "Friends of the cause sit around and write software," he says. "We have a vote database on every Democrat. The minute I get a vote, it is formatted and explained in the database, in categories, with attack themes. 'Perks.' 'Pay.' 'Turns back on working families.' I summarize it. I give it to the media people. They give it to the campaign manager. They've got their campaign in a box."

It's an expensive box. Biltmeyer charges $10,000 per study. Garvey, meanwhile, takes in between $20,000 and $25,000 for his five-tier onslaughts. This is comparatively cheap. David Hill of the Houston-based Hill Research Associates bills $100 per hour for projects that stretch out for months. "There's no way to make it go faster," sighs Hill, who shadowed Lawton Chiles for Florida gubernatorial hopeful Jeb Bush. "So much information keeps filtering in. It all requires follow-up work. You're constantly integrating new material. You can keep following trails until the sun goes down."

Such persistence is a virtual necessity, says Alex Castellanos of National Media Inc. "Boring, annoying, wonk-fact ads are bombing. If a politician is viewed as having his hand in the till, that's what really gets people going. But for that you have to go through campaign finance documents. Divorce papers. Tax records. You have to go on-site." That's where the research divisions of the party committees fall short. "We provide our candidates with public-record research," says Michael Meahan, spokesman for the Democratic Congressional Campaign Committee. "Funny votes and funny quotes. There's a limit to how much the committees can do."

In the past, candidates in search of juicier fare turned to private investigators—and the efforts often came back to haunt them. In 1990 Wisconsin gubernatorial candidate Jim Loftus was run out of town after news leaked that he had hired an investigator to look at Governor Tommy Thompson's relationship with dog track operators. Private eyes, too, have started to balk at political work. "I won't do it anymore," says Ken Cummins, a Washington P.I. hired by the Clinton campaign to look into allegations of impropriety surrounding Bush family finances. "I think a lot of firms feel the same way. The other side starts doing oppo on you. They look at your client list and phone records. They figure out who your principals are. You get investigated."

Research Professionals

This is where the new industry comes in. Imagine political consultants' relief at ceding the muckraking to a team of briefcase-toting professionals. "We really don't do much opposition research anymore," says Peter Lindstrom, research director of the Democratic Senatorial Campaign Committee. "We subcontract it out. We'd rather let the consultants do it." Dan Carroll, a former DNC [Democratic National Committee] research chief who left the committee to start his own oppo firm, agrees that "the difference is all in how you sell it. When I think of private eyes, I think of going through people's garbage, invading their privacy. If you throw around terms like 'private eye,' you can make points against a candidate.

"Imagine political consultants' relief at ceding the muckraking to a team of briefcase-toting professionals."

If it's an opposition research firm doing it, it's not as sinister sounding. The issue is how it's done and how it's spun."

Not surprisingly, most of today's opposition researchers see themselves not as gumshoes, but as gurus. Far from hiding behind trench coats, they promptly return reporters' phone calls, freely discuss current clients and are generally more than willing to supply examples of their own clout and guile. "We're not just looking for dirt," insists Hill. "We provide strategic insight on how to run a campaign." Adds Garvey: "We see ourselves as consultants first and researchers second. Campaigns are increasingly coming to rely on us to do their entire strategic plan."

And some other things, too. "We specialize in the public record," says Michael Segal of the Advanced Research Group in Cambridge. "Now, that public record might include con-

> *"The California Democrats accused Republican senatorial nominee Bruce Hershensohn of visiting a newsstand called Centerfold World."*

troversial records." That's one way of putting it. "We actually go into court-houses," brags Ray Strother of the Washington-based Strother Ltd., who has done work for Senators Lloyd Bentsen, John Breaux and Dennis DeConcini. "We check land transfers, police records, lawsuits. We look at credit records." Says Lindstrom: "I have found that the private consultants are less than scrupulous in the way this stuff gets used." All the same, he says he recommends the boutique firms to candidates "wanting to go above a basic level" of research. "I refer to it as spitballing," he says. "Sometimes it sticks. Sometimes it doesn't."

Muckraking Backfires

Despite a professed distaste for cloak-and-dagger tactics—"We'll leave that to the divorce lawyers," he says—one of the spitballers is Shawn Garvey. In 1992 the California Democratic Party hired his firm to dig up Republican scandal and intrigue in each of its thirty-eight state, legislative and congressional races. The results were not encouraging. Combing through arrest records at the county courthouse, Garvey's operatives stumbled across the name Carol Rowan in association with a DWI [driving while intoxicated] violation. Since their candidate David Roberti was running against a Carol Rowan for a state Senate seat, they blanketed the state with direct-mail flyers informing voters about the charge. It turned out to be the wrong woman.

They also accused state Assemblyman Bernie Richter, a conservative Christian, of trafficking in pornographic videotapes. Alas, the pornographer turned out to be one Bernie Z. Richter, who lived in an entirely different county. Finally, the California Democrats accused Republican senatorial nominee Bruce Hershensohn of visiting a newsstand called *Centerfold World* and a strip joint, The Seven Veils. "We learned that Hershensohn frequented all of these weird sex places and corner booth places," says Garvey: "We didn't analyze it. But I did tell [Democratic State Party Chair] Bob Mulholland, and it did get used." An angry Hershensohn denied the charges, but they stuck. "He was running as a right-winger, a moralist," says Karen Olick, chief of staff to Hershensohn opponent Barbara Boxer. "We were just pointing out the contradictions. And it worked."

Chapter 1

Marketing Ploys

The oppo specialists have developed elaborate marketing schemes to coax politicians into buying their product. If a potential client begs off an opposition study, citing hopes of a positive campaign, oppo researchers will hint at the evil designs of his opponent. The oppos will then offer to scour the candidate's own record for issues that could be exploited. If the candidate agrees to the "vulnerability study," the consultants will spend the next several months telling him about his weaknesses. After lying awake in bug-eyed alarm, the politician usually consents to a study on his opponent—if only for defensive reasons. "The vulnerability study is sort of an entrée to more research," admits Galetta. The term in vogue is "inoculation."

Plante elaborates on this principle. "I have to do a sales job to candidates," he explains. "You never want to be attacked by an opponent and not be ready for it. And sometimes the best response is an offense. As my candidates see the stakes involved, they begin to understand this." Plante, a Harvard-educated seminarian, points with pride to his efforts in the 1992 Wisconsin Democratic Senate primary. His firm did the oppo for Representative Jim Moody; local business magnate Joseph Checota hired the Wisconsin firm Carrier, Christofferson & Associates. "Jim Moody is a very fine person," Plante explains. "He didn't have an arrogant bone in his body. He said over and over again, 'I don't want to go negative.'" But after Plante's vulnerability study on Moody discovered a delinquent tax warrant for $4.13, he had little choice. "If you're weak in certain areas, you have to take that issue away from your opponent," he says. "You have to find similar weaknesses in their background. We suspected tax warrants on Congressman Moody would be a prime area of attack against him."

Moody empowered Plante to spend several weeks poring over Checota's economic interest statements, land records and Securities and Exchange Commission reports. "We found some grievous sins," says Plante. So the Moody campaign launched a pre-emptive ad campaign against Checota. The businessman fired back with negative ads of his own. "Over the course of a week, the two of them went from having almost all of the votes to having almost none of the votes," says Plante. The primary—and the race— was won by Russell Feingold, the candidate without an opposition researcher. But Plante doesn't seem to mind. "When the campaign started, [Checota's company] Universal Medical was traded at $22 per share," he says. "Just recently somebody faxed me an article. It's down to forty-seven cents a share. I feel proud to have been part of that campaign."

> *"Often just having the club is enough. It's like nuclear deterrence—you don't fire your missile, I don't fire mine."*

Strother has war stories of his own. "I try very hard not to use anything personal," he says. "Often just having the club is enough. It's like nuclear deterrence—you don't fire your missile, I don't fire mine." How does this work in practice? "You pick up gossip," he says. "A couple of years ago, the police responded to a wife-beating complaint against an opponent of ours. We followed it up, because we had done a vulnerability study on our guy, and it turned out he had a DWI arrest. Well, there was a tootsie involved. A new wife, and she was very angry. She would've talked. So one of our staffers met one of his staffers in a bar and whispered, 'We have this information. We don't intend to use it unless. . . .' And we were able to keep our opponent from talking about the DWI."

Investigations Everywhere

No wonder everyone is investigating everyone else. In December 1993, Oliver North signed a contract with the Arlington-based Terry Cooper Political Research Inc. to do some "exploratory" work for his Virginia Senate bid. Meanwhile, Dan Carol of Dan Carol & Associates spearheaded OLLIEPAC (Operation Last Laugh Independent Expenditure PAC), a group of "concerned citizens" that has joined together to do opposition research on North. All of the candidates for the RNC [Republican National Committee] chairmanship in 1993 hired "op shops" to investigate each other. Even the hopelessly amicable Bill Clinton, it seems, fell prey. The DNC hired Matt Dorsey, formerly with The Research Group Inc., to dig up dirt on opponents of the president's health care plan. "When the national health care campaign was formed, the decision was made to have an opposition research department that would track all the institutional opponents of the president's health care plan," explains Dorsey, speaking from DNC headquarters.

"There's not much difference between what we do here and what Shawn [Garvey] does on candidates. We're trying to expose ulterior motives, to diminish credibility.". . . Dorsey's oppo apparatus is wired in to the grass roots. "When a group in the field takes a hit from some opposition group, they'll call us up and say, 'Who are these guys?' We're never unprepared. We must have 350, 400 files on all these different groups." And no doubt they on him.

The Whitewater Affair Involved Corruption

by James A. Leach

About the author: *James A. Leach, a Republican from Iowa, has served in the U.S. House of Representatives since 1977 and is the chairman of the House Banking and Financial Services Committee, which began an investigation of the Whitewater affair in August 1995.*

I would like to take this opportunity to talk not of the issues of the day, but rather of the ethics of our time. In so doing, I would like to take as a starting point a scandal that has come to be dubbed "Whitewater" and suggest it is a central issue not because it is big, but precisely because it is small. In its very smallness, Whitewater evidences the shortcomings of public leadership in America today.

The German architect Mies Van Der Rohe once suggested that "less is more." The simplicity of design that hallmarked his buildings revealed great aesthetic character. Analogously, for individuals, truth of character is more generally revealed in small acts than large gestures.

What Is Whitewater?

Recently a colleague came up to me on the House Floor and exclaimed: "Jim, what is Whitewater? My stomach tells me something's wrong, but I've got no idea what you're talking about. Can you describe it in plain English so a plain American can understand?"

In a nutshell, Whitewater is about the arrogance of power—political conflicts of interest that are self-evidently unseemly. It all began in the late 1970s when an S&L [savings and loan] owner named James McDougal formed a 50-50 real estate venture with a young politician, the then–attorney general of Arkansas, Bill Clinton. In this venture called Whitewater, the S&L owner and S&L subsidiaries provided virtually all, perhaps all, the money; the governor-in-the-making provided his name.

Excerpted from James A. Leach, "Whitewater: Public Policy and Private Ethics," *Washington Times*, March 8, 1994. Reprinted by permission.

Over the years, the company received infusions of cash from the S&L [Madison Guaranty] as well as from a small business investment corporation that diverted, allegedly at the governor's request, federally guaranteed funds from a program designed for socially and economically disadvantaged people to the governor's partners and thence, in part, to Whitewater.

Some of these funds were used to pay off personal and campaign liabilities of the governor; some to purchase a tract of land from a company to which the state had just given a significant tax break. Whitewater

> *"Under the governorship of Bill Clinton, the first lady of Arkansas was hired to represent [Madison Guaranty] before state regulators."*

records have apparently been largely lost. A review of the numerous land transactions, however, raises questions of what happened to the money that came into the company and a review of the president's tax records raises questions about tax deductions that were taken and taxes that were not paid.

Under the governorship of Bill Clinton, the first lady of Arkansas was hired to represent the S&L before state regulators, the president of the S&L was placed on the state S&L commission, an attorney who represented the S&L was named the state S&L regulator, and the S&L was allowed to operate, despite being insolvent for an extended period, providing millions in loans and investment dollars to insiders and the Arkansas political establishment.

Under the governorship of Bill Clinton, the S&L was allowed to grow 25-fold until federal regulators forced its closing, at which time taxpayers picked up the tab for losses that amounted to approximately 50 percent of the institution's deposit base.

The S&L Debacle

The story of Whitewater is thus part and parcel of the story of the greatest domestic policy mistake of the century—the quarter-trillion-dollar S&L debacle.

In the largest series of bank robberies in history, which precipitated an industry bailout larger than the taxpayers provided Lockheed, Chrysler and New York City times a factor of 10, it is fair to ask: What happened? Who is responsible?

An answer to these inquiries requires an understanding that those accountable are not only a few negligent and corrupt S&L owners, but attorneys, accountants, state and federal regulators and assorted public officials. As wide-ranging as the responsibility is, however, it is a mistake to be so glassy-eyed as not to seek lessons for the future through a demand for individual accountability for breaches of law and ethics in the past.

Macro-economics aside, public responsibility for the S&L debacle is of a tripod nature, involving: 1) the conflict-ridden role of Congress in passing loose laws; 2) the ideological mistake of the Reagan administration in urging deregulation in an industry which requires responsible standards; and 3) the culpability of a small number of state governments, such as in California, Texas, Louisiana and Arkansas, which failed to rein in high-flying state-chartered, state-regulated institutions, which because of the federal nature of deposit insurance, precipitated a massive transfer of wealth from states with responsible governments to those without.

In Arkansas, it is impressive how the federal government was obligated to close more than 80 percent of state-chartered S&Ls in the 1980s and how large taxpayer losses were in relation to the state's S&L deposit base. The failure of the Clinton administration in Little Rock to fulfill its responsibility to police state financial institutions had the effect of increasing tax burdens on citizens of Arkansas as well as other states.

While taxpayers at the national level were forced to pick up the tab for the mistakes of politicians in whose elections they could not vote, citizens in states like Arkansas were doubly shortchanged. Not only did they have to share in eventual bailout costs, but when their home-based financial institutions frittered away the hard-earned deposit savings of their state to insiders, fewer resources were made available to potential homeowners and minority entrepreneurs.

Clinton Profited

What the Keating Five scandal was all about was the attempt of an S&L owner [Charles Keating, convicted of defrauding investors] to compromise through political contributions significant political players, in this case five senators, to influence regulators to keep an insolvent, corruptly run institution from being closed. What makes Gov. Clinton's involvement with the breaching of the vaults of an Arkansas S&L philosophically at least equal to, but in reality more troubling than, the Keating model is that not only did the institution's management organize conflict-ridden fund-raising endeavors for the key politician in the state, but through Whitewater it put the governor in a compromising personal finance position as well.

What is remarkable is the hypocrisy of the circumstance. Time after time in the 1980s, alleged defenders of the little guy in American politics found themselves advancing the interest of a small number of owners of financial institutions which were run as private piggy banks for insiders. The intertwining of greed and ambition turned democratic values upside down.

> *"An ethical lapse here and an ethical lapse there and pretty soon it adds up to a real character deficit."*

In our kind of democracy, ends simply don't justify means. Just as a conservative, who may despise government, has no ethical right not to pay taxes, a liberal has no ethical basis to put the public's money in his own or his campaign's pocket just because he may have the arrogance to believe he is advancing a political creed that is in the public's interest.

Why does all this matter?

Perhaps it would be appropriate to paraphrase Ev Dirksen [U.S. Senate minority leader, 1959–1969]: a few thousand here and a few thousand there and pretty soon it adds up to a real scandal. Put another way, an ethical lapse here and an ethical lapse there and pretty soon it adds up to a real character deficit.

I have never known anyone in public life better able to put embarrassing episodes behind him than Bill Clinton. Accordingly, I couldn't have been more surprised by the discombobulation of the administration at the minority's restrained request in November 1993 for hearings and full disclosure.

> *"Can a president demand that others play by the rules—i.e., obey the law—if he doesn't play by them himself?"*

As in most serious public scandals, coverups can prove as troubling as the crime.

The revelations that officials of the Department of the Treasury and Resolution Trust Corporation briefed key White House aides on potential legal actions that independent regulatory agencies might be obligated to take against the president and first lady subvert one of the fundamental premises of American democracy—that this is a country of laws and not men.

Violations of the Law

In America, process is our most important product. No individual, whatever his or her rank, is privileged in the eyes of the law. No public official has the right to influence possible legal actions against himself or herself. For this reason, agencies of the government as well as the White House have precise rules that govern their employees. Prohibitions against giving preferential treatment to an individual, losing independence or impartiality, making decisions outside official channels are standard and have patently been violated.

Seldom have the public and private ethics of lawyers in the White House and Executive Branch departments and agencies been so thoroughly devalued.

It is no surprise that Special Counsel Robert Fiske, Jr. initiated March 4, 1994, a series of subpoenas reaching into the White House. What these subpoenas indicate is the movement of an investigation from possible illegal acts committed by a president prior to taking office to possible illegal actions committed in office. Obstruction of justice is now clearly at issue.

It is also no surprise the special counsel reopened the investigation of the suicide of Vincent Foster, the deputy White House counsel. There are simply too many questions with too few answers.

The point of all this is that there is a disjunction in this administration between public policy and private ethics. Americans abhor privilege; hypocrisy gnaws at the American soul; it leaves a dispiriting residue of resentment.

Chapter 1

Presidential Hypocrisy

Can, for instance, a president credibly rail against Michael Milken [a billionaire junk-bond trader convicted of securities fraud] values if he has himself benefitted from Milkenesque deal-making?

Can a president credibly ask the people to pay taxes, let alone raise them, if he refuses to pay his own fair share?

Can a president credibly espouse open government if he applies a hide-and-seek standard to his own actions?

Can a president demand that others play by the rules—*i.e.,* obey the law—if he doesn't play by them himself?

Can a president credibly advance an ethic of national service if his own model is one of self-service?

Can a president credibly advocate campaign reform if his own campaign has been sullied by illegal contributions from an S&L which, with its failure, had the effect of causing deferred federal financing of a gubernatorial election?

Can a president credibly lead an ethical society if he doesn't set an ethical standard?

Can, in short, a servant of the people put himself above the people in personal and public ethics?

A Matter of Ethics and Trust

This is not to say the president is wrong on all issues; nor that the Democratic Party doesn't have some thoughtful models of integrity.

But it is to suggest that it is no coincidence that the word "trust" appears in the nation's motto as well as in the names of so many financial institutions. Both our political and financial systems depend on the trust of those whom they serve. The American people need to be able to count on the integrity of the institutions and processes that structure their lives, just as they need to have confidence in the probity of the individuals who lead and control these institutions and processes.

While government derives its original legitimacy from the consent of the governed, it can maintain that legitimacy only if the governors operate under the same ethics and rules of conduct as the governed.

Finally, a personal note. Some have asked why a mainstream Republican like myself would lead an investigation so awkward for the president. All I can say is that ethics is not an issue of the left, right or center. It is an American concern relating to the fabric and foundation of our society. As for motivation, I would simply paraphrase a great American who once carried the Republican banner, not to victory, but nonetheless with honor and integrity: Moderation in the pursuit of truth is no virtue; vigilance in the defense of public ethics no vice.

Ethical Behavior Has Improved

by Christopher L. Tyner

About the author: *Christopher L. Tyner is a former managing editor for* Ethics: Easier Said Than Done, *a quarterly publication of the Josephson Institute of Ethics in Marina del Rey, California.*

In recent years, a seemingly endless parade of political scandals involving reports of such matters as corruption, influence peddling, conflicts of interest, drinking, womanizing and adultery combine with the proliferation of ethics laws to create the impression that the moral fiber of American politics and politicians has deteriorated substantially. *Ethics: Easier Said Than Done* [ESTD] decided to consult former politicians, journalists, academics, and ethicists to shed some light on the current state of political ethics. After providing historical context, the consensus was that things are certainly not worse and that, in many ways, they are a good deal better. Still, there seemed to be much room for improvement.

Historical Context

In political ethics, apparently the good old days never existed. David Menefee-Libey, an assistant professor of government at Pomona College, points out "there has been a consistent pattern of elected and appointed officials engaging in corrupt action throughout American history. This is not anything new," he said.

According to Dr. Robert N. Roberts, author of the book *White House Ethics*, legislatures in the late 19th and early 20th century "were being bought and sold, literally. . . . There was no separation between private and public interest. We are much better off than we used to be." Professor Roberts credits the Populists and Progressives for cleaning up politics and making public administration a true profession. Government from about 1930 through the end of World War II, he says, "was amazingly free of corruption." What distinguishes this "renaissance of public administration," he says, "is the commitment of individuals who went into government to public service." But, he says, the old ways began to re-emerge in the Truman Administration with charges of improper conduct including conflicts of interest and influence. These kinds of charges persisted through Eisenhower's Administration. Things calmed down in the '60s but, Dr. Roberts says, the Watergate scandal in the early '70s "really touched everything off. . . . Conflicts of interest regulations took off like wildfire after Watergate; they spread through state and federal levels, and we're still on that tram."

Watergate was assuredly a watershed in contemporary American politics in two major respects. First, it spawned legislation regulating the political process as never before, and, second, it created a new generation of investigative journalists committed to playing a much more aggressive role than their predecessors.

Mr. Menefee-Libey points out that the Campaign Act of 1972 and subsequent amendments required federal candidates, for the first time, to disclose the sources and amounts of campaign contributions. As a result, there was a huge public record available to journalistic scrutiny. "The reaction of the press," he says, "was an explosion of stories based on this gold mine of information." And as the public became more knowledgeable about the inner workings of politics, the demand grew for more restrictive legislation limiting the amounts of contributions, requiring further disclosure of income and gifts and regulating conflicts of interest.

Post-Watergate Legislation

Ethics legislation has dramatically affected politics. In the past two decades a continuously growing body of regulations have imposed technical reporting requirements and a broad array of restrictions. While state and local governments have tended to lag behind federal efforts, legislative activity increased sharply in the late 1980s and it now seems inevitable that ethics laws will be a major part of the landscape at all levels of government.

Post-Watergate legislation falls into six major categories: 1) disclosure requirements regarding campaign contributions; 2) limitations on sources and amounts of campaign contributions; 3) prohibitions on the use of campaign funds for personal purposes; 4) disclosure of sources and amounts of earned income and gifts; 5) prohibitions on certain forms of income (e.g., honoraria) and limitations on gifts; and 6) general prohibitions of conflicts of interest. This vast body of regulations forces public officials to reveal actual and apparent improprieties and establish new, sometimes complex standards of behavior.

> *"It now seems inevitable that ethics laws will be a major part of the landscape at all levels of government."*

The disclosure rules have subjected public officials to unprecedented scrutiny by a highly motivated journalism corps who comb disclosure forms for evidence of relationships or transactions that cast doubt on the independence and objectivity of politicians. Under the appearance of impropriety test, all potential conflicts of interest are fair game. And, many public officials find themselves ensnared in the provisions of new laws that sometimes outlawed common practices.

Ronald Reagan's Administration

Former Attorney General Edwin Meese III, who is now a distinguished fellow at the Heritage Foundation, was subject to extensive criticism for what was attributed as a lack of ethical sensitivity. He believes that it is the combination of new and untried government ethics rules and aggressive media coverage that created an unfair impression that the Reagan Administration engaged in high levels of improper activity:

> One of the prime qualifications that the Reagan Administration had right from the start, going back to 1980, was that integrity among the people appointed by the president and among the federal work force was one of the primary requirements. [The Reagan Administration] was the first . . . in its entirety to be subject to the so-called Ethics in Government Act of 1978. . . . And so there was a good deal of new regulations, new requirements and necessarily, a breaking-in period for this additional body of law and regulation that subjected people to new forms to fill out, new questionnaires and new information to be disclosed. So obviously this took some getting used to, simply in terms of complying with the administrative requirements. But I think basically the '80s was a period in which ethics and integrity were a very highly prized aspect of the political scene.

Journalistic Change

Lance Morrow, a senior writer for *Time*, says that Bob Woodward and Carl Bernstein's Pulitzer Prize–winning reporting of the Watergate affair "reinvented the game" for "both good and for ill." It changed investigative reporting; "it put blood in the water and gave everyone a taste of blood."

CNN political commentator William Schneider agrees that changes in journalistic attitudes are a major factor in the tendency to believe that political ethics have gotten worse. "The old system . . . was that a lot of what happened in politics was overlooked or went unreported. There would be spurts of muckraking, but generally speaking, a lot of what went on in politics was winked at." He says the press exercised a great deal of discretion choosing not to report such things as heavy drinking and womanizing. "In the 19th century . . . there was open graft and bribery. There was a tremendous amount of womanizing all the way up to the White House. . . . No one noticed and no one cared. The press was essentially part of the club."

> *"The '80s was a period in which ethics and integrity were a very highly prized aspect of the political scene."*

But Watergate changed all that. Now, Mr. Schneider says, "reporters . . . know members of Congress rarely lose their seats, that election campaigns are not very serious and that the only way you can really destroy a member, particularly a member of the House [of Representatives] . . . is to get him on ethics charges. It is a weapon. Ethics has become a political weapon."

Mr. Meese thinks this kind of press coverage, as much as anything else, was responsible for the image that the Reagan Administration was replete with ethical miscreants. "If there was cynicism on the part of the public," he says, "it probably developed from the negative press reporting which I think reached an all-time high during the Reagan Administration, largely because most members of the press were opposed to the policies that President Reagan represented."

Washington Post reporter E.J. Dionne Jr. offers a slightly different perspective suggesting that the events of Watergate simply built on the momentum of political attitudes formed in the '60s which "created a much lower tolerance for hypocrisy and public corruption. . . . Together, the '60s revolution and Watergate created a much more skeptical, or as some people say, adversarial press. The result was much tougher reporting on everything from campaign finance reform to corruption and even occasionally to the personal lives of politi-

> *"What was acceptable in the past is not acceptable today. What is acceptable today, will not be acceptable 10 years from now."*

cians." Yet he believes the trend toward aggressive journalism "is being reversed and that's not entirely a good thing. I think journalism probably is less adversarial now than it was 10 years ago."

Ethics and Politics Today

The state of political ethics today is a complex picture. While there are indeed ethical violations galore, there is a sense on the part of most of our panel members that it is not as bad as it once was, that the numbers reflect the few, albeit highly visible, bad apples. They also argued that the continual revelations reflect higher standards on the part of our society, standards that journalists, however clumsily, are helping to uphold in their watchdog role.

[The late] former Congresswoman Barbara Jordan says that ethics in our nation's political arena is "evolving."

Indeed, what was acceptable in the past is not acceptable today. What is acceptable today, will not be acceptable 10 years from now. The refining fires of experience are recasting our nation's standards into higher and nobler forms.

Our panel warned that our nation's ethics should not be measured solely by the numbers of lapses—that is only part of the equation. A fuller picture would also have to include the majority of people whose acts don't make it into the newspapers.

While panel members did find today's ethical scandals perplexing, it was not their numbers so much as the magnitude of the havoc that today's complex ethical problems can leave in their wake that troubled them.

"The implications [of these ethical violations] are unusually grave," said Mr. Menefee-Libey. "It's the scale of the savings and loan scandal, or the aftermath of the 'Superfunds' scandal inside the Environmental Protection Agency . . . where you're talking about massive environmental contamination or hundreds of billions of dollars' cost—the scale of it is staggering and frightening."

> *"Given that there are over 17 million government employees, there are relatively few instances of corruption on the part of public officials."*

Some regard today's lapses as the inevitable fruit of human beings such as has always been and such as always will be. Others offer a more positive spin, arguing that newspapers and the public are sitting up and taking notice of what would have been yawned at two decades ago—and that this reflection of higher standards is cause for rejoicing.

Says Edward I. Koch, former mayor of New York and currently a partner with New York law firm Robinson, Silverman, Pearce, Aronsohn, and Berman: "We expect more from the people that we send to office and therefore when they are uncovered . . . as having violated standards, there is a greater sense of outrage. I'm not upset by that. I think that is OK. I don't agree with those who believe that the standards have fallen. I think the standards are higher."

In Good Shape

Michael Kinsley, senior editor at the *New Republic* magazine, agrees. He says the fact that newspapers are filled with stories of ethical lapses doesn't necessarily show that there are more of them or that the ethical violations are worse.

"It could show the opposite, that people are more attentive, that the outrage level is higher, and therefore, people are better behaved," says Mr. Kinsley.

And according to Dr. Robert Roberts, author of the book *White House Ethics*, given that there are over 17 million government employees, there are relatively few instances of corruption on the part of public officials:

> When you compare [the U.S.] to other countries around the world, I think we are really in very, very good shape ethically. Of course it's not going to appear (that there is less corruption) because what you're focusing on is individual cases taken out of the context of a tremendous amount of money being spent and a large number of government employees. . . . It is easy to report those things without putting it in proper context.

The *Washington Post*'s veteran political reporter David Broder says that today there are "far fewer hacks in politics than when I started out covering this beat 30 years ago. And more people . . . of ability and integrity."

Public Distrust

But if ethical standards are higher today, why is there such a high degree of public distrust in elected officials?

Mr. Dionne, a politics and ideas writer for the *Washington Post*, and author of the book *Why Americans Hate Politics*, explains the conundrum: "There is no

Chapter 1

real fit between whatever the ethical rules are and how well government performs," he says. So when government is not performing capably, people are "inclined to see corruption when it may not be corruption, but either ineptitude or blockages with the system, or a whole series of other things."

But Donald B. Robertson, former majority leader and later Speaker Pro Tem of the Maryland House of Delegates, argues that while we are further advanced in terms of the letter of ethics laws than we were 15 or 20 years ago, adherence to the spirit of the law is sometimes lacking. "We have the laws," says Mr. Robertson, "but I'm not sure we really have the mentality that I think we need to go with the laws in order to have a system work properly."

Ms. Jordan put it succinctly: "Ethical sensitivity cannot be superimposed from without. It needs to occur from within each individual."

Mr. Menefee-Libey feels that historically, political leadership used to involve more two-way communication in which politicians listened to the grievances of their constituencies. Today, politicians tend to operate from a marketing perspective in which market research "tells you information about voters . . . you don't need to talk to them, you don't need to find out what their grievances are," he says.

Media Revelations

Some argue that our nation's political ethics look bad because stories about ethical violations are so visible. "You say instantly this is terrible, because the papers are filled with terrible stories. . . . Let me just point out that it may be . . . better than it was in the old days when people didn't know what was going on. I think basically journalism has just become more independent and more aggressive. They don't cover things up," says Mr. Schneider.

Indeed, some are wishing the press would exercise a bit more discretion, and not rush into print every sordid detail they discover about the private lives of politicians. In fact, this is one of the central questions journalists are now debating—how far should they go in reporting the private lives of public figures?

"The press has certainly been a willing partner in revealing these things about public figures and focusing on characteristics of public figures that I don't necessarily think are particularly relevant to their actions as public figures. I mean, I don't think it's particularly important who someone sleeps with while they're in public office unless the people that they're sleeping with can expose them to their conflicts of interest," says Mr. Menefee-Libey.

> *"Some argue that our nation's political ethics look bad because stories about ethical violations are so visible."*

Some charge that the details of public officials' private lives are relevant for the public to know because they indicate character. But Mr. Menefee-Libey does not agree.

"Character is a complicated thing. There are lots of cases where we have people that are deeply flawed in their private behavior that are amazing public leaders. . . . I

54

find out sordid things about people that I think were great leaders like Abraham Lincoln or Franklin Roosevelt or other people . . . that they are privately unpleasant people [yet] are still great public leaders. On the other hand, we can find people who in their private lives seem to be impeccably moral [and] turn out to be lousy public leaders. I don't think that the correlation is that clear to me," says Mr. Menefee-Libey.

> *"There are lots of cases where we have people that are deeply flawed in their private behavior that are amazing public leaders."*

Mr. Meese says that the press sometimes creates stories from unproven allegations. "I think at times the press goes overboard in terms of playing up allegations . . . which are later proved to be false. And I think that because of this, some politicians have used the making of false allegations as a political tool to use against those with whom they disagree positionally."

Going Too Far?

Polls seem to confirm that journalism has a spotted reputation and some feel that the press itself should come under more intense scrutiny.

"I have a very low regard for journalism," says Mr. Koch.

> If the media had to observe the standards of people in public office many of them couldn't pass. . . . The reporters, journalists, editors, why is it that we don't watch what they do? In many cases they are more powerful than the local officials. We don't know what their economic interests are. We don't know what their net worth is. We don't know who they are visiting. Nobody covers them.

According to Mr. Broder, the public reaction to media stories revealing the private goings-on of public officials is that the press has gone too far.

"What I hear, and we do a lot of voter interviewing constantly [at the *Washington Post*], is none of us has led a blameless or totally moral life, and few of us would enjoy having every one of our actions subjected to intensive television and front-page scrutiny," says Mr. Broder.

Such stories have a direct effect on the public's faith in its leaders. According to Mr. Schneider,

> as a consequence it lowers the credibility of government. . . . So that if you say to people there is a fiscal crisis and we must raise taxes to take care of all these serious needs, the public's response is: "You want me to pay my taxes to those guys that I keep reading these outrageous stories about so that [they] can spend my money? Forget it!"

Attracting Quality Candidates

. . . Although today's political ethics are considered to be better, it is still difficult to attract good candidates. Most of the panel felt that a change has to take place in order to be able to attract good candidates—you have to pay legislators well so they will not need to seek outside funding.

"You've got to give them significant staff and research capabilities so that they really know something about the issues they are dealing with. [Having] some independence means that they don't always have to rely on the interest groups that tell them how things work. If they don't have independent research capabilities they can't legislate. In other words, you've got [to] professionalize," says Mr. Schneider.

However, the idea of a professional legislature is anathema to those who feel American politics revolves around that political footsoldier—the citizen legislator.

"When I would go on the radio and try to defend the pay raise, which I was favorable to, by saying you won't have as many conflicts of interest, there will be less corruption, they will be paid like professionals, they will consider themselves professionals, there was nothing but anger. People said: 'Wait a minute, what are you talking about professionals? These guys are citizen politicians. Politics is not a profession, it is a public service. You do it out of the goodness of your heart, you don't get paid for this.'" says Mr. Schneider.

> *"Although today's political ethics are considered to be better, it is still difficult to attract good candidates."*

Another ethical dilemma today is how to finance political campaigns—how to raise millions of dollars, without jumping into the pockets of the rich and powerful.

"The thing we don't talk about very much is that presidential campaign finance has been significantly cleaned up with public financing," says Mr. Dionne.

"I think there is also a possibility that the public is ambivalent about government; at the same time they want increased services and less taxes. And no administration is able to fill both of the objectives simultaneously," says Mr. Meese.

Alienated from Politics

Some experts say that the public feels alienated from politicians and the political process—that government has grown away from them.

"Because of the full-time Congress, because of the centralization of power in Washington, because Congress has become a bureaucracy and Congressmen are no longer a part of the communities, I think the public feels that they have little opportunity to influence the course of government because everything has been effectively federalized. And I think that is also one of the possible sources of cynicism to the extent that it is there," says Mr. Meese.

Lance Morrow, political writer for *Time* magazine, places at least some of the blame with the American populace. "To tell you the truth, I think people are getting very simple minded, literal minded, incapable of complexity."

Mr. Schneider is optimistic because we have this "muddling through system. There are excesses and abuses and all kinds of problems," he says, "but in the end something positive gets done.". . .

Goals for the Ethics Movement

Mr. Robertson offered two goals for the ethics movement that will lead the way into the next millennia:

> 1. We need, badly, to increase the level of sensitivity among elected officials to ethical issues. In Maryland we passed that 1979 ethics law. . . . Everybody patted themselves on the back and thought, well, we've really done the job. Now, the truth of the matter is that very many members of the legislature didn't really know what was in that bill, didn't understand the rationale behind it. I don't think we, and here I mean both in Maryland and nationally, have done enough to impress upon elected officials what their ethical responsibilities are.

> 2. I think we've got to enhance the concept of public service. . . . Too many elected officials . . . believe that their own re-election is their most important job. And I think we've got to try to get away from that. This, by the way, is something that I think has changed over the past 15 years. I think that mentality of re-election being the highest priority is much more pervasive today than it was when I was first elected.

Setting high standards and living up to them sets a powerful example and is a sure way to instill ethics into the system.

Albert H. Quie [a former member of the House of Representatives] argues that by setting a higher standard, others will follow suit. He tells how that worked for him with the issue of outside income.

"I think there will and should [be a complete disclosure of outside sources and amounts of income]. And I did that for years. I know it can be done. I publicized the contributions that everybody gave to me and made public my income tax returns for years. I went beyond the law—anybody who gives us anything, make it public. . . . I think the candidate who sets the highest standards is pretty likely to bring others along with him," says Mr. Quie.

Substance, Not Symbols

And Mr. Dionne says that the system will change when

> a candidate runs a very new kind of campaign that wins. . . . And I think that's possible. It's the center of my book. Americans want a debate about substantive things. They're tired of the debate purely on symbolic issues. And I think that if a candidate really joined real issues and attacked his foe or her foe for trying to run a campaign solely on symbolic issues, that could have something interesting happen.

In the end, according to Mr. Schneider, the American system of democracy works:

> Working through this messy, chaotic, irrational system, things improve, laws get written, the boundaries get better defined. So there is no straight-line progress. In other words, it's not that things get better and better, it's that something dramatic happens, there is a whole controversy, someone gets exposed, and somewhere in all of the excess progress is made.

Most Politicians Are Honest

by Sid Bernstein

About the author: Sid Bernstein, who died in 1993, was a columnist and chairman of the executive committee for Advertising Age, *a weekly magazine covering the advertising industry.*

Fun is fun, but what all of us have been hearing and reading lately is turning into something extremely serious. So I want to repeat exactly what I have said many times before: It is time to stop bashing Congress, the presidency, all the government officials in Washington as well as all the office holders and politicians in the states, cities and counties all over our 50 states.

A Self-Fulfilling Prophecy

It can be great fun and a wonderful way to let off steam to denounce all politicians as idiots and crooks, but I have a growing suspicion this attitude, as useful as it may be for speechmakers, stand-up comedians and huge chunks of ordinary citizens, is turning into one of those self-fulfilling prophecy situations.

This is not an original concern on my part; concern about our collective contempt for office-seekers and politicians has been voiced by scores of thoughtful people for many years. Businessmen, in particular, are notoriously unwilling to take the opprobrium that goes with attempts to win public office, unless it is in connection with some mildly unimportant post, such as membership on their library board or their village board of overseers.

That is bad enough. But even their unwillingness to help run the government as elected officials is, in my opinion, not as serious as the fact that an overwhelming proportion of our citizenry has such a poor opinion of those who run our institutions of government. No wonder why so many don't bother to vote.

A Reasonable Cross-Section

The simple fact is, as even a modest bit of intelligent thought will convince you, that our elected officials—either in national offices or in quite modest local ones—are a pretty reasonable cross-section of our population. As a body, they are considerably above average in intelligence, education, energy, ambition, reasoning ability and plain, ordinary salesmanship.

Of course, some of them may not deserve our approbation because of their moral or ethical qualities, and some may have notions about how to run our government or their jobs which do not coincide with our notions, so I do not for an instant suggest we abandon our constitutional right to criticize or condemn them.

Much of the same is true of the working force of men and women who make up our ever-widening bureaucracy—those job-holders who are supposed to carry on government's day-to-day activities, following the pattern set by their elected bosses.

I wouldn't dare suggest each one is a hard-working, dedicated employee, but by no means are all of them slothful nitwits. They, too, are representative of the general population. So

> *"Save a few words of praise for the majority of good, honest, committed bureaucrats."*

damn the bad ones, but save a few words of praise for the majority of good, honest, committed bureaucrats.

All I'm asking is that we cease pronouncing words like "Congress" or "politicians" with the intolerant tone that makes it all too clear that we are simply expressing contempt for nitwits and crooks.

Politicians Keep Their Promises

by Thomas E. Patterson

About the author: *Thomas E. Patterson is a political science professor at Syracuse University in New York and the author of* Out of Order, *an analysis of presidential campaigns.*

Reporters have a variety of bad-news messages, but none more prevalent than the suggestion that the candidates cannot be trusted. When candidates speak out on the issues, the press scrutinizes their statements for an ulterior motive. Most bad-press stories criticize candidates for shifting their positions, waffling on tough issues, posturing, or pandering to whichever group they are addressing.

After the 1992 election, I asked several of the nation's top journalists why they portray the candidates as liars. "Because they *are* liars," was the most common response, which was usually followed by an example, such as Bush's 1988 pledge not to raise taxes ("Read my lips") and Clinton's description of his marijuana experience ("I didn't inhale.").

Campaign Lies

Candidates do lie. But are they hardened, inveterate, cynical liars? Are they habitually prone to lying? Some campaign falsehoods are not only tolerated but applauded. While on the campaign trail, candidates are expected to say how great it is to be in Dubuque and to praise the people who have come to see them as the best crowd yet. They are supposed to call their host a great American and one of the country's finest public servants. Such lies are part of the hoopla of politics and help enliven it.

Some of the candidates' lies are more rhetorical than real. In the heat of the campaign, candidates can seemingly convince themselves that wild charges about their opponents are true. When George Bush called Democratic vice-presidential nominee Al Gore "the Ozone Man" and said his environmental positions were "crazy, way out, far out, man," he may have been trying to win votes, but it is also likely that he truly believed Gore's views to be "way out," and perhaps they were from Bush's own policy stance—a reluctance to pursue environmental goals that are incompatible with economic growth. Bush's comment, then, was more silly than cynical; it did more to tarnish his credibility than his opponent's.

Candidates at times stretch their will to believe so far that it goes beyond any reasonable standard of truth. Clinton was the best-funded of the Democratic contenders for nomination in 1992, and he used this advantage to buy Super Tuesday ads that attacked Paul Tsongas's modest proposals to control spending on federal entitlement programs. Clinton's ads were an attempt to scare retirees into believing

> *"Candidates at times stretch their will to believe so far that it goes beyond any reasonable standard of truth."*

that Tsongas planned to cut their Social Security benefits. Tsongas did not have sufficient funds to counter the exaggerated claims with ads of his own.

The night of the 1988 New Hampshire primary, a defeated Bob Dole was asked on national television whether he had a message for Vice President Bush. "Tell him to stop lying about my record," Dole blurted. Michael Dukakis said much the same thing about Bush during the general election. Bush inflated pieces of his opponents' records and turned them into broad allegations. Dole was tax-happy; Dukakis lacked patriotism and was soft on crime. But if Bush misrepresented their policies, Dole and Dukakis let him get away with it by not defending themselves adequately. Kirk O'Donnell, a Dukakis adviser, later said, "We had the opportunity to change the dialogue. We can take responsibility [for not doing it] on our shoulders." Partisan skirmishing is nothing new. Thomas Jefferson's opponents in 1800 tried to scare electors into believing that he would sell the country into France's hands if elected. Abraham Lincoln was called a "Liar, Thief and Baboon" by *Harper's Weekly*, and the Albany *Argus* described him as "the ugliest man in the Union"—a statement he used in his defense against charges that he was "two-faced": "I leave it to my audience," Lincoln said. "If I had another face, do you think I'd use this one?"

Hiding the Truth

Other campaign lies involve hiding painful truths that voters do not want to hear. Talk of an across-the-board tax increase was suicidal for a candidate until Ross Perot came along. With his own money on the line, he convinced some Americans that they would have to accept a hefty tax increase if they were serious about getting the federal deficit under control. Walter Mondale hurt his campaign when he said in accepting the 1984 Democratic nomination, "Let's tell the truth. Mr. Reagan will raise taxes, and so will I. He won't tell you. I just did."

There are some lies that candidates tell because the truth would destroy their career. These are falsehoods about the skeletons in their closets. When Gennifer Flowers made her [marital infidelity] charges, Bill Clinton could just as well have packed up and retired to Little Rock if he had told all. He said, "Her story is just not true," and during his appearance on *60 Minutes* he asked for understanding: "I think most Americans who are watching this tonight, they'll know what we're saying, they'll get it, and they'll feel that we have been more than candid. And I think what the press has to decide is, are we going to engage in a game of 'gotcha'?"

In such instances, a relevant question is the balance between the harmful effect of the lie on public morality and the damaging impact of the truth on the candidate and the interests he represents. Not everyone will agree as to how a candidate should act in these instances, but most people would concede that the nature of what is being concealed should weigh heavily in determining the public's response (a serious violation of the public trust would be a graver issue than a private indiscretion, such as marijuana use in one's youth).

All of the above forms of lying do not seriously harm the democratic process, except in severe cases. At no point in life is the truth always prized; nor is the truth always knowable. To expect candidates to bare their souls voluntarily or to say things that people do not want to hear or to rise above emotional subjectivity is to ask them to behave in a way in which no one behaves.

Breaking Promises

There is one type of campaign lie, however, that has no place in a democratic election. In terms of motive and context, this form of lying destroys the bond of trust between candidates and voters. It consists in making a promise to take a given course of action, to pursue a particular policy or program, that the candidate has no intention of keeping, and which is made not only to deceive the voters but to trick them into acting in a manner—voting for the candidate—that is contrary to their interests. Voters act on the promise and then get something else which they did not want. Such lies, if commonplace, turn free and fair elections into a sham.

"There are some lies that candidates tell because the truth would destroy their career."

The press makes such lies appear to be the norm. Candidates are said to change their positions as they campaign in different regions or talk with different groups, make promises they plan to break, make commitments that cannot be honored even if they try. Cynical manipulation is the story that is told of candidates' efforts to woo the voters. "The journalists' instinct," the sociologist Michael Schudson writes, "is that there is always a story *behind* the story, and that it is 'behind' because someone is hiding it."

Do candidates routinely lie when they make promises about the policies they will pursue? The importance of this question to the integrity of the democratic process has prompted scholars to investigate it. This research has involved extensive analysis, in which winning candidates' campaign promises were systematically catalogued and compared to what they did as presidents. At least four such studies have been conducted, each spanning a minimum of seven presidencies. Each of these studies reached the same conclusion: *Presidents keep the promises they made as candidates.*

Fulfilling Promises

The political scientist Gerald Pomper's exhaustive study of party platforms in nine presidential elections found that victorious candidates, once in office, attempt to fulfill nearly all of their policy commitments and succeed in achieving most of them. When they fail to deliver on a promise, it is usually because they cannot get Congress to agree; because the pledge conflicts with a higher-priority commitment; or because conditions have changed (as in the case of Reagan in 1980, who promised to settle the Iranian hostage crisis, which was resolved by the time he took office).

Another political scientist, Michael Krukones, reached the same conclusion after comparing the campaign speeches and in-office performances of eleven recent presidents. In yet a third study, Ian Budge and Richard I.

> *"[Several] studies reached the same conclusion:* **Presidents keep the promises they made as candidates."**

Hofferbert found "strong links between postwar (1948–1985) election platforms and governmental outputs." A fourth study, conducted by American University's Jeff Fishel, concluded that presidents in the period 1960–1984 signed executive orders or submitted legislative proposals corresponding to a large majority of their campaign pledges; in the case of legislative proposals, Congress enacted most of them (Johnson's 89 percent was the high; Nixon's 61 percent was the low).

These studies are less conclusive than they might appear. Candidates focus on consensual issues, sidestep some controversial issues, and frame many of their positions in general or ambiguous terms. The studies also do not distinguish the candidates' promises in terms of their scope or impact. These considerations do not, however, invalidate the general conclusion that presidential candidates make important promises and act on them when elected. Candidates are not empty vessels who have no ideas about policy and no plans about what to do with political power. The record of campaign pledges largely reveals a trail of promises kept.

Commitments to Interests

Why would it be otherwise? It is not logical to run for the presidency and ask afterward what the job entails. Candidates for the presidency want to govern, and to do so they need the support of the interests they have committed themselves to during the campaign.

Even a cursory review of recent presidencies refutes the press's claim that campaign commitments are empty promises. Ronald Reagan the president did what Ronald Reagan the candidate promised in 1980: he cut taxes, increased defense spending, opposed abortion, reduced government regulation of business, and slowed the escalation of domestic policy spending. There was one major promise that Reagan failed to keep: the balancing of the budget. He made an effort to do so in his first term but misjudged the severity of the recession that had begun under Jimmy Carter, and he erred in his belief that the revenue generated by the economic stimulus of a steep tax cut would offset the revenue loss directly attributable to the cut.

Jimmy Carter was accused by the press in 1976 of "waffling on the issues" and, ironically, was ridiculed by the press when, as president, he compiled his nearly two hundred campaign promises in a book and proceeded methodically to keep them.

Though George Bush is remembered best for a promise he broke, he did pursue the lean, business-centered economic policies, including global free trade measures, that he advocated in his 1988 campaign. On social issues he stayed true to his pro-life position on abortion and his commitment to a tougher criminal code. And during a presidency that labored under severe budgetary restraints, he persuaded Congress to appropriate significant new funding for two programs he emphasized in his 1988 campaign: HeadStart and the war on drugs. These were two of the three components of Bush's education policy (HeadStart assisted preschool children from disadvantaged backgrounds and the larger war on drugs contributed to drug-free schools); the third was freedom of choice for parents in the selection of the school their children would attend, which was also promoted by Bush while in office.

> *"Jimmy Carter . . . compiled his nearly two hundred campaign promises in a book and proceeded methodically to keep them."*

Perhaps George Bush even intended to keep his 1988 pledge of "no new taxes." He held out for two years against pressure from Congress, conceding when it became necessary to avert a budget crisis, and then only after forcing congressional Democrats to accept a deal that included a lid on discretionary domestic spending. At the time, the move was lauded by many in the press. "The President," said the Washington *Post* in an editorial, "did the right thing."

Clinton's Promises

In 1992 the votes were barely counted when Bill Clinton instructed his transition team to begin the process of implementing his campaign promises. Some commitments did fall by the wayside, including his pledge to open the nation's shores to the Haitian boat people and his promise to raise fees on the ranching and mining interests that lease federal lands. But Clinton kept, or took initial steps to carry out, a significant number of his promises: humanitarian relief to Bosnia, a tax increase on upper-income taxpayers, an end to the ban on abortion counseling in family-planning clinics that receive federal funds, deep and broad-based spending cuts, health-care reform, a family-leave program, banking reform, an economic stimulus package, tougher ethical standards for presidential appointees, tax incentives for small firms, economic assistance for Russia, a college-loan program, a job training program, among many others.

> *"Interests . . . can cause trouble for a president who fails to honor his commitments."*

Press accounts of Clinton's early months in office made it appear otherwise. The news focused on the promises he broke and, more so, on the instances where he was forced to negotiate with Congress. Each compromise was reported as a headlong retreat from principle. This perspective is unfair and inappropriate. American presidents are not like European prime ministers, who operate with a ready-made legislative majority. The president and Congress are separately elected, and share legislative power. For a president to adhere rigidly to his position is to invite deadlock and risk failure. Moreover, compromise in a system of checks and balances is not perfidy; it is a founding principle of American democracy. James Madison in the *Federalist*, no. 48, described this process of accommodation as the proper alternative to the "tyrannical concentration of all the powers of government in the same hands." There is nothing in either the practice or theory of American government that suggests presidents can or should unilaterally dictate policy.

Constrained by Commitments

The press sends the wrong message. Its claim that candidates make promises in order to win votes is true, but that is only part of the truth. They make them, *and* work to keep them. What journalists fail to take into account is the constraints affecting these commitments.

Candidates are not free to make any promise they might wish to make, and they must declare commitments they might wish to avoid. They are constrained by the interests that support their party and whose support they need. The Democrat Clinton offered promises to lower-income taxpayers, educators, the unemployed, minorities, gays, labor, and other groups that are aligned with the Democratic coalition. For his part, Bush made commitments to business, high-income taxpayers, religious fundamentalists, and others more closely aligned with the GOP. The assertion that presidential candidates are only reeds in the wind ignores their natural leaning toward constituent groups, and therefore toward certain courses of action.

Another basic truth about the candidates' pledges is that they have a stronger incentive to keep them than to break them. Interests that receive promises during the campaign have ties to Congress and to bureaucratic agencies that can cause trouble for a president who fails to honor his commitments. There is no following that is loyal despite broken promises. Bush paid dearly even within his own party for breaking his 1988 promise of "no new taxes."

Personal Causes

Finally, candidates have personal philosophies and causes that guide their choices. Political leaders have policy goals in which they believe and which constrain what they are willing to say. The economic program that Bill Clinton began working to implement the day after his election was the same one that he had described in his first major campaign speech on the subject, which he had delivered late in 1991 at his alma mater, Georgetown University. His speech contained the economic proposals that were later expressed in his acceptance speech at the Democratic convention in July 1992, and he explained those same ideas in the televised presidential debates during the general election. The policies were built on Clinton's experience as Arkansas governor, his association with policy experts such as Robert Reich, and his own sense of how to deal with the nation's problems. When Clinton was challenged by a reporter during the general election about one of his economic commitments, he replied: "It is not a promise I cooked up for the election. It is the work of a lifetime."

The Whitewater Affair Did Not Involve Corruption

by Gene Lyons

About the author: *Gene Lyons writes a column for the* Arkansas Democrat-Gazette *and reviews books for* Entertainment Weekly. *He is the author of* Widow's Web, *a 1993 book about a celebrated murder in Arkansas.*

The Great Whitewater Political Scandal and Multimedia Extravaganza has always played very differently here in Little Rock than in, say, Washington, New York, or Los Angeles. To read the great metropolitan newspapers, observe the grave demeanor of network TV anchors, and heed the rhetoric of the politicians and radio talk-show hosts who have made the issue their own, one would gather that the republic teeters on the brink of a constitutional crisis. The dread "gate" suffix of Nixonian legend has been applied. Melodramatic charges of bribery, corruption, cover-up, even of suicide and murder, fill the air (although at the time of this writing the focus has shifted to "improprieties" in Washington). There has even been loose talk of presidential impeachment.

Small Failures

All this over a failed $200,000 dirt-road real-estate deal up in Marion County and a savings and loan flameout that cost taxpayers a lousy $65 million—the 196th most costly S&L failure of the 1980s, nationally speaking, and one that accounted for about 7 percent of the roughly $1 billion tab bankrupt institutions ran up right here in little old Arkansas. For the longest time, it was hard for most Arkansans to take all the bellyaching over Whitewater and Jim McDougal's Madison Guaranty very seriously.

Apart from a superficial acquaintance with both Clintons shared by thousands of Arkansans, I know none of the characters in the Whitewater saga personally. (My wife gave Clinton a little bit of money and went to Wisconsin for a week on his behalf as an "Arkansas Traveler" at her own expense. But that's her business.) What little I have written over the years has been mostly critical. Indeed,

I cherish a videotape of myself in a short-lived guise as the poor man's Andy Rooney on a Little Rock TV station back in 1988 predicting that the governor had won his last election.

It angers me, though, that Whitewater has brought back all the old stereotypes, what the *Arkansas Times* magazine once called the image of "the Barefoot State." Barefoot, hell. To hear the national press go on about it, under Clinton poor little Arkansas became a veritable American Transylvania: a dark, mysterious netherworld populated by a mob of ignorant peasants and presided over by a half dozen corrupt tycoons in collusion with the Clintons as the Count and Countess Dracula. Scarcely a Whitewater story has appeared in the national press that hasn't made references to the state's uniquely "incestuous" links between business, government, and the legal establishment—concepts utterly foreign to places like Washington, D.C., and New York City, of course.

> *"Even Arkansans long weary of Clinton's amoeba-like style of leadership . . . can't recognize the caricature of either the man or his milieu in the national press."*

Even Arkansans long weary of Clinton's amoeba-like style of leadership—his indecisiveness, his downright genius for equivocation, his habit of launching more trial balloons than the National Weather Service—can't recognize the caricature of either the man or his milieu in the national press. And we're not just talking about such off-the-wall publications as the *American Spectator* or the *Wall Street Journal* editorial page. In the *New Republic*, author L.J. Davis accused Bill and Hillary Clinton of a nefarious plot to void Arkansas usury limits for the benefit of the First Lady's banker clients. Problem is, the deed was done through an amendment to the Arkansas constitution by public referendum during the term of Republican Governor Frank White—a banker.

How the Story Broke

So how did we get here? Well, at the expense of shocking you, dear reader, it all began with the *New York Times*—specifically with a series of much-praised articles by investigative reporter Jeff Gerth: groundbreaking, exhaustively researched, but not particularly fair or balanced stories that combine a prosecutorial bias and the art of tactical omission to insinuate all manner of sin and skulduggery. Accompanied by a series of indignant editorials, Gerth's work helped create a full-scale media clamor in December 1993 for a special prosecutor. Testimony in Senate hearings showed that the Resolution Trust Corporation's Whitewater investigation began in direct response to the *Times* coverage; the hearings *themselves* resulted in large part from the Clinton Administration's panicky reaction to reporters' queries about the RTC probe, Gerth's among them. Absent the near-talismanic role of the *New York Times* in American journalism, the whole complex of allegations and suspicions subsumed under the word "Whitewater" might never have made it to the front page, much less come to dominate the national political dialogue for months at a time. It is all the more disturbing, then, that most of the insinuations in Gerth's reporting are either highly implausible or demonstrably false.

Let us return briefly to those thrilling days of yesteryear—specifically the 1992 primary season. On March 8, 1992, Jeff Gerth's initial story about Whitewater appeared on the *Times* front page under the headline CLINTONS JOINED S.&L. OPERATOR IN AN OZARK REAL-ESTATE VENTURE:

> [In 1984], Madison started getting into trouble. Federal examiners studied its books that year, found that it was violating Arkansas regulations and determined that correcting the books to adjust improperly inflated profits would "result in an insolvent position," records of the 1984 examination show.

> Arkansas regulators received the Federal report later that year, and under state law the securities commissioner was supposed to close any insolvent institution.

> As the Governor is free to do at any time, Mr. Clinton appointed a new securities commissioner in January, 1985. He chose Beverly Bassett Schaffer. . . .

> In interviews, Mrs. Schaffer, now a Fayetteville lawyer, said she did not remember the Federal examination of Madison, but added that in her view, the findings were not "definitive proof of insolvency."

> In 1985, Mrs. Clinton and her Little Rock law firm, the Rose firm, twice applied to the [Arkansas] Securities Commission on behalf of Madison, asking that the savings and loan be allowed to try two novel plans to raise money.

> Mrs. Schaffer wrote to Mrs. Clinton and another lawyer at the firm approving the ideas. "I never gave anybody special treatment," she said.

> Madison was not able to raise additional capital. And by 1986 Federal regulators, who insured Madison's deposits, took control of the institution and ousted Mr. McDougal. Mrs. Schaffer supported the action.

Gerth's original story was praised in the *American Journalism Review* as containing 80 to 90 percent of what the press knows about Whitewater today. Rival reporters complained, though, that the 1992 article lacked a "nut paragraph" summing up what the Clintons had done wrong and why it was important.

More *Times* Articles

The insinuations became clearer in subsequent Gerth stories in the fall of 1993. Following the *Washington Post*'s October 31, 1993, revelation that the RTC had made a referral to the Justice Department naming the Clintons as (perhaps unwitting) beneficiaries of possible criminal actions, Gerth and Stephen Engelberg, another *Times* reporter, wrote lengthy articles that appeared on November 2 and December 15. The first dealt mainly with the still-unsubstantiated claims of former Municipal Judge David Hale that Bill Clinton urged him to commit federal bank fraud by lending $300,000 to Jim McDougal's wife, Susan. (Gerth and Engelberg neglected to point out that David Hale—no Clinton intimate but a courthouse pol first appointed by Republican Governor Frank White—had set up thirteen dummy companies with the same mailing address as his own, evidently without pressure from the Clintons.) Elsewhere, the November 2 piece was pretty much a rehash of the original 1992 article, with a few characteristically misleading tidbits added for emphasis. "By 1983, Mr. McDougal's bank was in trouble with Arkansas regulators," the *Times* informed readers. "The state's banking commissioner, Marlin S. Jackson, ordered the bank to stop making imprudent loans. Mr. Jackson, a Clinton appointee, said in an interview last year that he told Mr. Clinton at the time of Mr. McDougal's questionable practices."

> *"Gerth and Engelberg's December 15, 1993, story . . . all but accused both Clintons, Jim McDougal, and Beverly Bassett Schaffer of criminal conspiracy."*

Now, what Jackson told the *Los Angeles Times* (which also turned the tale inside out but did give fair context) was that the governor had urged him to ignore politics and be the "best banking commissioner you can [be]." Jackson had acted on this suggestion, with the result that the Clintons' own note was called.

The real bombshell was Gerth and Engelberg's December 15, 1993, story, which all but accused both Clintons, Jim McDougal, and Beverly Bassett Schaffer of criminal conspiracy to keep Madison Guaranty afloat regardless of the cost. But the implication in that account that has shown the most staying power involves a supposed quid pro quo involving Hillary Rodham Clinton. It centers on an April 1985 political fund-raiser Jim McDougal held and the suspicion that he may have illegally siphoned Madison Guaranty funds into Bill Clinton's campaign coffers. "Just a few weeks after Mr. McDougal raised the money for him," the *Times* noted darkly, "Madison Guaranty won approval from Mrs. Schaffer, Mr. Clinton's new financial regulator, for a novel plan to sell stock."

Alleged Favors

"The search for new capital," Gerth and Engelberg continued,

> took Madison to the offices of Mrs. Schaffer, who had the ultimate authority to approve any such stock sale. One of the lawyers employed by Madison to argue its case before the state regulators was Mrs. Clinton.
>
> Within weeks, Mrs. Schaffer wrote a letter to Mrs. Clinton giving preliminary approval to Madison's stock plan.
>
> The sale never went forward. But this fall the [RTC] asked the Justice Department to examine a number of Madison's transactions, and federal officials say the state's approval of the stock plan was among the matters raised by investigators.

The *Times* also quoted McDougal to the effect that Bassett Schaffer was his handpicked choice as Arkansas securities commissioner.

The theory implicit in Gerth's *Times* stories may be summarized as follows: when his business partner and benefactor McDougal got in trouble, Bill Clinton dumped the sitting Arkansas securities commissioner and appointed a hack, Beverly Bassett Schaffer. He and Hillary then pressured Bassett Schaffer to grant McDougal special favors—until the vigilant feds cracked down on Madison Guaranty, thwarting the Clintons' plan. This is the Received Version of the Whitewater scandal as it first took shape in the pages of the *New York Times*—what all the fuss is ultimately about. And it bears almost no relation to reality.

Distortions and Selective Reporting

The distortions begin with the headline of the original Gerth story in the *Times*: CLINTONS JOINED S.&L. OPERATOR IN AN OZARK REAL-ESTATE VENTURE. This headline was misleading because when Bill and Hillary Clinton entered into the misbegotten partnership to subdivide and develop 230 forested acres along the White River as resort property in 1978, Jim McDougal wasn't involved in the banking and S&L businesses at all. He was a career political operative—a former aide to Senators J. William Fulbright and John L. McClellan. In the meantime, McDougal had done well in the inflation-fueled Ozarks land boom of the Seventies. But it wouldn't be until five years later— by which time the Whitewater investment was already moribund—that he bought a controlling interest in Madison Guaranty.

Details, details. Gerth wrote that McDougal quickly built Madison "into one of the largest state-chartered associations in Arkansas." Wrong again. Among thirty-nine S&Ls listed in the 1985 edition of Sheshunoff's *Arkansas Savings and Loans*, Madison ranked twenty-fifth in assets and thirtieth in amount loaned. These errors of detail might be forgiven if Gerth had in fact uncovered a conspiracy between the Clintons and the Arkansas securities commissioner to treat Jim McDougal leniently. The appearance of conspiracy, however, was created not by the actions of the alleged parties but by selective reporting.

> *"Gerth wrote that McDougal quickly built Madison 'into one of the largest state-chartered associations in Arkansas.' Wrong again."*

Consider, for example, Gerth's treatment of the appointment of Beverly Bassett Schaffer as Arkansas securities commissioner in his March 8, 1992, article: "After Federal regulators found that Mr. McDougal's savings institution, Madison Guaranty, was insolvent, meaning it faced possible closure by the state, Mr. Clinton appointed a new state securities commissioner. . . ." The clear implication is that *in response* to a Federal Home Loan Bank Board [FHLBB] report dated January 20, 1984, suggesting that Madison might be insolvent, Clinton in January 1985 installed Bassett Schaffer as Arkansas securities commissioner for the purpose of protecting McDougal.

Bassett Schaffer's Appointment

So how come he waited an entire year? In reality, the timing of Bassett Schaffer's appointment had nothing to do with the FHLBB report, which there's no reason to think Clinton knew about. (The Clintons had no financial stake in Madison Guaranty, although that, too, has been obscured.) The fact is that Bill Clinton *had* to find a new commissioner in January 1985 because the incumbent, Lee Thalhiemer, had resigned to reenter private practice. Appointed by Republican Governor Frank White and kept on by Clinton, Thalhiemer says he told Gerth this in an interview, and describes the *Times* version as "unmitigated horseshit."

Bassett Schaffer strenuously insists that to this day she has never met McDougal, never heard Bill Clinton mention his name, and does not be-

> *"If McDougal shoved any funny money in the Clintons' direction . . . the Arkansas Securities Department sure found an odd way to reward him."*

lieve he influenced her appointment—and told Gerth so. She had actively sought the job from the moment she learned that Thalhiemer was quitting (he confirms recommending her to Clinton). She herself had volunteered in Clinton's 1974 congressional campaign and had worked for him full time on the Arkansas attorney general's staff while in law school. And her brother, Woody Bassett, also a Fayetteville attorney, was a personal friend and supporter of Bill Clinton.

The claim that Jim McDougal was behind Bassett Schaffer's appointment rests entirely on the word of McDougal himself, a victim of manic-depressive illness whose lawyer filed an insanity plea in a 1990 bank-fraud trial in U.S. District Court, in which McDougal was ultimately found not guilty. In his original 1992 article, Gerth had acknowledged McDougal's history of emotional illness but described him as "stable, careful and calm." By 1993 mention of those difficulties had all but vanished from the pages of the *New York Times*—despite the fact that the supposed recipient of Bill Clinton's largess was living in Arkadelphia in a trailer on SSI [supplemental security income] disability payments. Also unmentioned, for what it's worth, was that McDougal had long since recanted his accusations against Clinton and taken to blaming the whole mess on Republican partisans in the RTC.

Madison Guaranty's Insolvency

But did Bassett Schaffer help McDougal anyway? Did the Arkansas Securities Department, as Gerth asserts, have proof of Madison Guaranty's insolvency in early 1985? Did Bassett Schaffer have the legal authority to shut it down?

Consider the allegation that Madison was insolvent and Bassett Schaffer failed to respond. True, the 1984 FHLBB report did argue that Madison Guaranty had overestimated its profit from contract land sales—not including Whitewater—by $564,705. "Correcting entries will adversely effect [*sic*] net worth and result in an insolvent position." But is this proof of legal insolvency? Hardly. In the first place (although Gerth neglected to point this out), the title page of the document from which the *Times* reporter took the one brief passage he cited stipulated that it had "been prepared for supervisory purposes only and should not be considered an audit report." More significantly, federal auditors later accepted Madison's position on contract land sales, and the putative adjustments were never made. Indeed, on June 26, 1984, six months after the report Gerth cited, and six months *before* Bassett Schaffer took office, Madison Guaranty's board of directors met in Dallas with state and federal regulators. They agreed to enter a formal "Supervisory Agreement" with the FHLBB that spelled out detailed legal and accounting procedures designed to help the S&L improve its financial

> *"I never saw [Basset Schaffer] take any action that was out of the ordinary."*

position. In a letter dated September 11, 1984, the FHLBB gave Madison formal approval of a debt-restructuring plan that "negat[ed] the need for adjustment of $564,705 in improperly recognized profits" and dropped all references to insolvency. Arkansas officials also called Gerth's attention to an independent 1984 audit that also refuted Madison's insolvency. In his story the reporter neglected to mention either document.

If McDougal shoved any funny money in the Clintons' direction—either through Whitewater or an April 1985 campaign fund-raiser—the Arkansas Securities Department sure found an odd way to reward him. No sooner did Bassett Schaffer receive the FHLBB's 1986 report on Madison than she recommended stringent action. On July 11, 1986, she and a member of her staff flew to Dallas to meet with FHLBB and Federal Savings and Loan Insurance Corporation [FSLIC] regulators for a showdown with Madison's board. McDougal himself was not invited. McDougal was stripped of authority, and federal officials agreed to supervise the failed thrift until the FSLIC found money to pay depositors. When, a year later, Bassett Schaffer received an audit for 1986 (and a revised audit for 1985) officially reflecting that Madison Guaranty was insolvent, she wrote the FHLBB and FSLIC a letter, dated December 10, 1987, strenuously urging them to shut down Madison and two other Arkansas S&Ls. Fifteen months later, federal regulators (whose tardiness cannot be blamed on pressure from a state governor) finally locked Madison's doors.

Nothing Illegal

There is not the slightest evidence, then, that Bassett Schaffer inappropriately delayed taking action against Madison. Nor, it seems, did she bend the law when asked by Hillary Clinton to approve a stock sale by the ailing thrift.

Remember the dark hint of misdeeds in Gerth and Engelberg's December 15,

1993, story: "Just a few weeks after Mr. McDougal raised the money for [Governor Clinton], Madison Guaranty won approval from Mrs. Schaffer, Mr. Clinton's new financial regulator, for a novel plan to sell stock." Now, what made Madison Guaranty's plan "novel" is hard to say. The vast majority of state-regulated S&Ls in 1985 issued stock. Even so, the adjective, with its implication of wrongdoing, has recurred mantra-like in virtually every Whitewater roundup article since.

For Hillary Rodham Clinton to have ventured anywhere near Madison in any capacity was a damn fool thing to do. But the fact is that her entire involvement in the "novel" stock issue consisted of the mention of her name in a letter written by a junior member of the Rose Law Firm expressing the opinion that it would be permissible under state law for Madison Guaranty to make a preferred stock offering. After studying the applicable statutes and consulting with her staff, Bassett Schaffer agreed. "Arkansas law," she wrote in a two-paragraph letter dated May 14, 1985—the now-famous "Dear Hillary" missive—"expressly gives state chartered associations all the powers given regular business corporations . . . including the power to authorize and issue preferred capital stock." Bassett Schaffer had issued the narrowest sort of regulatory opinion. Had she ruled otherwise, Madison Guaranty would have had no difficulty finding a judge to reverse her. Anyway, no application was ever filed.

> *"When it became apparent that Clinton would run again in 1990, Nelson became a Republican and won the 1990 gubernatorial primary."*

The Arkansas Securities Department's power to close ailing S&Ls was mostly theoretical. Unlike the feds, Bassett Schaffer's office had no plenary authority to shut S&Ls down and seize their assets. Nor did Arkansas law make any provision for the state to pay off depositors of bankrupt S&Ls. That duty belonged to the FSLIC. "We acted in unison at all times," says Walter Faulk, then director of supervision for the FHLBB in Dallas. "I never saw [Bassett Schaffer] take any action that was out of the ordinary. Nor, to be perfectly honest, could she have gotten away with anything if she did. To my knowledge, there is nothing that she or the governor of Arkansas did or could have done that would have delayed the action on this institution."

Jeff Gerth's Connection to Arkansas

When I asked him about the discrepancies and omissions in his reporting, Jeff Gerth stood his ground, alternately argumentative and defensive, and did not wish to be quoted. He argues, for example, that he never literally wrote that Jim McDougal had *in fact* gotten Bassett Schaffer the job, merely that he'd claimed to. Her denial struck him as beside the point. In other instances, he pleaded limitations of time and space.

The perception that Gerth most resents is the one most talked about in Arkansas: his reliance upon the hidden hand of Sheffield Nelson—Clinton's 1990 Republican gubernatorial opponent and a legendary political infighter. The *Times* reporter insists that Nelson did no more than give him Jim McDougal's phone number and later introduce him to former Judge David Hale, whose defense attorney is Nelson's associate. Nelson, the Republican nominee for governor again in 1994, tends to be coy about his role. But he has given other reporters a thirty-eight-page transcript of an early 1992 conversation between himself and McDougal, then embittered by what he saw as Clinton's abandonment.

Indeed, Jeff Gerth, Sheffield Nelson, and the *New York Times* go way back. As long ago as 1978, Gerth wrote a well-timed exposé of Nelson's mortal foes Witt and Jack Stephens—the billionaire natural-gas moguls and investment bankers who ran Arkansas like a company store during the Orval Faubus era (1955–67). The Stephens brothers owned a small gas-distribution company in Fort Smith that was paying them at a better rate than other gas-royalty owners. But what made Gerth's piece significant was its timing: it appeared shortly before a Democratic primary in which the Stephenses' nephew, U.S. Representative Ray Thornton, was eliminated in a three-man race for the U.S. Senate. Gerth had promised local reporters he'd uncovered a scandal that would knock Thornton out of the race. Some observers think the *Times* article about the business dealings of Thornton's uncles did swing just enough votes in Fort Smith to keep him out of a runoff election won by Senator David Pryor.

Nelson's Gas Ventures

A few more highlights from Sheffield Nelson's political biography may help underline his motives for helping reporters portray the Clintons in the worst possible light. Hired out of college as Witt Stephens's personal assistant, Nelson was later installed as CEO of Arkansas-Louisiana Gas Co. (Arkla), controlled by the Stephens family and the state's principal natural-gas utility. (It was his subsequent refusal to use Arkla pipelines to carry gas from other Stephens-owned companies to buyers east of the state that eventually provoked a lifelong blood feud of Shakespearean malevolence.) Until 1989 Nelson was a Democrat, impatiently biding his time until the end of the Clinton era. But when it became apparent that Clinton would run again in 1990, Nelson became a Republican and won the 1990 gubernatorial primary over an opponent funded by Stephens interests. Bill Clinton then proceeded to humiliate Nelson 58 percent to 42 percent in the general election.

> *"Imagine the uproar had your tax dollars bailed out the Clintons rather than an embittered Republican politician."*

Clinton owed his 1990 triumph in part to the fact that his Public Service Commission conducted an inquiry into a business deal involving Nelson and a friend of Nelson's named Jerry Jones. It seems that back when Nelson was CEO of Arkla, he'd overridden the objections of company geologists and sold the drilling rights to what turned into a mammoth gas field in western Arkansas to Arkoma, a company owned by Jones, whom Nelson had brought onto Arkla's board of directors. The price was $15 million. Jones found gas almost everywhere he drilled. Two years after Nelson's departure, Arkla paid Jones and his associates a reported $175 million to buy the same leases back as well as some other properties. Jerry Jones then proceeded to buy the Dallas Cowboys and win two Super Bowls. The election-year probe of the Arkla-Arkoma deal resulted in millions of dollars of refunds to rate payers, which wasn't necessarily the point. It also earned the President a permanent spot on Sheffield Nelson's enemies list. The result, it's no exaggeration to say, has been Whitewater.

Another Land Deal

The talents of investigative reporters poring over Whitewater documents might be better spent looking into another McDougal real-estate venture. Sheffield Nelson and Jerry Jones put up a reported $225,000 each in return for a 12.5 percent share of McDougal's ill-conceived luxury retirement community on Campobello Island, New Brunswick, Canada. It was New Deal Democrat McDougal's odd conceit that wealthy vacationers and retirees would be moved by sentimental memories of FDR's [Franklin Delano Roosevelt] summer retreat (remember *Sunrise at Campobello?*) to purchase lots on a resort island that is in fact damp, cold, foggy, and remote. The Campobello project not only failed but helped pull Madison Guaranty down with it. Gerth and the *Times* have left that aspect of the Madison Guaranty story unexplored—even though, unlike Whitewater, the name of Campobello Properties Ventures is mentioned prominently and repeatedly in the very FHLBB examination report that Gerth quoted in his original March 8, 1992, article. Also unlike Whitewater, the Campobello project *did* put a big chunk of Madison Guaranty's scant capital at risk—some $3.73 million, to be exact, at a time when the FHLBB examiner contended that the S&L was actually $70,000 in the hole.

At last report, that particular picturesque stretch of Canadian coastline belonged to the Resolution Trust Corporation. Nelson and Jones, however, actually made a profit. In 1988, the FHLBB, then supervising Madison Guaranty's assets, bought the boys out for $725,000—leaving them a profit of $275,000. No doubt there's a plausible explanation, although William Seidman, chief of the FDIC [Federal Deposit Insurance Corporation] and the RTC at the height of the S&L crisis, told the *Fort Worth Star-Telegram* that "I can't believe it. It's an extraordinary event. It smells. It could be legit, but I doubt it." Gerth says the Campobello deal holds no interest for *Times* readers. But imagine the uproar had your tax dollars bailed out the Clintons rather than an embittered Republican politician feeding damaging allegations to the *New York Times*.

Chapter 2

Is the Legislator-Lobbyist Relationship Improper?

Legislators and Lobbyists: An Overview

by Greg D. Kubiak

About the author: *Greg D. Kubiak is a Washington, D.C., political writer and syndicated columnist. As an aide to former Oklahoma senator David Boren, Kubiak drafted congressional campaign reform legislation that was introduced to, and approved by, the U.S. Senate in 1993. Kubiak is the author of* The Gilded Dome: The U.S. Senate and Campaign Finance Reform, *from which this viewpoint is excerpted.*

In 1992, members of the U.S. Senate received an annual salary of just over $125,000. Yet the cost of running a successful race for election to that body averaged $4 million. Senators running for reelection must raise roughly $12,000 each week during each year of their six-year term to amass an adequate campaign war chest. To the average American, such funds must surely seem extravagant and such a fund-raising capacity exhaustive.

Even after being adjusted for inflation, the four Senate election (six-year) cycles between 1982 and 1988 saw an increase in the cost of winning a seat in the U.S. Senate—from 51 percent to 166 percent. In other words, when the seven elections from 1976 to 1988 were calculated by what the winning candidate spent (in 1976 dollars) to get elected, the results were as follows: the 1982 elections cost 100 percent more than in 1976; the 1984 elections cost 51 percent more than the 1978 elections; the 1986 elections cost 166 percent more than the 1980 elections; and the 1988 elections cost 54 percent more than 1982 spending.

Money Follows Power

Moreover, money follows power. On February 11, 1986, the *Wall Street Journal* ran a story entitled "Some Ways and Means Members Saw a Surge in Contributions During Tax Overhaul Battle." The piece, written by Brooks Jackson and Jeff Birnhaum, looked at individuals on the tax-writing committee, such as Rep. Wyche Fowler (D-Ga.). Fowler, who had only a 27 percent approval score from the pro-business barometer of the U.S. Chamber of Commerce (and, conversely, a 67 percent approval from the AFL-CIO [American Federation of Labor–Congress of Industrial Organizations]), raised over $57,000 in one day from Texas contributors affiliated with Quintana Petroleum Corporation of Houston at an event arranged by a Washington business lobbyist. Interested in tax provisions favorable to the drilling industry, Fowler, like others, received immense financial support from interests unaccustomed to contributing to liberal Democrats. (Over 40 percent of Fowler's 1985 receipts in his bid to unseat Sen. Mack Mattingly (R) in the 1986 race came from PACs [political action committees].) Then Congressman Judd Gregg (R-N.H.) told

> *"The 1986 elections cost 166 percent more than the 1980 elections."*

the *Wall Street Journal* that being on a prestigious, influential committee was "like night and day, being on the Science Committee before and being on Ways and Means now," in terms of raising money.

Indeed ABC's *20/20* reported in the midst of the markup of that tax bill that then Senate Finance Committee Chairman Bob Packwood (R-Ore.) was the top recipient of political action committee (PAC) money the previous year. Out of $966,016 in PAC money, $344,326 came from the insurance industry, $105,700 came from the banking/finance industry, and another $93,565 came from labor unions; all had a substantial stake in the tax bill.

A public interest lobbyist, Fred Wertheimer of Common Cause, told *20/20*,

> The system legalizes buying influence. . . . When I give you, a member of Congress, a substantial amount of money, we both know that you've accepted money from me and you know I have something in mind. . . . They [PACs] are buying a lot more than access. But even if that was all they were buying, what kind of system do we have, where you get access to your representative if you can put up a bunch of money?

People with money are ready, if not eager, to fill with money the outstretched hands of incumbents who come to them months, even years, before their elections. PACs are the most obvious, visible, and powerful force in providing money. And they do it for a reason.

Functions of PACs

In a 1985 interview about PACs, Tom Baker of the National Association of Home Builders, one of the largest such committees, told CBS News why contributions to incumbents were good investments. "We want access. We want to be able to get in the door and be heard."

But newspaper columnist Mark Shields reverses the viewfinder. In a 1991 column, he explained that PACs are not the principal villain in the corrupt system.

> PACs . . . are frequently victims of legalized extortion at the hands of incumbents who sit on congressional committees, the decisions of which can directly affect the fate, fortune, and future of the PAC's membership. Failure to con-

tribute carries with it the risk of loss of access to the fund raiser/ lawmaker and
no chance to please your members' taste.

PACs, which numbered 4,170 in 1990, became "the ultimate whipping boy in
the debate over reform," according to a May 1990 advertisement in the *National Journal*. The ad, placed by the National Association of Business PACs
(NABPAC), was part of a public campaign to remind Congress and the public
that—as a result of a previous reform bill—PACs "have stimulated millions of
Americans to become involved in our political system."

PACs cover a wide range of occupational and special interests, a spectrum beyond the categories of animal, vegetable, and mineral. There are committees for
avocado farmers, Native Americans, rum distillers, Walt Disney employees,
right-to-life advocates, sellers of Avon products, Ohio psychologists, and Veterans of Foreign Wars. Individually, they represent no threat to democracy.

But what has been their collective effect on congressional behavior and electoral competition? Whereas in the 1974 election cycle, PAC contributions only
made up about 17 percent of a House member's receipts, twelve years later that
figure doubled to 34 percent. The actual dollar amount contributions of PACs to
Congress grew from $12.5 million in 1974 to $149.9 million in 1990, nearly a
1,200 percent increase.

Seeking Influence

Such facts might not indicate cause for major concern to those who believe an
open system of government must allow for political activism in the form of financial assistance. However, if the system is truly "open," why is the staggeringly disproportionate share of that $149.9 million—a ratio of 11 to 1—going
to incumbents?

The answer lies in the fact that special, monied interests—PACs, lobbyists,
political fund raisers, and wealthy individuals—want "more than just good government" in return for their contribution, as a Senate leader once said.
Some may want an appointment, say,
ten minutes with the senator, to discuss a tax provision. Some may want
a vote against a nomination in the
committee of a senator. Some may

> *"People with money are
> ready, if not eager, to fill
> with money the outstretched
> hands of incumbents."*

just want an "insurance policy" of sorts, the ability to see the member of
Congress when they need him or her. People who give a $25 donation to a political candidate's bean supper fund-raising event may want "good government." However, people who write a $1,000 check to a congressman's
campaign committee probably want access.

Over the course of several years as a Senate aide, I came to discover that for
many in Congress, raising money is seen as a sport. The strategy, the hunt, the
catch, and the victory are immensely enjoyable, as though it were sportfishing
or a baseball game.

Contributions to Congressmembers Buy Their Influence

by Skip Kaltenheuser

About the author: *Skip Kaltenheuser is a writer and lawyer in Washington, D.C.*

Money in politics, passed by gloves both iron and velvet, surrounds a Congress that, as Barry Goldwater puts it, is "paralyzed with the fear of alienating" interest groups. Paralysis benefits the status quo and rockets the deficit. This should be our top domestic issue.

It isn't, of course, because campaign finance is Washington's hottest growth industry. Congressional races in 1992 cost $678 million, a 52 percent increase over 1990. Everyone is related to or friends with someone who milks the cash-based lobbying machine, or aspires to do so. It permeates the society scene, and even the Fourth Estate [the national media], with its own conglomerates' political action committees (PACs) and media seers who pick up speaker fees from lobbying groups.

Most important, it offers incumbents an incredible advantage. In 1990 the General Electric PAC gave money to 19 United States House candidates who faced no opponents, and to 70 more who had won past elections by margins of more than 3-to-1. Incumbents are reluctant to tamper with such a system.

PAC Contributions

From 1982 to 1985 AT&T enjoyed tax loopholes that garnered a huge rebate instead of having to pay taxes on $25 billion in profits. Its million or so in PAC contributions fell far short of the point of diminishing returns. The late Phil Stern, campaign reform champion and author of *Still the Best Congress Money Call Buy*, analyzed congressional votes and showed a stunning correlation between increasing levels of PAC money given and the percentage of recipients

Skip Kaltenheuser, "The Low Art of the Thinly Disguised Bribe," *Christian Science Monitor*, March 14, 1994. Reprinted by permission of the author.

who "vote right." The cash arms race escalates because the potential gain is astounding.

Consider President Bill Clinton's task in revamping an $800 billion-a-year health industry. Its 200 political action committees gave $60 million in PAC contributions to congressional candidates, plus individual contributions, during the 1980s.

In the mid-'80s, the American Medical Association's PAC dumped hundreds of thousands of dollars of "independent expenditures" (a clever sidestep around contribution limits) to attack a couple of popular congressmen who sought ceilings on Medicare fees. The failed attempt to dump them was viewed as a victory because, as the PAC chairman said, it sent "a message to everyone in Congress who won by 51 percent."

"When these political action committees give money, they expect something in return other than good government," Senate Minority Leader Bob Dole once wryly observed. Senator Dole, whose thrift-and-fortitude lectures are Sunday morning TV fixtures, gave Mr. Stern his favorite illustrations of money calling the tune. For example, in 1982 Dole chided Democrats like Rep. Dan Rostenkowski (D) of Illinois for assisting 333 wealthy Chicago commodity traders over questionable use of a tax loophole. He even com-

> *" 'We're looking closely at this,' is often code for 'It's on the block, open your wallets.' "*

plained to the Internal Revenue Service. Traders bumped up largess to Dole by a factor of six. Dole abruptly reversed, approving a proposal that took traders off the IRS hook, worth an average of $866,000 to each trader.

Not just cynics wonder how often lawmakers make noise about what's right just to get contributions flowing so they can afford to do what's wrong. "We're looking closely at this," is often code for "It's on the block, open your wallets." When markers are called in they can be as subtle as a pass not caught or a ball fumbled. Don't count on a toothless Federal Election Commission, crouched under the thumb of those it watches, to follow the play.

A Symphony of Influence

PACs and trade associations are dominated by members who are most active because they seek the most. When the economic marketplace doesn't pan out, they gild their pitch in a political bazaar focused on the short term. It's a poor formula for rational decisions, and often tilts toward losers. Cases made on money, not merit, breed inefficient and unfair results.

It isn't just PACs. The top 1 percent of income earners provide the vast bulk of campaign cash, giving more to candidates than do PACs—huge amounts in "soft money" to national and state parties, and toward charities associated with legislators. They orchestrate a symphony of influence.

Yet this system is defended as a great equalizer which enables little guys to pool money in democracy's "marketplace." One columnist lauded it as "an inherently messy brawl of competing egos, ambitions, factions, and interests."

Lobbying groups like the National Association of Manufacturers (NAM) purport to include the interests of small entities, but that's questionable when they conflict with better-heeled members. For example, the NAM advocates patent changes that clearly favor large multinationals over smaller firms.

In any case, if campaign money gives voice to the small player, it's a squeak compared to the operatic booms of those who can focus large amounts, including couples who pay $100,000 to attend fund-raising parties.

Years ago, I asked a top staffer of former U.S. Sen. Alan Cranston (D) of California how he coped with the flood of lobbying cash. His deadpan reply: "People think if they give you a lot of money, they're buying influence. But all they really buy is access." Charles Keating must have thought the fiction of a wall between influence and access funny. Taxpayers were less amused as they bought his and other savings and loan fiascoes to the tune of $150 billion, plus interest on the increased debt, after thrifts bought all the access they needed to hang themselves.

The Thinly Disguised Bribe

Some legislators collect most of their funds out of state, choose committee assignments based on fund-raising potential, run their own PACs, and use surpluses to salt state legislators who draw congressional borders. The tyranny of the tin cup forces senators to spend most of their time fund-raising, averaging perhaps $10,000 a week over six years, with roll-call votes suspended during the "cocktail hour primaries." Fancy job titles disguise the low art of the thinly disguised bribe.

Stern felt such influences fell outside the voter constituency the Founding Fathers had in mind, and saw no road back save "disinterested" public money. Private cash would be limited to small, pre-primary, in-state voter contributions to qualify candidates for "citizen financing." Independent expenditures, and expenditures by those refusing spending limits, could be neutralized by increased public financing for those in the system, who would also get cost breaks for the broadcast of substantive messages.

The cry that taxpayers must not be soaked to fund politicians is phony. The cost is minuscule next to, say, the

> *"Fancy job titles disguise the low art of the thinly disguised bribe."*

cannibalization of industries because corporate raiders could deduct interest on takeover debt, or the urban misery catered by the National Rifle Association. No system produces perfect decisions, but we're in a percentage game where the deficit has shrunk our margin for error.

Before its 1993 fall recess, the Congress offered proposals for reform that earned kudos but no passage. Meaningful improvements can be slyly gutted in conference. Even now, loopholes are cavernous. For example, there's debate over limiting an individual's aggregate federal political contributions to

$25,000 or $50,000. That's per year, and they can be doubled by a spouse and further increased by offspring who aren't minors. The House would allow "bundling," (the wallop of unlimited accumulation of individual contributions), for groups that do not lobby, despite well-known criteria for recipients that leave no doubt about the expected quid pro quo. So it goes. Flowing money finds the leaks.

Civic Decline

The currency devaluation of our vote destroys confidence in government and eats at our collective ethics. Desperate people sadly abdicate civic rights and responsibilities in favor of term limits, or look to an ever-ironic billionaire for shelter.

Voters weary of the shell games. Who figures the National Wetlands Coalition for a group of oil companies? Some groups conceal members (even NAM members can't get an NAM membership list). "Housewife," the most frequently listed occupation of large contributors, reveals nothing.

What mentality does all this cultivate? A small U.S. high-tech company was bewildered at hearings when former Sen. Robert Packwood (R) of Oregon ran interference against it on behalf of Mitsubishi, the Japanese conglomerate. Not now. Recent allegations of special arrangements to ward off criticism of Mitsubishi are surprising only in degree. Once practices that are criminal in other branches of government are accepted as commonplace, limits start to drift.

> *"Once practices that are criminal in other branches of government are accepted as commonplace, limits start to drift."*

Our system saps public confidence, cripples innovative government, and excuses legislators from making difficult choices.

Demagoguery tempts as politicians are left to succeed not with better ideas but by engineering the failure of the opposition. That guarantees a downward spiral for America.

Legislators-Turned-Lobbyists Act Improperly

by Fred Barnes

About the author: *Fred Barnes is the executive editor of the conservative mag-azine* Weekly Standard *and a commentator on the public television show* The McLaughlin Group.

As they left the floor of the House of Representatives last June, members were accosted in the cloakroom by an ex-con. He also happened to be a former colleague—Larry Smith, who represented Miami in Congress from 1983 to 1993.

Fresh from serving three months for income-tax evasion and filing a falsified Federal Election Commission report, Smith was back in his former haunt—as a registered lobbyist. He was buttonholing old associates on behalf of his new client, the Cuban American National Foundation. Later, Smith joined forces with one of Washington's premier public-relations firms, the Kamber Group. Explained company chairman Vic Kamber: "He didn't murder or rape anyone. He paid his dues."

Smith's case may be colorful, but it is hardly unique. In Washington there are scores of ex-members of Congress—retired or defeated—who have become highly paid lobbyists for trade associations, business interests, political pressure groups, even foreign governments. These superlobbyists have what other lobby-ists don't: ex-members' right of unlimited access to the House and Senate floors, cloakrooms and gyms.

They peddle influence in ways that would have been unthinkable a generation ago. After Senate Commerce Committee Chairman Howard Cannon (D., Nev.) was defeated for re-election, he occasionally managed to sit on the dais during hearings. Although not a registered lobbyist himself, Cannon worked for a law firm that did lobbying.

Once, the services of former legislators weren't so coveted in Washington. But as the federal government claimed an ever bigger chunk of the economy (about 22 percent in 1994), corporations, trade associations and labor unions decided they needed more help in dealing with government regulators and bureaucrats. Former Senators and House members have been only too happy to guide clients through the forest of federal regulations that they helped create. These lawmakers-turned-lobbyists are Democrats and Republicans, liberals and conservatives. Steve Symms was an apple grower in Caldwell, Idaho, when he ran for Congress on the anti-Washington slogan "It's time to take a bite out of government." Symms, a Republican, served eight years in the House and 12 in the Senate denouncing big government. Retiring in 1992, he set up shop near the capital—as a lobbyist.

Special Access. The massive turnover in Congress last fall triggered a new round of job-seeking by departing members. Most were Democrats, but Republicans were more successful because Congress is now GOP-controlled. Even former Sen. David Durenberger (R., Minn.), under federal indictment for filing false statements to the Senate, was hired as a part-time consultant by APCO Associates, a public-relations firm that does some lobbying. (Durenberger has denied any criminal wrongdoing.)

Former Congressmen often can get through to key people when other lobbyists cannot. "There's that personal relationship," says former Rep. Tim Penny (D., Minn.). "You're going to take their call, let them come by for a cup of coffee or talk to them on the House floor."

In his early days as a Senator in 1987, John McCain (R., Ariz.) remembers he was walking off the Senate floor with former Sen. William Hathaway (D., Maine). "Next thing I know, he's lobbying me hard," recalls McCain.

Former Rep. Tony Coelho (D., Calif.) says as House whip he had to run former members out of the House chamber because of brazen lobbying. After leaving office in 1991 under an ethical cloud in the savings-and-loan scandal, Coelho joined a prestigious investment-banking firm. He now makes $1 million a year. Although he is not a registered lobbyist, Coelho acknowledges that clients (whom he refuses to identify) seek his guidance on how to maneuver in Washington. "It happens all the time," Coelho told the New York *Times.* "I will give them my best advice, based on 25 years in government."

> *"Former Senators and House members have been only too happy to guide clients through the forest of federal regulations."*

Old Congressional relationships are often exploited by former members to gain special indulgence. Sen. Paul Laxalt (R., Nev.), who retired in 1986, had his friend Sen. Jesse Helms (R., N.C.) help arrange an appearance by a trade expert last summer before the Senate Republican Steering Committee. His mission: to attack international trade legislation. Laxalt, who said it was not lobbying but a "briefing session," represents textile tycoon Roger Milliken, a fierce opponent of the legislation.

Former Rep. Tom Tauke (R., Iowa) leads the government-affairs office of NYNEX, the regional telephone company in the Northeast. To get his messages out, he had friends in Congress book private rooms on Capitol Hill, where he hosted luncheons to discuss telecommunications issues. These were attended by important Congressional aides.

Defeated for renomination in 1992, Rep. Carroll Hubbard (D., Ky.) was hired as a consultant by the Washington-based Independent Bankers Association of America. "In law, it's not what you know, it's who you know," he told *Public Citizen* in 1993. Hubbard later pleaded guilty to theft of government property, obstruction of justice and conspiracy to impede the Federal Election Commission. In November he was sentenced to three years in federal prison.

Better Pay. Until the last decade or so, former members of Congress routinely returned home when their Congressional careers ended. But that was before the big money arrived. Now some never consider returning to their districts. "Going home wasn't an option," says Laxalt. "A former Senator practicing law in a small state like Nevada would likely confront one conflict of interest after another. I wasn't independently wealthy. I had to make a living."

> *"Ex-lawmakers who are only 'moderately successful' at lobbying earn $250,000 to $400,000 a year. (The salary of Senators and Representatives is $133,600.)"*

Former Sen. Warren Rudman (R., N.H.), a Washington lawyer who doesn't lobby, estimates that ex-lawmakers who are only "moderately successful" at lobbying earn $250,000 to $400,000 a year. (The salary of Senators and Representatives is $133,600.)

Just getting a client through a Senator's or a Representative's door pays handsomely. When he was a Senator, Rudman recalls, he once, as a courtesy, met with a former House member and the agribusiness group he was escorting around Congress. Rudman later learned that the former Congressman had charged the agribusinessmen $75,000 to $100,000 for a week-and-a-half's work.

No wonder legislators are willing to quit midterm to take major lobbying positions. Rep. Bill Gradison (R., Ohio) resigned only months after he was reelected with 70 percent of the vote in 1992 to run the Washington-based Health Insurance Association of America. He had been a key member of the House Ways and Means Committee, which writes tax legislation. According to *National Journal* research, the former Congressman's salary was more than $544,000 in 1993.

In 1994 Rep. Glenn English (D., Okla.), a high-ranking member of the House Agriculture Committee, left the House in midterm to head the National Rural Electric Cooperative Association. His predecessor's pay: $231,000.

For most former Senators and Congressmen, lingering in Washington comes naturally. "If you played baseball for 15 years and decided to give it up, you'd probably look into coaching and managing," says Ed Jenkins (D., Ga.), another high-ranking member of the House Ways and Means Committee who left Congress in 1992. "You know the operation. You know the team. And the owner is more likely to look for a former player." With a former Congressional assistant, Jenkins has set up a major Washington lobbying shop.

A federal law barring ex-members from lobbying the House or Senate for one year after retirement is supposed to limit the activities of superlobbyists. However, the law has little effect because they can lobby the Executive branch from day one.

Rep. Beryl Anthony, Jr. (D., Ark.) bounced 109 checks at the House bank and was defeated for renomination in 1992. A former member of the House Ways and Means Committee and the brother-in-law of then-deputy White House counsel Vince Foster, Anthony was quickly signed up by the Washington office of Winston and Strawn, a Chicago law and lobbying firm whose clients included major participants in last year's health care debate.

Dispensing Dollars. Some former lawmakers bring more than just access to the lobbying business. Under current law, they can use unspent campaign kitties to contribute to people they will be lobbying. The Center for Public Integrity, a Washington watchdog group, has documented a number of such arrangements:

• As a member of the House, Rep. Norman Lent (R., N.Y.) was a partisan Republican. As a partner in his Washington lobbying firm, however, he is clearly bipartisan, having dispensed $14,298 of his unused campaign funds to 24 House members, seven of them Democrats.

• Former Rep. Marvin Leath (D., Texas) retired in 1991 and became a lobbyist. Taking with him his leftover campaign funds, he paid $131,717 in taxes to the IRS, then distributed $19,900 to assorted House and Senate candidates.

• Rep. Ronnie G. Flippo (D., Ala.) left Congress in 1990 after a losing race for governor. He took with him $485,009 in unused campaign funds, set up a Washington lobbying firm and donated $27,850 in 1991 to Congressional incumbents of both parties.

> *"[Former legislators] can use unspent campaign kitties to contribute to people they will be lobbying."*

Moneyed foreign interests are some superlobbyists' best clients. Former Rep. Wayne Owens (D., Utah) registered as an agent of Jordan. Former Rep. Toby Moffett (D., Conn.) is the Angolan government's lobbyist.

Few former Congressmen have labored as vigorously for a foreign client as ex-Rep. Michael Barnes (D., Md.), the chief lobbyist for President Jean-Bertrand Aristide of Haiti. Barnes has notable connections. He was chairman of the House Foreign Affairs Subcommittee on Latin America and ran President Clinton's campaign in Maryland in 1992.

For his work lobbying for the ousted Haitian leader, Barnes's law firm was paid handsomely by Aristide. Barnes worked tirelessly in presenting Aristide's case, talking to dozens of members of Congress. His biggest success, however, may have been with the White House, which switched from uncertain support for Aristide in January 1994 to backing his September return and sending troops to make it happen. The Haitian operation has cost American taxpayers nearly $1 billion.

Perhaps the most outrageous lobbying arrangement was entered into by former Reps. David Bowen (D., Miss.) and John Murphy (D., NY.). Bowen did not run for re-election in 1982 after serving five terms. Murphy, a seven-term veteran, was retired by the voters in 1980 after he was caught taking an "illegal gratuity" in the FBI's Abscam sting. He served 20 months in federal prison. Murphy and Bowen helped set up G.B.M. Consultancy Limited in 1992. Their client: Hassan Tatanaki, a Libyan national who was performing services for the benefit of Muammar Qaddafi's

> *"Increase the period during which former members can't lobby Congress from one to five years."*

dictatorship. Their contract: $450,000, plus $225,000 in expenses. Their mission: to arrange for a "normalization" of Libyan relations with the United States. Libya has paid millions to buy friends in Washington. It wants to free up its assets, which have been frozen in the United States since 1986 as a result of its sponsorship of terrorism.

Because G.B.M. had not obtained a required Treasury Department license, these lobbying efforts were illegal. Murphy was fined $10,000 and Bowen was fined $20,000. That kind of punishment hardly deters foreign governments and their agents from covertly seeking influence.

What can be done to curb the scandal of ex-members of Congress who lobby? These measures should help:

• Increase the period during which former members can't lobby Congress from one year to five years, thus making the bridge from lawmaking to influence peddling far more difficult.

• Apply the same ban to lobbying the Executive branch.

• Tighten the rules on what constitutes "lobbying" to include such services as providing "strategic advice" and conducting "seminars."

• Make former Congressmen abide by the same rules that govern everybody else in the lobbying game. This would eliminate the use of Congressional facilities for lobbying.

The election of the 104th Congress offers a historic opportunity for change. The new Republican leadership, under House Speaker Newt Gingrich (R., Ga.) and Senate Majority Leader Robert Dole (R., Kan.), has promised serious political reform. The people who elected these new leaders have every reason to hold them to their word—especially when it comes to putting their own house in order.

Gifts from Lobbyists Influence Legislators' Actions

by Frank R. Lautenberg

About the author: *Frank R. Lautenberg has served as a Democratic U.S. senator from New Jersey since 1983.*

Editor's note: The following viewpoint is from an October 7, 1994, speech in the U.S. Senate supporting passage of the Lobbying Disclosure Act of 1993, a bill subsequently defeated by the Senate.

As Members of Congress, we are often frustrated by our inability to solve problems. Some of us decided that a major reason for that inability was the structure of our own institution. So we decided to fix our own house, clean up our own act, and regain some of the public faith and support that government has lost.

We may have made the problem worse. We hoped to reform the campaign finance system. We did not. We hoped to simplify and modernize the organization of the Congress. We did not. We hoped to pass legislation bringing the Congress under the same laws as the rest of the country. We did not. We hoped to reduce the influence of special interest lobbyists by requiring greater disclosure of their activities and eliminating their ability to ply Members with food and entertainment and trips. And now it looks like we will not.

There may be some who oppose this last reform on the list because they honestly have problems with the language of the legislation. But when we offer to fix the problems they have identified, we are told, "Oh, thanks. But I just found a few more."

The People's Voice

My constituents do not want to listen to me tell them why we did not do something. They want me to listen to them and do something about their prob-

Frank R. Lautenberg, "Should the Conference Report on S. 349, the Lobbying Disclosure Act, Be Approved?" (Pro response), *Congressional Digest*, December 1994.

lems. That is what the gift ban lobbying reform bill is all about. Making it easier to hear our constituents instead of the special interests who buy us dinner and give us tickets to events and take us on trips. Their voice, amplified by their power and access and wealth, make it hard for us to hear the voice of the people we were elected to represent.

Let us pass these bills. We have offered to fix what may be the legitimate problems some have found in the legislation. Let them accept the offer and let us get on with our business. The business of building this country rather than tearing it down.

Let me explain why a gift ban is so necessary. Right now, our constituents do not believe we represent them. They think we are being influenced by the special interests—that they give us gifts in order to secure our support for their views.

And make no mistake about it. That is the motive for the gifts if not their effect. We do not get free tickets to concerts or sporting events because we are charming companions. We do not get taken out to dinner or flown away for free vacations because people like us. We get those things not because of who we are but because of what we are: Members whose actions and votes influence public policy and can mean a difference of millions of dollars for a company and contracts for lobbyists.

Undue Influence

I am not claiming that my colleagues are being "bought and sold" for a dinner or a round of golf. That is not my argument at all. I do, however, make two arguments. First, the public believes there is undue influence being exerted. It may be an example of post hoc reasoning; it may be a valid concern. But it is a fact. During House debate on this issue, one Member said, "I cannot be bought for a cup of coffee." I agree. But why can he not buy his own cup of coffee? What kind of sacrifice would that involve? We accept other sacrifices as part of the price of being in public life. We surrender, for example, a lot of our privacy; we lose control of our own schedules and lives; we give up many things in order to serve. This gift ban does not ask us to give up anything. It simply demands that we pay for everything. That is the sort of sacrifice people make in the private sector. It is the least we in public service can do.

> *"Our constituents do not believe we represent them. They think we are being influenced by the special interests."*

But there is a second argument in favor of this bill. It is not just an appearance problem. Gifts do not buy our votes but they do influence our actions. Not because we got a gift. But because we spend an hour or two at a game or a restaurant with the lobbyist who uses that time to subtly make sure we are aware of the arguments which favor their position. There is nothing wrong with them making their case. What is wrong is giving them a special route of communica-

91

tion, an extended period of access, a unique opportunity to make their case. Most constituents are fortunate if they can get a 15-minute meeting to discuss their concerns directly with a Member of Congress. Lobbyists are paid to make sure they have a lot more time than that. Gifts which must be enjoyed together is one way to get the time; develop access; exercise influence.

I know that this bill will not cure everything that is wrong with the way Washington works. As others point out, we may be buying our own dinner, but we will still be getting checks for $10,000 from PACs [political action committees] and $1,000 from individuals. I wish we had changed the campaign finance law. But our failure there does not mean that we ought to fail here. A gift ban will have an effect in and of itself. It will change the way business is done, alter the relationships which too often affect legislation, eliminate the excesses which so pollute the public perception of politics.

> *"Gifts do not buy our votes but they do influence our actions."*

The Law Is Flawed

Let me make one final point: The gift ban and the lobby disclosure bill have been properly joined together. You cannot have one without the other. Current law designed to disclose lobbying activity is fatally flawed because most lobbyists are not required to register. We can't find out what they are doing and how much they are spending to get it done. I think that information is essential; it certainly would be interesting to know how much was spent on the lobbying effort designed to convince Senators that this bill would chill free speech. I think the people of this country would be interested in knowing that it was the very lobbyists they think have too much power who used that power to fool them and defeat this bill. There is an irony there which we ought to appreciate. And there is a lesson there we ought to learn.

Congressmembers Are Too Solicitous of Lobbyist Contributions

by Martin Schram

About the author: *Martin Schram, author of* The Great American Video Game: Presidential Politics in the Television Age, *is a syndicated columnist and a regular panelist on* Reliable Sources, *a CNN television program.*

Bathed in the rose-orange hues of a springtime sunset, the Capitol dome gleamed in deceptive brilliance as the U.S. Senate voted in May 1994 to ban itself from taking freebies from lobbyists. No gifts, no junkets, no winings-and-dinings. Soon to be gone, forevermore.

Bathed in the white-hot TV light that is now the official afterglow of every Washington newsmoment, Common Cause crusader Fred Wertheimer was more than glowing—he was gushing— about the 95 to 4 vote. "This will *fundamentally change* the way business is done in Washington and on Capitol Hill," he declared.

Bathed in the light gloss of perspiration, a passel of self-proclaimed populist senators dashed off the Senate floor, out the Capitol door, down the street, and into the special non-taxpayer-supported offices of their campaign committees. There they reached for their phones and began conducting their twilight ritual: dialing for dollars.

No Fundamental Change

Nothing in their overwhelming vote was going to *fundamentally change* their daily quest for campaign cash from the lobbyists who represent the special interests their committees oversee. If that Senate vote dealt with any kind of change, it was just chump change—a ban on baubles, bangles, and bright shiny beads. It said nothing about quasi-bribes, the very legal solicitations that senators and representatives undertake each day.

Make no mistake: The senators and representatives who are now posing as populist reformers by banning themselves from taking small gifts are still campaigning for re-election under rules that permit (some would say "compel") them to solicit (some would say "shake down") special interests for contributions. American folklore is rife with tall tales (handed down from Will Rogers to Mort Sahl to Johnny Carson to Jay Leno) about lobbyists with bulging wallets who prowl the Capitol corridors, buying (or at least renting) legislators for the price of a campaign contribution. But the truth is that it works mainly the other way.

> *"You have to work every day for six years to raise enough money to run for re-election."*

Every day, our elected officials dial up lobbyists and lawyers who control the PACs (political action committees) of the special interests (corporations, labor unions, and citizen do-gooders) whose fates and fortunes are under the jurisdiction of their congressional committees. The legislators are not dialing to swap pleasantries. They are calling, quite simply, for money: $5,000 or $10,000 or even $15,000 if they are soliciting the maximum amount for a primary, a primary runoff, and a general election. It is about as close to soliciting bribes as payments of money can legally be. Every senator and representative and lobbyist knows the law. So no one mentions any specific piece of legislation. They know the rules. But they also know how to play the game.

Playing the Game

Sen. John Glenn, D-Ohio, is sitting comfortably at a private phone in the posh offices of the Democratic Senatorial Campaign Committee. He has just voted to ban himself from taking trinkets from lobbyists. Now he is asking lobbyists to give him big bucks— $5,000 and $10,000—and the irony does not escape him.

"There is this dichotomy that drives you crazy," Glenn says. "We'd just voted in these new ethics rules that say we can't accept a hamburger from the lobbyists. But we can ask them for $5,000 from their PAC and $1,000 from him and his wife. It's just plain crazy."

Understand where Glenn is coming from: Three decades ago, he was astronaut John Glenn, circling the world in a semi-crouched position, jammed into a cramped space capsule the size of a golf bag, while the world held its breath. But now Glenn, who remains an Eagle Scout by Washington standards, finds himself jammed into another uncomfortable position. He feels forced to pander.

"Its gotten so gosh-darned expensive to campaign that you have to work every day for six years to raise enough money to run for re-election," he says. "If you haven't come into someone's home via television, you're not going to get their vote. So here we are, spending an inordinate amount of time each day, not doing the people's business but just raising money."

The reason? The cost of campaigning for Congress has skyrocketed to sheer lunacy. Sen. Dianne Feinstein, D-Calif., who raised $8.1 million to win her Senate seat in a special election in November 1992, now finds she must raise a reported $22,000 a day—yes, each day!—to amass the $10 million she figures she'll need to keep her seat. The system by which we now finance our democratic process virtually forces Feinstein and her colleagues to quit doing the public's business for hours each day so they can dial for dollars.

Shaking Down the Money Trees

Collegiality, of course, is the official rule in the House and Senate. But the competition gets fierce, back in the cloakrooms, when members joust for committee assignments. Yes, some still look to match their expertise—but most are seeking a committee that will provide an enriching experience. Enrichment, in the form of campaign contributions, comes with the turf for those who get seats on the House Ways and Means and Senate Finance committees, tax-writing panels where lobbyists anxiously work the corridors daily. But all committees that oversee major industries—banking, commerce, energy—prove lucrative for the campaign contribution needs of their members.

The greening of the members of the Senate Banking, Housing, and Urban Affairs Committee stands as a living, self-renewing monument to the price we pay for the system by which we underwrite democracy. The extent to which special interests from banking, Wall Street, real estate, and insurance underwrote the campaigns of senators who oversee their industries is meticulously documented in *Open Secrets: The Encyclopedia of Congressional Money and Politics* by Larry Makinson and Joshua Goldstein of the Center for Responsive Politics (where I am a senior fellow). Their analysis shows that contributions are bipartisan—the special interests are far more interested in influence than ideology.

> *"The thing that gets [lobbyists'] attention—and their PAC money—is whether the representative or senator has the clout."*

A conservative—Sen. Alfonse D'Amato, R-N.Y.—was the Banking Committee's champion shaker of the banking and financial money trees. D'Amato received $1,143,033 for his winning 1992 campaign from banking, finance, real estate, and insurance interests. A liberal—Sen. Christopher Dodd, D-Conn.—received almost as much from the same special interests: $967,075. A moderate—Sen. Arlen Specter, R-Pa.—collected $844,347 from those whose business is overseen by the Senate Banking Committee.

Contributions to members of the parallel committee in the House—Banking, Finance, and Urban Affairs—also illustrate the corrosive influence of special interests. Consider Rep. Charles Schumer, liberal Democrat from New York: It was his House Judiciary Committee work on crime-fighting issues that put him in the news spotlight so frequently—but it was Schumer's seat on the House

Banking Committee that put him in the chips as he raised $407,746 in 1992 campaign contributions from banking, finance, real estate, and insurance interests. Schumer was the committee's number-two recipient of money from industries it oversees. The champion shaker was Rep. Tom Campbell, R-Calif., who got $842,114 from these industries for his unsuccessful Senate race.

The Way It Works

Some members of Congress make their own solicitation calls, and others have an aide solicit for them, but lobbyists say it makes little difference. The thing that gets their attention—and their PAC money—is whether the representative or senator has the clout to make a difference to their special interest.

House Ways and Means Chair Dan Rostenkowski, whose desire for dollars was chronicled in a 17-count indictment [prior to his defeat in the 1994 election], never called to ask for money, lobbyists say. "And yet we all lined up to give him all the money he wanted," concedes one of Washington's most prominent lobbyists. Senate Minority Leader Bob Dole also shuns the chore of dialing for his own dollars. Dole's aide makes the call; then if the contribution is promised, Dole calls later, just to say thanks.

But many of Washington's grandest congressional celebs do make their own calls. Sen. Orrin Hatch, the ever-dapper, ever-conservative Republican from Utah who holds positions of influence on the Senate Labor, Finance, and Judiciary committees, makes his own solicitation calls—and does not like to take no for an answer. Lobbyists from finance and industry hold Hatch in high regard but cite him as a member who, while always proper, can be most persistent, even if he is not always persuasive.

A typical call from Orrin Hatch to a lobbyist from the world of finance and industry goes like this (we won't put the words in quotation marks, because no one was taking notes; but lobbyists swear this is the way it sounds from their end of the phone):

Hi. Orrin Hatch here. How are you doing? Have you heard about the fund-raiser I'm having? I need $10,000 from you. (The lobbyist says that's more than the PAC can afford.) *But I need it.* (The lobbyist says the PAC doesn't give that kind of money anymore.) *But this is ME!*

> *"Have you heard about the fund-raiser I'm having? I need $10,000 from you. . . . But this is ME!"*

Rep. Henry Waxman, a liberal Democrat from California, is both a major power on the House Energy and Commerce Committee and an influential voice of reform. But he says that while he's pro-reform, he can't afford to be shy about picking up the telephone and making some calls to raise money. He raises money for himself and for his colleagues, and he does it just the way everyone else does—by calling those who have particular interests before his committees. As chairman of the subcommittee on health and the environment, Waxman has been adept at getting maximum allowable contributions from some lobbyists whose special interests rarely coincide with Waxman's more progressive politics. And when Waxman doesn't get the full $5,000 contribution he requested from a health interest group he rarely supports, he'll usually come away with $3,000. "I'm sure they are thinking, 'Well, most of the time Waxman won't be doing us any good, but sometimes he'll do what he can'—so they contribute something," Waxman says.

> *"[Companies] can use the bundle loophole and give as much as they want."*

It is also instructive to look at Waxman's quick rise to power in the House. Working squarely within the system and the law, Waxman created his own PAC and contributed some $24,000 to the 1978 campaigns of his House Energy and Commerce Committee colleagues. These recipients were, in turn, duly grateful, and they voted to make Waxman a subcommittee chairman, bypassing the more senior moderate who was in line for the job, Rep. Richardson Preyer. D-N.C., who eventually retired.

Showdown at the K Street Corral

Campaign Finance Showdown Nears; House, Senate Leaders Deadlocked Over Limiting PAC Donations.
                                    —*Washington Post* headline, June 27, 1994

All along Washington's K Street, the lawyers and lobbyists who mass-produce loopholes—it's the capital's only local industry—know this "showdown" fuss is bogus. The law limits contributions by a PAC to $5,000 per election, and well-intentioned reformers want to cut that in half. But these limits aren't hard to get around: In 1992, 21 senators and 29 representatives received campaign contributions from an individual corporation or special interest that exceeded $20,000 (twice the legal limit), and one received $130,405—13 times the legal PAC limit from a single special interest! It's all perfectly legal—through a loophole called bundling, in which a company or other special interest has its executives write out personal checks to a candidate's campaign, then wraps the checks as one big bundle of joy to make sure the candidate can measure just how grateful he or she should be.

Since 1907, it has been illegal for companies to give direct contributions. But they can create PACs through which they can give in limited amounts. Or they can use the bundle loophole and give as much as they want. Securities firms have been the most energetic corporate bundlers; seven securities firms made the *Open Secrets* list of 1992's biggest bundlers for needy senators. Lobbyists are understandably proud of their bundling loophole and know it won't be effectively closed by any "showdown" compromise.

Ironically, Capitol Hill's 1992 recipients of the biggest and second-biggest bundles from a single special interest were two liberal first-termers. Sen. Barbara Boxer, D-Calif., received $130,405; Sen. Carol Moseley-Braun, D-Ill., received $83,190. They topped all of corporate America's traditional pals because women's rights groups got their activism together and outbundled the big boys.

The women's rights PAC, called EMILY's List (for "Early Money Is Like Yeast"), bundled almost $1 million in reported large contributions of $200 or more; EMILY's List actually takes credit for bundling as much as $6 million when individual small donations are included. But lest the liberals and women's rights advocates get swept away by their success, the sobering fact is that their money (be it $1 million or $6 million) is dwarfed—and will always be dwarfed—by the total from corporate America.

Right behind the bundles received by Boxer and Moseley-Braun, for instance, was D'Amato's $62,051 bundle from Bear, Stearns & Co. He also got a $32,600 bundle from Goldman, Sachs & Co.; $28,450 from Morgan Stanley & Co.; $24,605 from Merrill Lynch; $23,600 from Smith Barney; $22,990 from Coopers & Lybrand.

Just Say No to PACs (with a Wink)

Bundling and other schemes to organize individual contributions enable high-minded politicians to refuse publicly to take PAC contributions—but still get plenty of special interest money. Sen. John Kerry, a liberal Democrat from Massachusetts, has taken a firm stand against taking money from PACs. But Kerry, a vocal supporter of campaign reform, has taken gladly from special interests, according to Makinson and Goldstein. About 30 percent of Kerry's contributions of $200 or more came from individuals representing special interests voted upon by the Senate Commerce, Science, and Transportation Committee on which Kerry sits. His contributions included $239,125 from entertainment and communications firms regulated by that committee; among them: Time Warner, Walt Disney Co. and the Disney Channel, Continental Cablevision, and MCA Inc.

"As viewed by the lobbyists, heavy-handed hits from senators and representatives are a bad problem that has gotten worse."

About 27 percent of his contributions of $200 or more came from individuals representing special interests before the Senate Banking, Housing, and Urban Affairs Committee on which Kerry also sits. He received $853,441 from finance, insurance, and real estate interests. Kerry also received $670,205 from Washington lawyers and lobbyists—individuals who no doubt represent interests before his committees.

Senators and representatives also need not stop shaking the lobbyists' money trees just because a lobbyist's PAC has maxed (that's Washingtonspeak for having contributed its maximum legal contribution). They then ask the lobbyist to host a fundraiser at his or her home or office and invite other lobbyists to come for cocktails and check-writing. Or, if the member of Congress has enough Capitol clout, for dinner.

Washington lawyers work at hosting these affairs where fellow lobbyists can meet-and-greet members of Congress with the sort of indefatigable energy that lawyers in other cities employ inside courtrooms. According to fellow lobbyists, attorney Thomas Boggs of Patton, Boggs, and Blow—son of the late House Majority Leader Hale Boggs and retired Rep. Lindy Boggs of Louisiana, brother of ABC's Cokie Roberts—is the undisputed champ at hosting a meet-and-greet. "I must get one invite a week from Tommy to come to a meet-and-greet in his office," says one lobbyist.

> *"Even in the doldrums of June, one lobbyist received 34 requests for funds in one week."*

Lobbyists' Lament

As viewed by the lobbyists, heavy-handed hits from senators and representatives are a bad problem that has gotten worse. The solicitations pour daily into the K Street office of Neal Gillen, a well-connected and well-respected lobbyist for the cotton industry, by phone, by fax, by midday mail. His cotton industry PAC is quite modest in size. But there is nothing modest about the volume of solicitations he receives.

"It never stops," Gillen says. "About half of my faxes these days are solicitations. The worst are the guys who call and ask you to host something at your home—a fund-raiser dinner. They say, 'My campaign is tapped out, and I've got to raise money to get out a mailing.' Mostly I just say no."

Some years ago, Gillen and fellow lobbyist Clarence Martin of the American Psychological Association tried to find a humorous way to bring some law and order to the shakedown system. They drew up a bill that made it a violation of federal law for senators or representatives or their staffs to solicit funds from anyone registered as a lobbyist with Congress. Figuring that members might not see the humor in a threat to send legislators to the calaboose, they decided the bill should be sponsored by two representatives: one had the surname Love, the other Kindness. But their visions of "The Love and Kindness Bill to Protect Lobbyists" came acropper because of unforeseen difficulties. They discovered that Love was no longer in Congress—and then Kindness didn't take kindly to the idea. "He threw us out of his office," Gillen laughs.

Even in the doldrums of June, one lobbyist received 34 requests for funds in one week. One celebrated lobbyist says the solicitations have gotten so out of hand that lobbyists now play a little trick on senators and representatives. Because the law prohibits politicians from soliciting contributions from offices supported by federal tax dollars, the politicians go to special facilities set up by their party's campaign committees to do their dialing.

"When we get a call from a senator or representative, we need to know if it is a call about legislative business, or a solicitation for money. So we have our secretary tell the senator or representative, 'He's on the phone now, but if you give me your phone number, he'll call you right back—just as soon as he gets off the phone,'"says the lobbyist.

"Now, if we see that the senator is calling from a 224 exchange or the representative is calling from a 225 exchange, we know it's from the Capitol and we call right back. But if they leave a 675 or 863 or 479 number, we know they're in their campaign fund-raising office. And then, well, we often don't get around to returning their call."

Looping the Loopholes: Public Funding

There is only one way the American people can end the abuses by which special interests now invest in campaigns and reap huge profits on their investments at our expense. We must be willing to support a new system of democratic financing of congressional campaigns—with public financing as the centerpiece. We will discover that we have bought ourselves a bargain.

Here's why: Special interests do not think of it as *contributing*—they consider it *investing*. And they are investing so grandly in political campaigns because they have calculated that they'll reap grander profits in return, in the form of legislative decisions—an unwarranted subsidy here, an undeserved tax break there. What Americans must recognize is that the tax money that the government spends to finance all or most of the Senate and House campaigns will cost us millions less than what our government is now spending on subsidies, tax breaks, and assorted bonanzas that are often just paybacks to the special interests.

> *"It will cost the federal treasury $500 million a year— about $5 per taxpayer, each year—to finance all congressional campaigns."*

Various proposals for public financing have gained credence in recent years. The Working Group on Electoral Democracy, an organization of grassroots organizers and researchers, advocates "democratically financed elections" based upon total public funding of campaigns. To qualify for public financing in a primary election, House candidates would need to demonstrate their initial public support by raising 1,000 contributions of $5 each; Senate candidates would need to raise 2,000 contributions of $5 plus 250 additional contributions from each of the state's congressional districts.

Two experts, Jamin Raskin and John Bonifaz, worked up some detailed cost figures for such a system in an article published in the *Columbia Law Review* in May 1994. They say it will cost the federal treasury $500 million a year—about $5 per taxpayer, each year—to finance all congressional campaigns. Their plan, however, would require TV and radio stations to provide free time to candidates.

My own view is that we shouldn't ask the stations to donate their revenue-producing product when we don't require newspapers, cable TV, airlines, phone companies, and even button- and bumper-strip makers to do the same. Some counter that TV and radio broadcast stations are different because they use public airwaves. That's true, but no longer really relevant. Years ago a community had only public airwaves—no cable channels—and station owners had a real monopoly. In today's cable-wired world viewers choose from among scores of TV cable channels. So why penalize a broadcast station owner and give every cable station owner a free ride?

> *"This system is just no good—period. . . . There's a never-ending chase for money."*

TV ads account for a third or less of most campaign spending, so double or even triple that $500 million figure to pay for broadcast media ads and taxpayers would still get a bargain rate for democracy—we would be paying $1 to $1.5 billion a year. That's a lot of money, but it pales when compared to the $500 billion that the General Accounting Office says we'll pay over the next 40 years to bail out the savings and loan [S&L] industry. We're paying that price because in the '80s, members of Congress became too willing to look the other way when their S&L contributors decided to get richer quicker.

New Lines of Support

As fund-raising pressures force senators and representatives to spend more and more time dialing for dollars, a strange phenomenon is starting to take hold: The idea of public financing, in full or in part, is gaining new receptivity and even glimmerings of sound support. Politicians don't like to talk about such matters publicly. They know the public rates them even below car dealers and journalists. And they know that a voter's reflex reaction will be to shout: "I don't want one dollar of my taxes going to some politician's campaign!" But the pols also know how many billions of tax dollars go to the special interests who are their prime contributors.

On the rare occasions when you hear a pol speak out for public financing, you'll usually find you're listening to a liberal. So you won't be surprised that liberal Henry Waxman, though himself a masterful raiser and dispenser of private funds, is a strong advocate of some form of public financing. "This system is just no good—period," says the California Democrat. "There's a never-ending chase for money. We need to get the idea of raising money off the minds of the members of Congress."

But you might be surprised to hear a cautious moderate like John Glenn, not given to impetuous pronouncements, declare that it is time for a change:

> It's difficult and obnoxious to have to run the way we do now, having to spend every waking hour worrying about raising money. I think we should be at least doing something for the Senate and House races like we do for the presidential

races— maybe a [federal income tax] checkoff or some way of providing matching funds to candidates.

And you should be astounded to hear Sen. Larry Pressler, a conservative Republican from South Dakota, begin to rethink the unthinkable. "I'm not for public financing in any way," he begins, adding: "Campaign reform has gone nowhere—backwards, in fact, in my view." But after we talk about the time wasted dialing for dollars, and why big givers are really giving, Pressler shifts slightly. "You may be right," he says. "I'm sort of on an intellectual odyssey, struggling with this. I have to rethink this. We have to do something."

The Beat Goes On

The irrepressible Sen. Alfonse D'Amato is surrounded by influential lobbyists. They are wining-and-dining in one of Washington's fine private clubs, as these lobbyists do regularly, inviting one official as their guest. It is a time for light banter and heavy candor. Not dealmaking, but a time when all sides can learn which positions have been taken just for public show, which ones can be bartered, and which ones are bottom line.

On this evening D'Amato informs his hosts that this is their last get-together. After all, he says, the Senate just banned lawmakers from accepting free wining-and-dining from lobbyists— "and I ain't paying for bleep."

To which one of the lobbyists creatively constructs a new loophole: "Hey, Al, YOU can pay for it with the money our PACs give to your campaign committee."

D'Amato thinks it over and replies: "So it's your money anyway? OK! OK!"

Political Action Committees Benefit Politics

by Herbert E. Alexander

About the author: *Herbert E. Alexander is a political science professor at the University of Southern California and is the director of the Citizens' Research Foundation in Los Angeles.*

Political action committees, better known as PACs, are the most visible and controversial manifestation of the campaign finance reforms of the 1970s.

Today, a vast array of groups attain a measure of political activism at the federal level through their PACs. While the individual voter is seldom powerful enough to present a particular viewpoint before the government and the public, an association of many individual voters usually will be heard and may be respected. PACs act as an institutionalized outreach by providing a process to gather contributions systematically through groups of like-minded persons for whom issues are a unifying element in their political activity.

Raising Money

In the 1993–94 election cycle, PACs of all kinds raised $391.0 million and spent $387.4 million. Their cash reserves at the end of 1994 totalled $98.8 million. They contributed $189.4 million to 1994 candidates for the Senate and House of Representatives. Some 3,954 PACs were registered with the Federal Election Commission at the end of 1994.

The growth of PACs since the federal campaign laws of the 1970s took effect merely adds a new testament to an observation first made by Alexis de Tocqueville during the young French nobleman's visit to the United States during the 1830s.

"In no country in the world," de Tocqueville wrote about the fledgling nation, "has the principle of association been more successfully used or applied to a

Herbert E. Alexander, "The PAC Phenomenon," in *Almanac of Federal PACs, 1996–1997* (Arlington, VA: Amward Publications, 1996). Reprinted by permission of the publisher.

greater multitude of objects than in America." And, he concluded with admiration: "There is no end which the human will despairs of attaining through the combined power of individuals united into society."

While PACs are a relatively new phenomenon, they really fit naturally into the larger stream of American political life which has often witnessed the creation of new forms of association to further people's interests and goals.

Simply stated, a PAC is a political arm organized by a corporation, labor union, trade association, professional, agrarian, ideological or issue group to support candidates for elective of-fice. PACs raise funds for their activities by seeking voluntary contributions which are pooled together into larger, more meaningful amounts and then contributed to favored candidates or political party committees.

> *"While PACs are a relatively new phenomenon, they really fit naturally into the larger stream of American political life."*

Essentially, PACs are a mechanism for individuals who desire to pool their contributions to support collective political activity at a level higher than any individual could achieve acting [alone]. The PAC's donors are thus simultaneously exercising speech and association rights which are both protected by the First Amendment.

Constitutional Difficulties

Lawmakers who advocate restrictions or prohibitions of PAC contributions in federal elections acknowledge the constitutional difficulties that are inherent in their proposals. A reform measure introduced in 1995 by Sens. John McCain (R-Ariz.) and Russell Feingold (D-Wis.), and endorsed by President Bill Clinton in his 1996 State of the Union message, contains a "fallback" provision that would lower the PAC gift limit of $5,000 per candidate per election to $1,000 if another provision that would ban PAC contributions altogether is found unconstitutional. Supporters of anti-PAC legislation have trouble with the logic of their proposals which recognize the rights of citizens to engage in political speech and to associate freely with like-minded individuals, but would make it unlawful to engage in both First Amendment–protected activities simultaneously.

PACs also help facilitate fundraising for office seekers who would find it difficult, costly and inconvenient to solicit each of the PAC's donors on an individual basis. Corporations and labor unions, for example, are better equipped to raise money because they have access to large numbers of employees or members, an internal means for communicating with them, and specific political goals.

Our nation has always had special interests. The "mischiefs of faction," as they were called by James Madison, were discussed at length in the *Federalist Papers*. Madison realized that a major challenge to a free democratic government was to allow these groups the freedom to disseminate their political views while ensuring that no single faction could dominate the government. His answer was to let "ambition counteract ambition." This simple declaration is the essence of pluralism: that democracy works best when many conflicting, competing groups present their ideas in the political arena and ultimately before the voters.

PACs Are Not Monoliths

However, most of the criticism of PACs has questioned Madisonian assumptions about political groups. PACs are viewed by their detractors as well-ordered monoliths, neatly queuing up for favors from an obedient Congress whose members depend on large PAC contributions for re-election.

This viewpoint incorrectly assumes that PACs dominate the financing of congressional campaigns. Although all PACs, including labor and environmental, did account for a significant share of campaign fundraising by 1993–94 congressional candidates—some 31.3 percent of the funds raised by House candidates and 14.6 percent of the funds raised by Senate candidates—they by no means monopolized such giving. (These percentages are based on fundraising from all sources, including personal loans and gifts which candidates made to their own campaigns. Thus, the percentage for the Senate may be skewed by California Republican candidate Michael Huffington's personal expenditure of $27 million, as well as other self-contributing candidates.)

PACs are not major contributors to presidential campaigns, accounting for only about one-half of one percent (about $900,000 of the total 1992 presidential prenomination receipts, the least amount contributed since 1976). No private funding is possible in the general election period, although some PACs spend money directly in parallel campaigning and by making independent expenditures.

The assertion that PACs act as a monolith also crumbles upon inspection. In assessing the influence of PACs, it is important to remember that they represent many different, and sometimes competing, interests. The differences in structure, purpose, procedures and processes among corporate, trade association, labor union and other membership PACs and single-issue PACs are immense. Some allegations focus on corporate PACs as if the business community acts as one. It does not. Some PACs serve "high tech" industries, others' interests are of the "smokestack" variety; some favor high tariffs, others do not; the steel PACs and the aluminum PACs represent industries that compete, as do the banks and the thrifts. Because of competition or divergent interests, the business community does not march wholly in the same direction.

> *"PACs . . . represent many different, and sometimes competing, interests."*

How PACs Began

The history of PACs can be traced back to the time of World War II. Since 1907, federal law prohibited corporations and national banks from making money contributions in connection with federal elections. When the wartime

Smith-Connally Act of 1943 extended that prohibition to labor unions, the Congress of Industrial Organizations set up a separate fund to solicit voluntary contributions from union members for the purpose of making contributions to political candidates. This, most observers agree, was the first PAC. Other labor organizations followed in the CIO's footsteps and, by the late 1950s and early 1960s, they were joined by some business and professional groups which also established PACs.

It was not until the 1970s, however, when Congress enacted the Federal Election Campaign Act and its amendments that PACs, other than those formed by labor unions, began to flourish. A key provision in the federal law enabled corporations to use their general treasury funds to pay the costs of establishing and administering PACs and to pay the costs of soliciting contributions from their stockholders, executive and administrative personnel and members of their families. In similar fashion, labor unions were permitted to use money collected as dues payments to set up and administer PACs and pay the costs of soliciting contributions from members and their families.

Filling Needs

In contrast, ideological and single-issue PACs, without an organization to sponsor them, must pay their own administrative and solicitation costs with the political money they raise from their supporters. The increasing importance of PACs is related to the decline of another mechanism of political action: the major political parties. Party influence has diminished successively since the Civil Service replaced party-controlled patronage as a means for filling government jobs; since government-sponsored social services replaced those which urban party organizations had used to attract the allegiance of voters; [and] since television led attention to be focused on individual candidates independent of their parties. Compared with their period of greatest influence in the late 19th and early 20th centuries, parties now find themselves in a greatly weakened condition.

In some measure, PACs have filled this void, too. They represent loyal constituencies, they fund primary and general elections and, some would say, they even "discipline" the votes of Members of Congress.

Further, there are socio-economic factors which have influenced the development of PACs. One factor is that, more than ever before, there are today definable groups—business, labor, single-issue and ideological—

> *"There are today definable groups—business, labor, single-issue and ideological—which are seeking government attention."*

which are seeking government attention. More demands are made for government action to meet needs, correct injustices and render advantages and entitlements. Since the growth of government programs affects still more citizens, the response—both pro and con—is the formation of still more groups.

106

Each subgroup has the effect of fragmenting larger groups, thus weakening the force of the front-runners. In time, no one's voice is heard effectively, with the exception of those with large resources making political contributions, or those scoring dramatic impact through demonstrations or other attention-getting devices.

Changes in Politics

Pluralism has become more extensive: the more groups there are, the more diffusion takes place and the weaker the impact of any single one. Modern technology triggers more ways to communicate and, consequently, more clamor for access. So many are now standing on tiptoe that few can see any better. As a result, many groups find it more efficacious to form their own PACs and make direct contributions to candidates rather than rely on a political party to be the intermediary between themselves and the public office seekers, something which would tend to diffuse their message. Generally, PAC contributions provide direct access to candidates, both challengers and incumbents, on a one-to-one basis.

The growth of PACs has been helped along by the dramatic shift from neighborhood politics to nationalized socio-economic and interest group politics. Corporations and labor unions, for example, are socio-economic units replacing geographic precincts. The workplace and the vocational specialty have come to attract the loyalty of the politically active citizens, replacing loyalties once enjoyed by the political parties. PACs are better able to adapt to these changes than are political parties. This is because PACs can focus on single issues or give priority to emerging issues and still survive with limited but devoted constituencies, whereas parties must attain broad-based consensus in order to survive.

Money and Influence

As PACs have gained influence, they have become increasingly the object of criticism. Poll data indicates that a majority of Americans feel that too much money is spent on elections, and that those with money to spend on elections have too much influence over government. Critics suggest that contributions give PACs undue influence over election results; that PACs favor incumbents and thereby decrease the competitiveness of election campaigns (71.3 percent of all PAC contributions in the 1993–94 election cycle went to incumbents); and that PAC sponsors enjoy extraordinary access to office-holders and exert decisive influence on legislative decisions, making it difficult for lawmakers to represent the interests of the public as a whole. And some critics further argue that PAC contributions are inherently corrupt, serving as legalized bribery of candidates for public offices. Such critics argue that election finance reform should

> *"As supporters of PACs point out, men and women who are elected to federal office are not easily manipulated by outside influences."*

move in the direction of further restraining PACs.

While it is true that the percentage of congressional campaign funds contributed by PACs has increased steadily since 1972, contributions from individuals remain the single largest source of political funds, albeit a declining one in recent years.

But, as supporters of PACs point out, men and women who are elected to federal office are not easily manipulated by outside influences. To the contrary, Congress is filled with people who were drawn to careers in public service in large part by their strongly held political and ideological beliefs.

However, there is one common understanding among PAC supporters and detractors: PAC growth has been substantial and PACs will continue to be controversial as major suppliers of political campaign funds.

Lobbyists Provide a Useful Service

by Thomas Hale Boggs Jr.

About the author: *Thomas Hale Boggs Jr. is a lawyer and lobbyist in Washington, D.C.*

Shakespeare's "kill all the lawyers" has been replaced with "kill all the lobbyists." Journalists at most major publications have joined the chorus. In an editorial, for example, [the *New York Times*] described the "threat that corporate influence and big-time lobbying represent to enlightened populism."

I agree that the system needs to be changed. Campaign finance reform, stricter lobbying disclosure rules and post-employment restrictions for Government officials and employees would serve the democracy well. But few commentators ever stop to consider the legitimate role lobbyists play in policy-making.

Critics charge that the use of lobbyists by special interests is unfair, that if members of Congress respond to the influence of special interests, they are somehow acting contrary to the benefit of their constituents as a whole.

Clients' Own Special Interests

All interests are special and every individual and organization seeks to advance its own special interests. In the last quarter of 1992 alone, the House Clerk listed more than 6,000 registered lobbyists, who were supported by tens of thousands of additional personnel. These individuals fight for the interests of 40,000 registered clients, including religious organizations, foreign governments, the Boy Scouts, doctors, gambling organizations, trial lawyers, consumers, environmental protectionists, baseball players—the list goes on and on.

To cite a few of my firm's activities, is it unfair to: Lobby for Federal assistance to Chrysler to save thousands of jobs? Seek a regulatory structure to keep newspaper publishers from being forced out of business by legal monopolies? Help defeat a constitutional amendment on flag burning? Seek legislation making it easier for homeless people to vote?

Lawyer-lobbyists advocate the position of their clients. Our first role is to determine the proper forum—the courts, Congress or a regulatory agency—in which the client can seek to achieve its goals.

When the issue involves Congress, we prepare substantive materials explaining the issue and the likely impact on the member's district: How many jobs are at stake? What's the likely impact on the local economy? We help to identify and mobilize grassroots constituents who agree with our client's position. We build coalitions among these diverse groups.

The Lobbyist's Power

Facts are the first source of a lobbyist's power. Forty-three percent of House members have served less than five years. Newspapers cannot give them the substantive detail they need. Congressional staffs are overworked and underpaid. Lobbyists help fill the information vacuum.

The second source of the lobbyist's power is money. In 1992 House races, including uncontested seats, major party candidates spent $369,000 on average. That's less than $1 per voter. Citizens see more advertising for hamburgers and beer than for political candidates. The problem with the campaign finance system lies not in the amount spent but in the incursion on a member's time that fund-raising entails. In a $500,000 campaign, the member may have to make 4,000 phone calls at two calls per contribution to get an average contribution of $250.

Lobbyists help by raising money from clients, colleagues and allies. And the help brings influence, connections and returned phone calls. But anyone can give or raise money. A lawyer cannot become a truly effective lobbyist without strategic skills and information, which can be shared with the member of Congress.

The first source of power—facts—is essential to the democratic process. The second—fund-raising—we all could do without. Meaningful campaign finance reform would reduce this source of power.

To take the fund-raising burden away from the candidate, and with it the need to rely on lobbyists' assistance, we should strengthen the parties and make them the primary recipients and distributors of campaign funds. We could begin with a transition period when candidates could raise a fixed amount, which would be matched by the party. As the parties grew stronger, candidate fund-raising could be phased out.

> *"Congressional staffs are overworked and underpaid. Lobbyists help fill the information vacuum."*

Many observers advocate public financing and permanent campaign-spending limits—ill-advised proposals, in my opinion. Public financing requires spending limits, and such limits would protect incumbents blessed with name recognition, franking privileges and free media time. Voters need more information, not less. Candidates, particularly challengers, spend money to get their message to the people.

Other reforms are needed. Lobbying disclosure rules only require the reporting of meetings with a member of Congress to influence him or her about pending legislation, along with very limited information about the legislation involved. The rules should be amended to include contacts with executive branch officials. A central repository should be maintained with uniform reporting requirements for all types of contacts. More detail should be required on the subject involved.

> *"The democratic process works best when all 'special interests' are heard and all information is available to policymakers."*

Some limitation on post-government employment lobbying should be maintained. But the restriction cannot be so Draconian as to limit the talent available to the legislative and executive branches.

Overcoming Gridlock

A third source of lobbying power has waned with time. In the 1980's, lobbyists were needed to bridge the gap of divided government. On occasions when gridlock was overcome, lobbyists usually played a significant role in bringing factions of the two parties together. Conversely, lobbyists in the 80's could use gridlock by championing partisanship in order to obtain the opposition of the White House or Congress to the proposals of the other branch.

But the American people spoke clearly in November 1992: no more gridlock. Public officials and lobbyists alike should get that message.

The system has some problems. Too much time is spent raising money, and lobbyists play too important a function in that regard. But the democratic process works best when all "special interests" are heard and all information is available to policymakers. Lobbyists serve an important role in the process.

Lobbyists Benefit the Legislative Process

by James M. DeMarco

About the author: *James M. DeMarco, a graduate of Notre Dame Law School, is an attorney in Evanston, Illinois.*

Much has been written concerning the expanding role of the federal government in American political history. With the Industrial Revolution, the expansion of interstate commerce and rail transportation, and the need to counter post-reconstruction backlash in southern states, the federal government found its law-providing role expand. Administrative agencies performed much of this new federal work, and the role the federal government had in the economy gradually shifted from that of enabler to that of manager.

Growth of Lobbying Groups

With the rise of federal managerial control, groups evolved to represent the industrial interests affected (i.e., chambers of commerce, labor unions, etc.). By the 1950s, organized industrial interests found themselves lobbying regularly in Washington for their respective interests. Over time, the federal role in everyday life has grown, stemming from the vast array of federal programs established during the New Deal and continuing through the Great Society. Traditional industrial lobbying groups have become unable to represent to Congress the opinions of national constituencies on all issues. A vast array of new interest groups, focused on the much more specific and complex issues faced by Congress, has arisen to lobby Congress for their constituents' needs.

Congress continues to pass increasingly generalized statutes, which have led to expanded federal law and a larger role for administrative agencies. Today, administrative agencies enforce the legislature's intent by fleshing out the details of Congressional policy. Because administrative agencies must follow the general guidelines of their enabling legislation, parties interested in a particular issue have an increased incentive to lobby Congress for protection of their in-

Excerpted from James M. DeMarco, "Lobbying the Legislature in the Republic: Why Lobby Reform Is Unimportant," *Notre Dame Journal of Law, Ethics, and Public Policy*, vol. 8, no. 1, 1994, pp. 610-17. Reprinted with permission.

terests at the policy-making level. Thus the broadening scope of federal statutes has led to an increase in organized interest groups who lobby to affect the overall focus of legislation. In sum, the increased complexity of federal law and the rise of administrative agencies have precipitated increased lobbying of the federal legislature.

The increase in specific programs to deal with complex needs has caused a corresponding increase in groups interested in individual issues. Large lobbying groups work for national constituencies, but their methods are similar to those used by smaller, more narrowly focused lobbying groups. To see how influential these groups are, and what kinds of influence they exert in the House of Representatives, one needs simply to look at their methods of operation.

Lobbyists Play Multiple Roles

Contrary to popular opinion, lobbying groups generally do not trade campaign funds for votes. Bribery and influence-peddling are much more myth than reality in the current American political scene. Lobbying groups operate, as the numerous training manuals on how to lobby suggest, openly and under close scrutiny.

The role of a lobbyist is to influence legislation as an active representative of constituents. There are various specialties within the field of lobbying. The stereotypic lobbyist, known in the industry as the contact person, maintains contact with legislators to remain a familiar face and recognized voice when a legislator considers relevant legislation. Most of a contact person's work is done not by glad-handing but rather by telephone and letter contact. Communications via letter and telephone are means to provide information to legislators.Contact people maintain connections most strongly with legislators most open to influence.

> *"Contrary to popular opinion, lobbying groups generally do not trade campaign funds for votes."*

Other forms of lobbying involve organizing grass-roots support for a particular legislative program, watching the legislative calendar to keep constituents informed of important Congressional activities, developing a lobbying strategy, and, importantly, making sure legislators are apprised of both relevant facts and a group's opinion on major issues.

Lobbyists Build Coalitions

Lobbying activities mirror the coalition building of a legislature. Individual representatives find they have much better success when working with others toward a common interest. When a particular lobbying group hopes to enact or to oppose a piece of legislation, it assembles a cadre of groups with similar interests to increase their effect. Synergy among lobbying groups increases not only the resources available for a project but also the claim of representation of popular interest. Once popular support for (or against) a measure is organized, the lobbying system operates symbiotically with the legislative system: key players are contacted, information on the issues is shared, legislators are polled for support, administrative agencies are contacted for support, testimony is given, and the legislative process runs its course. The central role of lobbyists in this process is to enable legislators to form opinions by offering information.

Lobbyists focus their attention on those most important to their group's success. Because of the specialization of the House in its committee

> *"Groups use money to keep friendly voices in power, not to keep powerful voices friendly."*

system, lobbyists need only contact a handful of representatives concerning passage of particular legislation or administrative oversight. Thus lobbyists can concentrate their efforts rather than going to the expense of contacting 435 representatives. The structural relationship that intimately connects lobbyists with specific representatives may lead to legislative capture.

Grass-Roots Organizing and Fund Raising

Lobbyists use press and advertising campaigns and grass-roots measures such as mass-mailing to muster support for their viewpoint. A classic example of this method is the work on the Cable Reform Act of 1992. Groups supporting the Cable Bill, including the Association of Network Broadcasters and the Consumer Federation of America, aired many advertisements on network television asking for mail-in campaigns in favor of the bill. At the same time, cable regulation opponents advertised warnings (on cable channels) about the potential effects of the legislation. Regulation supporters succeeded in generating enough popular support for the bill that it passed overwhelmingly, becoming the only bill to overcome a veto during President George Bush's administration.

The history of the Cable Reform Act illustrates another aspect of lobbying, namely, campaign spending. Conventional wisdom suggests that special interest groups and PACs [political action committees] spend money on political campaigns so to ensure that a legislator will favor them in the future. In fact, the converse is true. Lobbying groups expend personal and financial resources to support legislators who have shown them support in the past. Groups use money to keep friendly voices in power, not to keep powerful voices friendly. Money interrelates with access, not with voting. Indeed, many works describing the methods of lobbying mention campaign contributions only briefly.

Lobbyists Act in Symbiosis with Congress

Lobbying works not to control Congressional voting but rather to complement the work of Congress. Lobbying groups aid Congress by demonstrating the desires of the public and private organizations whose goodwill substantially affects significant portions of the public. Lobbyists share important information with lawmakers. Lobbying groups act as secondary access points to Congress, thereby increasing the amount of public influence exerted in Washington. The effect of lobbying should be positive, so long as lobbying activities are open and above-board.

Also contrary to popular myth, lobbying groups generally avoid using underhanded methods of influencing legislators, mainly because such methods are highly ineffective. Because the two primary activities of a lobbying group are information-sharing and generating popular support, credibility is of primary importance for effective lobbying. If a group loses its credibility by misstating facts or by using unethical methods of influence, legislators will mistrust that group's influence and popular support will evaporate.

Lobbyists survive in Washington not on the power of the money they spend, nor on the connections they maintain, because individual Congressional representatives are too independent from lobbyists to allow them to hold too much power. Lobbyists succeed by demonstrating the importance of the viewpoints they represent and the measure of support that exists for their positions. PACs and other quasi-public groups maintain a counterbalancing view against powerful public-interest lobbies and other opposing interests, and vice versa. This multiple presentation of interests empowers Congressional representatives to make better-informed decisions. Thus, lobbying

> *"[Lobbyists'] multiple presentation of interests empowers Congressional representatives to make better-informed decisions."*

generally aids Congressional decision-making rather than hindering it. If lobbying groups ever effectively counter public demand and thereby capture Congressional policy, they succeed by taking advantage of a Congressional system that places power in the hands of only a few representatives. Lobbyists do not maintain the stranglehold that most people think they have on Congress. The hands around the Congressional neck are its own.

Chapter 3

Is Scrutiny of Politicians' Character and Conduct Warranted?

Chapter Preface

Allegations of sexual misconduct can taint, or even terminate, a politician's career or term in office. In 1992 and 1994, Bill Clinton's image became tarnished in the minds of many Americans after allegations surfaced that as Arkansas governor he had had an extramarital affair and had sexually harassed a woman in his Little Rock hotel room. In 1995, Bob Packwood resigned after serving twenty-seven years as a U.S. senator amid charges that he had sexually harassed several female staff members.

Accusations such as these raise the question of whether sexual behavior is a proper litmus test of politicians' character and ability to serve the public. Many Americans believe that sexual conduct is less important than other criteria—or is even totally irrelevant—in judging a politician's character. For example, according to a May 1994 *Newsweek* poll, while 28 percent of Americans thought that Clinton's involvement in the Whitewater affair (an investigation into Arkansas real-estate and savings-and-loan deals) was "very important" in judging his presidential capabilities, only half as many (14 percent) thought his extramarital sex life was "very important." Television commentator Roger Rosenblatt offered another perspective when he said, "You could have a guy who's the worst son of a bitch on earth, and because he never cheated on his wife, he looks moral."

Other observers believe that sexual conduct is wholly relevant to a politician's character and that such behavior should not be so easily dismissed. In the words of author Thomas C. Reeves, "Sexual misbehavior can be, depending on the facts, a significant indicator of character. If [a politician's] record includes, say, adultery [or] fornication . . . , let us face those facts." Authors Larry J. Sabato and S. Robert Lichter write, "Philandering matters to many voters. The American people should be the judge."

Many media experts agree that whether sexual behavior is a legitimate character issue or not, scrutiny of politicians' sexual conduct will likely continue. The viewpoints in the following chapter address issues of politicians' character and conduct.

A Politician's Character Is Crucial

by Meg Greenfield

About the author: *Meg Greenfield is a columnist for* Newsweek *magazine.*

I propose we get rid of the term "character issue" in our political chitchat. My purpose is not to get rid of the subject itself. On the contrary, it is to enlarge its sweep and acknowledge its importance. "Character issue" tends to set the subject aside, makes it sound marginal, implies that it is but one on a list of qualifications we need to inspect—along with the candidate's position on NAFTA [North American Free Trade Agreement], say, and his attitude toward campaign-financing reform. But we don't elect disembodied opinions. We elect men and women (and they appoint other men and women) who have to operate, to see that some things happen and others don't. The kind of people they are— their values, their strong points, their weaknesses, their intelligence, their characteristics as people, in short—is what makes them good or bad at public office. It is everything.

Segmented Views

That is not the way it's thought of now. As reflected in the press and in public discourse, character has come to mean several other things. A durable and wrongheaded one is behavior *outside* the public arena, that is, in private life or relationships with individuals who are not part of the political picture. It is this segmented way of viewing public people that accounts for the basic argument when a politician is charged with sexual or other misbehavior in his personal life. The segments are weighed against each other, so that you will hear people say that although Politician X (President Bill Clinton this week, various senators other weeks) has been accused of doing some scabrous thing or other, he is good on health care or defense, and since this is what really matters, why not let him get on with it.

The Relevance Argument

What we have here is one variation on the larger, even all-enveloping, "relevance" argument. People who charge a political figure, whether it is Bill Clinton or Clarence Thomas or Bob Packwood or Gary Hart, with personal transgressions (1) are routinely told that they must show how this is relevant to the public business the political figure is expected to conduct and (2) are always able to do so. This last is because we are all very elastic and opportunistic and resourceful in our ability to find reasons to support our preferences in politics. There has been a lot of hooting in the Paula Jones affair [stemming from Jones's accusation that Clinton sexually harassed her in 1991] about how right and left have changed sides. Why this is considered surprising or even novel I cannot fathom. Right and left habitually change sides on what were thought to be large issues of principle when their political interests change.

Politicians—at least those feeling the heat of charges arising from some aspect of their personal conduct, family or social life, etc.—make a fetish of arguing that whatever they are accused of does not meet the relevancy-to-public-office test. They make a mistake here. When they attempt to cordon off private conduct this way, they let their misdeeds be taken as the sum total of their character or of "the character issue": good on the deficit, rotten on the character issue. They should instead be insisting that everything goes into the character profile and that position papers on issues do not make up the whole of their public life any more than the personal scandal of the moment defines their character.

It is a tired old truism in Washington that the scandals of the past couple of decades, whatever their nature and whatever the political party of those who perpetrated them, were marked by this one common phenomenon: the accused got into much more trouble for what they did after the lapse was discovered than for the lapse itself, never mind how grave. You may sometimes see as much about the character of your average political person, in other words, in the way he or she responds to the charges as you will in the nitty-gritty of the misdeed itself. What I am saying is that an ability to withstand adversity, not to panic, to take responsibility for one's behavior and not lay it off on others and so forth are virtues in a public person that count right along with the spectacular scandals in totting up the overall score on character. I think people tend to set great store by these and even to forgive political people for personal misbehavior on we're-all-only-human grounds if they show themselves mature and responsible in the aftermath of disclosure and in their ordinary conduct of office. But, of course, this bank account has limited, nonrenewable funds in it, and the public won't let any official make repeated withdrawals from it. That's abuse.

> *"Politicians . . . make a fetish of arguing that whatever they are accused of does not meet the relevancy-to-public-office test."*

Chapter 3

Beyond Journalists' Questions

For us in the news business there is a separate set of rules. Is it true? Is it fair (as a representation of overall conduct)? And, yes, is it something on which a public figure must yield his right of privacy even though for others it would be regarded a private matter? On the last of these questions I think there is an ascending scale for the loss of privacy, with the president being entitled to least: practically everything about him is relevant. But finally the judgment we must make goes well beyond all these questions. It concerns what makes a *suitable* character for a person in high office.

> *"The mature, not to say sane, adult political leader has integrated public and private conduct and public and private values."*

This requires more detachment and sophistication than we are often willing to bring to the subject. It concerns weighing what kind of virtues and what kind of, well, vices are helpful in getting the nation's public business done. I don't say that personal squalors of the kind we have been regularly informed of in our public people in contemporary times are justifiable, let alone good. But I do say that, especially in executive office, getting things to happen at all can call on resources of craftiness, slipperiness, toughness, artful dodging and a lack of sentimentality verging on cynicism in the reading of others that you sure don't get in a Barney. The trouble is that most of our public leaders, including our presidents, pretend to *be* Barney . . . I love you, you love me, we're a blah, blah, blah. Their critics and often we in journalism seek to define their character, their essential self, by the worst of their failings. They respond by pretending to be that big, overstuffed, purple bag of eternal selflessness and cheer.

Governing isn't talk, it's doing. So is character. Character isn't something that happens after office hours. And it isn't grown men and women behaving, or pretending they behave, like nonexistent, ideal children. The mature, not to say sane, adult political leader has integrated public and private conduct and public and private values. Character is something we should be thinking about. But we haven't been thinking about it the right way.

The President's Character Should Be Scrutinized

by Thomas C. Reeves

About the author: *Thomas C. Reeves is a history professor at the University of Wisconsin-Parkside and the author of* A Question of Character: A Life of John F. Kennedy.

The president and first lady today face several allegations that challenge their basic integrity and, indeed, their public identities. Mounting evidence about the private and financial conduct of Bill and Hillary Clinton, while in Arkansas and in the White House, could shatter the popularity of the first couple and severely damage, if not destroy, the Clinton presidency.

Potential Infractions

Few would deny that the alleged financial chicanery involving the Whitewater Development Corp. and Madison Guaranty Savings and Loan is a serious matter. And the apparent suicide of Deputy White House Counsel Vincent Foster and the clandestine confiscation of documents in his possession have caused deep concern across the political spectrum. A study by the conservative *American Spectator* lists possible legal infractions by the president that could result in disqualification from federal office, 178 years in prison and more than $2.5 million in fines. His wife conceivably could serve 47 years in prison and pay more than $1.2 million in fines. The facts in this case began to be determined by a special investigator in 1995.

Equally damaging, if true, are charges by four Arkansas state troopers that the Clintons were both involved in extramarital affairs while in Arkansas and are, in fact, crude, dishonorable, foul-mouthed politicos—far from the pillars of virtue and compassion believed by millions of Americans. Testimony by Gennifer Flowers, who claims to have had a 12-year affair with Bill Clinton, and by Paula Jones, who says that Clinton sexually harassed her in 1991, would in themselves make a mockery of the president's lofty rhetoric about morality and personal trust.

Of course, the Clintons have strongly denied illegal or immoral activity, and it is important to remember that they have been convicted of nothing. Careful investigation may clear the air completely. Indeed, all of us, regardless of ideology, and for the good of the country and the world, should hope that the president and first lady are who they say they are—innocent victims of a small group of people seeking financial and partisan gain.

The Character Issue

There are many, moreover, who argue that "Troopergate" is irrelevant; that a chief executive's sexual conduct, before or during his presidency, is a personal matter of little or no consequence. Conservative writer Dennis Prager has declared, "the evidence is overwhelming that whether a man or woman has had an extramarital affair tells us nothing about his or her ability to be a good and moral leader." *Time* magazine's Lance Morrow has dismissed the "character issue [as] the sex lives of politicians," a story that was "basically junk." In *New York* magazine, Joe Klein wrote of a president's "zone of privacy" and contended that only "twerps and moralists" are concerned about sexual hijinks. "The world is a subtle, dangerous place; leadership requires something more complex than Sunday school morality."

> *"Very few are willing to dismiss the character question completely, especially when it comes to national political figures who wield immense authority."*

And yet very few are willing to dismiss the character question completely, especially when it comes to national political figures who wield immense authority. Wilbur Mills, Gary Hart, John Tower, Clarence Thomas and Robert Packwood are among those whose private lives have been publicly scrutinized in recent years.

Character has been a part of every presidential contest in our history. As well it should, for presidents, of course, have vast power and are role models for people all over the world. As Bill Clinton himself has acknowledged, we need presidents who have outstanding integrity and deserve our confidence. In short, presidents should have good character.

Marital Fidelity

But what does sexuality have to do with character? And why should we be concerned about the marital fidelity of someone in the Oval Office? Franklin D. Roosevelt had a mistress and was one of our greatest presidents. John F. Kennedy indulged his satyriasis constantly and remains our most popular chief executive. On the other hand Richard Nixon was faithful to his wife and was forced to resign from office. Jimmy Carter was by all accounts a moral man but a dud in the White House.

Character is not a mysterious concept; it has been discussed at length from the ancient world to the modern day and has been linked to politics since Plato. Good character begins with integrity and includes such qualities as compassion, generosity, prudence, courage, loyalty, responsibility, temperance, humility and perseverance. Marital fidelity is part of this package for the obvious reason that it involves many of these attributes.

It has often been asked, "If a wife cannot trust her husband, why should anyone?" A California man responding to the Troopergate story put the question this way:

> A public man who dishonors his wife by infidelity, who then lies about his conduct, is not only wrong, but he also cannot be trusted. He cannot secure the trust of the people because he dishonors the basic governing unit of civilization, the family. If he uses the agents of government to abet his wrongful acts, he seals the mistrust of the people.

We are not discussing mere personality, which is the bearing and behavior of a person at the surface. (Crooks may seem charming and jovial, while saints can appear misanthropic.) Character is what you are at the deepest level of your being and it is linked to your basic values and beliefs. In the Western world character includes the Judeo-Christian precepts of right and wrong deeply imbedded in our culture and recognized by the majority of Americans.

Americans have long reflected on classical and biblical virtues. The first Anglicans, for example, had a strong knowledge of right and wrong, and Puritans, Quakers and others devoted much of their energies to righteous living. During the Enlightenment, Americans wrote at length on the relationship between good character and judicious political leadership. The Declaration of Independence said of King George III: "A Prince, whose character is thus marked by every act which define a Tyrant, is unfit to be the ruler of a free people." Thomas Jefferson paid tribute to George Washington's "perfect" character, saying at one point that the "whole art of government consists in the art of being honest."

> *"Good character begins with integrity and includes such qualities as compassion, generosity, prudence, courage, [and] loyalty."*

A Question of Degree

Of course, certain acknowledgments must be made about the complexity of the concept. For example, presidents are politicians, and one cannot expect a St. Francis or a Mother Teresa in the White House. As in most things, it is a question of degree. Character must be judged not only by a high standard but also, in this case, by a reasonable standard that takes into account the things even the best American politicians are expected to do. Harry Truman had good character, but he also knew how on occasion to cajole, threaten, lie and compromise on principle.

We also should distinguish between the trivial and the significant when thinking about character and the presidency. Examples of the former might include onetime extramarital flings (Grover Cleveland, Franklin Roosevelt, Dwight D. Eisenhower), the admission of having lust in one's heart and the claim to have smoked but not inhaled marijuana. A consistent pattern of lying, thievery, cowardice, disloyalty or irresponsibility is another matter.

> *"Harry Truman had good character, but he also knew how on occasion to cajole, threaten, lie and compromise on principle."*

Moreover, good character is only one quality an admirable president needs. It is also exceedingly helpful to have intelligence, breadth of knowledge, solid political skills, managerial competence, first-class advisers, public relations expertise and lots of luck. Jimmy Carter, for example, lacked six of these seven additional advantages. To repeat, character is extremely important, but it is not everything. It is significant because what you are plays a major role in determining what you do.

Then too, there is the obvious truth that good people can do bad things (one thinks of Woodrow Wilson), and bad people can do good things (Lyndon Johnson comes to mind). It is the overall tendency that matters.

It also is possible to grow in office. Chester A. Arthur was transformed from a crooked spoilsman into a dignified and decent statesman when the assassination of James A. Garfield summoned him to the White House in 1881.

Kennedy's Tarnished Character

Kennedy, Bill Clinton's role model, deserves special attention, for as most sophisticated people know, or should know, his character was far less admirable than his family and the hagiographers have led us to believe. In recent years, scholars and journalists have had to revise a great deal of Kennedy's pre–White House history. He was not, for example, brilliant, studious, ambitious, athletic, religious, prudent or particularly courageous. He consistently lied about his poor physical health, and his insensitivity toward others—especially women—is appalling.

Kennedy was largely a reflection of his ruthless, ambitious, charming and lecherous father. From the beginning, Joseph P. Kennedy was the major figure in his feckless and sickly son's political career. Quite naturally, the imprint of the elder Kennedy's grievously flawed character may be seen everywhere in Camelot.

President Kennedy showed courage and prudence at times during [his term known as] the Thousand Days. His handsome appearance, inspired rhetoric and promotion of his wife's good taste charmed much of the world. Toward the end, with his father incapacitated by a stroke, Kennedy seems to have absorbed a bit of the high-mindedness then in the air and was beginning to shed his father's deep cynicism.

But JFK was seriously deficient in integrity, compassion and temperance. For example, he backed clandestine, ruthless activities in Cuba, Laos and Vietnam largely because he was oblivious to the moral arguments against them. His reckless sexual escapades, associations with organized crime and use of drugs compromised his character and his high office. The potential for blackmail and public scandal was very serious. Had Kennedy lived, he might have been impeached.

There is a clear connection between character and conduct. It is neither priggish nor unwise to seek presidents who uphold such values as honesty, fidelity, responsibility, fairness and respect for others. Nothing prohibits us from finding another Washington or Lincoln. And why shouldn't we make every effort to do so?

Media Scrutiny

Much of the responsibility lies with the media. Many Washington insiders knew of Kennedy's lack of principle and infidelity but chose to look the other way. More recently, Clarence Thomas, John Tower and Robert Packwood have received far more rigorous scrutiny than, say, Ted Kennedy, Jesse Jackson and the Clintons. The reason, of course, is ideological. (Compare the media's treatment of Dan Quayle and Al Gore.) No reporter has dared to ask the first lady about the state trooper allegation that she had an affair with Vincent Foster. The matter is hardly unimportant.

In-depth investigations of presidential aspirants ought to begin early, even before the primaries. Perhaps an independent, bipartisan commission could be created to supervise the collection and evaluation of research. (I would hesitate to include the leading lights of academia on the ground that these days they are less capable of objectivity than journalists.) We need to know who presidential candidates—and their spouses—really are. The awesome power and the inspirational qualities of the office demand it. If the vile and vicious people described by the Arkansas state troopers are now in the White House, we could be in a lot of trouble. Millions, of course, are already troubled by the morality revealed in the administration's wholehearted endorsement of radical feminism and gay and lesbian demands. At this moment we need to know if "Slick Willy" is a cruel caricature or a reality. Rigorous research and impartial reporting can tell us.

> *"It is neither priggish nor unwise to seek presidents who uphold such values as honesty, fidelity, responsibility, fairness and respect for others."*

The response to the Troopergate allegations in the January 1994 issue of *American Spectator* and corresponding research published in the *Los Angeles Times* was not encouraging. Paul Duke and his colleagues on the PBS television program *Washington Week in Review* simply dismissed the 11,000-word *American Spectator* article, moderator Duke calling author David Brock one of the

125

year's "losers" and describing the story as "slimy." *New York Times* columnist Frank Rich contended that if everything said by the troopers was correct, the charges "would make the president seem all too pathetically ordinary." In Rich's world, apparently, married people regularly engage in serial sex, lie and scream obscenities at each other.

An Example for Americans

In fact, few Americans deny the value of such age-old virtues as truthfulness, resoluteness, self-control and moderation. In one public opinion survey of presidential character, 79 percent of respondents said they favor a president whose private and public life is exemplary, and 62 percent agreed that "a president should give a perfect example for all Americans, at all times."

We owe it to ourselves and to the entire world to ensure that this nation's highest public official has sufficiently good character to inspire us by example as well as by oration. The effect could be salutary in many ways, including the badly needed restoration of confidence in American institutions, our political system in particular.

From every angle, it simply is sensible to want a president who has good character as well as high intelligence, experience and political skill. One important measure of character is, and has been for centuries in this country and elsewhere, a person's willingness to honor marital vows and, in general, show sensitivity and respect for the opposite sex.

Sexual Harassment by Politicians Should Be Condemned

by Karen Houppert and Jennifer Gonnerman

About the authors: *Karen Houppert is a staff writer and Jennifer Gonnerman is a contributor for the* Village Voice *weekly newspaper.*

The Packwood Papers make for strange reading—and just how strange is something the mainstream press has only hinted at. The diaries released in September 1995 have the flavor of a cheap '60s thriller (call it *Advise and No Consent*), with the Republican junior senator from Oregon casting himself as the swinger protagonist bragging about his sexual exploits and political one-upmanship. Bob Packwood imagines himself as a politico James Bond who surmounts every obstacle through sheer ingenuity and wit. What distinguishes this trashy tale, however, is that with his assiduous chronicle, our hero blindly engineers his own downfall. "I'd like to change and have Cathy retype the diary so it shows something different but it turns out the typeface is different and somebody can tell it," Packwood gripes into his dictaphone on September 23, 1992. Whatever drove him to do that, when he knew by then that his nemesis, the Senate Ethics Committee, intended to read that very entry?

The Media's Omissions

One could marvel endlessly at such a psyche. For the most part, however, the press has dismissed Packwood's gauche peccadilloes, and his equally gauche cover-up attempts, in the easiest way: he was stupid. Splashing across front pages for a brief two days with nary a follow-up analysis, reports on the scandal portrayed Packwood as a jaw-dropping aberration of life on [Capitol] Hill—a dolt, a fool, a moral idiot. Focusing on the diary-tampering and the ethical and legal questions raised by Packwood's dealings with lobbyists and Senator X (presidential hopeful Phil Gramm), the media failed to engage the sexual ha-

Karen Houppert and Jennifer Gonnerman, "Senator Snitch," *Village Voice*, September 26, 1995. Reprinted with permission.

rassment issue head on. News accounts focused on the bizarre private proclivities of a supposedly straight-arrow senator, but the media seemed not to notice the most valuable gift the diaries had to offer—a sustained peek at the larger context in which Packwood operated. Packwood did not stupidly assume he was invincible—he had every reason to assume he was invincible, since he'd been carrying on the way he did for more than 20 years without a single repercussion.

> *"[Packwood's] colleagues on the Hill, the laws they made, and his own senior female staffers all conspired to protect him."*

The diaries and documents are a rare window on the world of Washington power, the culture of complicity that makes Packwoods possible. As the diaries show, he got away with it because his colleagues on the Hill, the laws they made, and his own senior female staffers all conspired to protect him. It's not as if his activities were secret. This was a man capable of cocking his head and squawking "Kiss!" at the woman operator of the private Senate elevator, then forcing her up against the wall to get one, after all.

"I remember one staffer had the senator banging on her door in the middle of the night," Complainant-7 told the committee. "I think we talked in the women's bathroom. I just remember two or three of us talking about it and saying, Well, what can we do, what do we do?"

But they had nowhere to turn for help. C-7 was sure everyone in the office knew what was going on, but no one in a position of authority would act. "I feel that there was some cognizant recognition of what was going on," she said. "I can't believe they didn't know about it. It was just too prevalent."

The Elite's Behavior

If Packwood's behavior was well known to his staff, it must also have been known to countless pages, interns, aides, representatives, and senators. Sexual harassment of this magnitude may go unchecked, but as Washington's long and scandalous history attests, it does not go unnoticed. Packwood has taken his place in a rogue's gallery that includes Wilbur Mills, Clarence Thomas, Teddy Kennedy, Mel Reynolds, Christopher Dodd, even Barney Frank. Judging by the absence of reproof from his colleagues, few of the lessons of those cases have been learned. The only senator who accuses Packwood of abusing power, ironically, is John Danforth, one of Clarence Thomas's [accused of sexual harassment by Anita Hill] staunchest defenders. When Danforth tells Packwood he senses no repentance, the senator from Oregon wails, "I said, *Blank*, [name omitted], what did I do wrong?"

Packwood's bafflement is emblematic of a larger failing among Washington's male elite, an inability to evaluate their own behavior—only the response to it in the public sphere. It is the same sort of confusion one sees in the diaries when Packwood has a steam room chat with Ted Kennedy, whose biggest concern about allegations that he has witnessed a "rape situation" seems to be that they made his approval ratings plummet overnight. To an ethics committee question about whether his behavior brought discredit on the Senate, Packwood responds, ". . . if it happened and *it becomes public* [emphasis added], it brings discredit on the Senate." But with the Senate's image so recently tarnished by the Hill-Thomas hearings, this committee's members weren't buying. It is not whether the actions go "undiscovered or unpublicized," the report admonishes. "It is the behavior which is discrediting, and it is no less so if only its victims know of it."

Packwood's Escapades

Packwood has tried mightily to portray his sexual escapades as mere antics, the folly of a naive and perhaps lonely man. They were far more than that. Take the case of Julie Williamson, Packwood's Clatsop County campaign chair, who was alone in her office and on the phone when Packwood walked in and started kissing her neck. She finished her call and told him never to do that again. He wasn't listening. "Somehow he grabbed me and was holding me and stood on my feet and then pulled my head back—like this—by my hair and was giving me this really ugly, big, wet, yucky kiss," Williamson told the committee. *Big*, *wet*, and *yucky* are comical-sounding words, but as her description continues, the humor fades. "I remember that with one hand he was pulling my hair and that it hurt and that while—that somehow he was struggling with his other arm to get under my skirt . . . and he was trying to get off my panty girdle. . . ." She kept struggling and either got away or he released her. She ran into the front office and he stalked out. Then "he stopped at the threshold to the hallway and turned around and said, 'If not today, then someday.'" This is attempted rape, capped by a threat.

Packwood's supporters have also claimed there were no professional ramifications for the women involved, that there was no quid pro quo (the smoking gun of sexual harassment charges), no threats or promises that tied hiring, firing, or advancement to sexual favors. The ethics report indicates otherwise. Repeatedly.

> *"Packwood has tried mightily to portray his sexual escapades as mere antics, the folly of a naive and perhaps lonely man."*

In the mid-'70s Jean McMahon went to Senator Packwood's campaign-trail hotel to interview for a speech-writing position. When she arrived, he went after her, chasing her around a table, pulling her to him, and kissing her. McMahon fled, although (and this says something about the power of Washington) she still wanted the job. "It wasn't really until a couple of days later that it sank in that he wasn't serious," she told the committee. "I remember calling up his office in Portland saying, does anybody want this speech, and there's a draft here, thinking there was some staff person waiting for it. And the reaction was, what speech, we never heard of this."

The McMahon and Williamson incidents fit the pattern that emerges in Packwood's own account of his sexual antics. There is the ordinary strutting and crowing about his sexual prowess, but these come up in connection with his successes—the affairs, short and long, and their, to him, satisfying numbers. What's most Packwoodian and has, rightly, fascinated both the public and the media, doesn't involve sexual triumph by any recognizable measure—rather, it's the infantile lunge to steal a kiss. This is Packwood's singular compulsion— he seems to have done it at every opportunity, however unlikely and inappropriate. This is also his even more singular source of satisfaction; these aren't passes but thefts, and they have nothing to do with the disinhibiting effects of alcohol. Their sole point seems to be violation. Early in the morning, stone sober, Packwood jumpstarts the work day by grabbing a young female staffer—or an elevator operator or, for all we know, some hapless woman on the D.C. subway—and shoves his tongue in her mouth.

> *"Until 1995, a person accusing a senator of sexual harassment had less recourse than any other employee in the country."*

Lacking Recourse

Packwood's activities went on for decades, beginning long before Anita Hill and other high-profile cases that have eased the way for women who want to speak out about sexual abuse. Even if Packwood had been exposed, however, Congress had erected a legal fortress around its members. Until 1995, a person accusing a senator of sexual harassment had less recourse than any other employee in the country.

Workers for private companies seek relief by filing a suit in federal court under Title VII, the provision of the 1964 Civil Rights Act that bars discrimination based on sex and that, since the early 1980s, has been the backbone of sexual harassment litigation. They can sue for damages, their jobs back, or lost promotions or income. But staffers on the Hill have no such option. "You simply couldn't file a complaint in court against a senator," explains Margaret Olney, an attorney representing one of Packwood's accusers. In fact, the Senate and House, in passing laws against harassment, granted themselves immunity from prosecution. Until 1995, when, under a proviso in Newt Gingrich's Contract With America, Congress agreed to be held to the same laws and standards that govern the rest of us, Packwood and his ilk truly were untouchable. His victims had no access to civil court.

What this meant is that the only recourse remaining for women on Packwood's staff was their superiors. And many of Packwood's senior staffers were women. It is in this respect that the diaries are most dismaying, as they detail the way that senior women not only countenanced, but collaborated in, the exploitation of other, less powerful women in the service of protecting their senator—by their silence, their refusal to give help to those who sought it, and their active assistance in Packwood's various defensive strategies. While most of the young victims provide substantial evidence that they reported the senator's assaults to more seasoned staffers at the time, these staff heavies have consistently tried to put a different spin on events.

In the fall of 1990, a young woman recently hired as Packwood's press secretary was working privately with the senator in his office at the end of the day. He was called to a vote and told her to wait for him to get back. "That's when Pam, his secretary, came in and told me I might not want to be there when he returned. . . . She didn't put it into words. She just gravely looked me in the eye and said, 'You're new here. I'll let you know, you shouldn't be here when he returns.'" The staffer, who took that to mean she might not be safe, left the office. (Pam Fulton later told the committee she was simply referring to the senator's drinking problem and was concerned that if he found someone to hang around the office and drink with him, he would stay there till all hours instead of going home.) Soon thereafter, she told deputy chief of staff Lindy Paull what happened. "[Paull] sighed and rolled her eyes and said . . . 'Gosh darn him,' and kind of laughed, said, 'You'll have to avoid him for a while. It will fade.'"

Blaming Victims

Packwood's response to these charges is standard blame-the-victim fare—for which he marshaled enormous staff support. Referring to his press secretary, Complainant-1, Packwood said she wore short skirts and low-cut blouses to work. "There's substantial evidence that C-1 behaved toward me in a way that would suggest to me that she wanted a romantic relationship," Packwood told the committee. (In another deposition, he'd said it would be too strong a characterization to say that she wanted a romantic or sexual relationship with him.) To reinforce his character assault, Packwood called on the loyalists among his staff.

> *"Packwood's response to these charges is standard blame-the-victim fare."*

Bobbi Munson, who works in his press office, submitted a statement asserting that C-1 "flattered and flirted with Senator Packwood. . . . She was obviously interested in Senator Packwood in a romantic way and would throw herself at him." Richard Grafmeyer, tax counsel to Packwood's Senate Finance Committee, went even further: "She would touch his knee or arm, touch him on the shoulder and laugh heartily at his jokes even if they were not that humorous. If he said something funny, C-1 would act like it was the most hilarious thing she had ever heard. *She was all over him* [emphasis added]." Packwood even submitted a letter to the committee in his defense from a victim's ex-husband: "Mary has many fine qualities, and is honest in most situations," it said.

"But in any circumstance with the potential for a feminist interpretation, her perceptions become quite distorted."

Packwood's most stalwart defender was Elaine Franklin, his chief of staff. Franklin came to work for him in 1981, attracted by his support for feminist causes, and she appears in the Packwood Papers as both his protector and enabler.

In 1985, a campaign worker named Judy Foster-Filippi drove Packwood home from a dinner party in Oregon. She claimed he launched one of his kissing attacks before he left the car. "The next day I called Elaine Franklin, told her what had happened the night before and asked her if . . . there was more to working for Bob Packwood than I had thought," Foster-Filippi later testified. "She cooled me down and told me not to worry. She said she could not imagine what had gotten into him and that she would talk to him."

> *"The Ethics Committee's recommendation to expel Packwood . . . is an unmistakable 'No More!' to business as usual in the capital."*

One can only imagine how many times Elaine Franklin must have had that conversation. Indeed, when news of the aforementioned press secretary's "problem" with Packwood reached Franklin, she pulled C-1 aside to talk to her before she left for her new job. "Ms. Franklin told me that she knew I had had problems with the senator once and warned me again that I should not talk to anyone when I arrived at my new office in Oregon," C-1 told the committee. The day C-1 left, "She [Franklin] said, 'you know, you can't tell anyone about this.' She asked me three times, 'Have you ever told [your] husband about this?' And I lied three times and said no, because . . . she could be pretty scary sometimes and I was afraid she might try to do something."

Even after C-1 started her new job, she says Franklin repeatedly harassed her at work and demanded to know the name of a former roommate in whom she had confided. At one point C-1 broke down in sobs. She said, "Elaine, I'm not going to give you her name and I don't want you to call me anymore. You're beginning to scare me." Franklin's response: "How do you think Bob Packwood feels?"

Packwood Resigns

He feels a lot worse now. The Ethics Committee's recommendation to expel Packwood and its prompt release of the report is an unmistakable "No more!" to business as usual in the capital. The message goes first to Packwood, of course, who blatantly lied to committee members, tampered with the diaries after he knew they would be called as evidence, and in a final arrogant act, indignantly demanded open hearings. But the message is also addressed to those inside the Beltway [Washington, D.C.], mired in the muck of daily politics, who fretted over the committee's 10,000-page-report as if it were the blind-item gossip column from hell, full of blanked and coded names that they scramble to decipher. Are they in here? Are their friends? Their enemies?

Few of the specifics make waves for the rest of us. Who among us puzzles over who *Blank #1* is, or *S-2* or *C-3*? The beyond-the-Beltway public could not care less if this particular senator tattled on that one, or that staffer bad-mouthed her boss to this one—what matters is the cumulative impact. When the incidents portrayed in these diaries and documents are tallied, they paint a devastating portrait of the culture of power in all its abusiveness. And like Richard Nixon, the senator from Oregon was nailed not because he did it but because he insisted on setting it all down for posterity.

Once committee members were faced with Packwood's own written evidence of his transgressions, they wanted to put as much distance as possible between themselves and the senator. Of course they booted Packwood. [Packwood announced his resignation in September 1995.] He left them no choice. He stepped outside the brotherhood, wrote about his exploits, and ratted on himself and all of Washington.

It's hard to pinpoint why. None of the news accounts truly captures the bizarre nature of these diary entries, which read like a peeper's glimpse into the private life of a powerful man but have been written, clearly, with some future reader in mind. Describing a staffer he was preparing to screw on the floor of his office Packwood writes, "Well, I won't bore you with all the details of the evening. . . ." Eventually he cuts to the chase or, rather, the remarkably creepy capture. "Just as I was about to insert I said, 'I love *Blank*'. . . She said, 'Then please, put it in. . . .'"

> *"These diary entries . . . read like a peeper's glimpse into the private life of a powerful man."*

Who is the "you" that he is so thoughtfully sparing? If Packwood is subject and *she* is object, then who is his audience? Is it some imaginary private constituency? Perhaps nothing is more illustrative of Packwood's complete immersion in the arrogance that is Washington than his certainty that we, dear readers, would walk away from his journals thinking as highly of the man as he does of himself.

Investigative Reporters Have Harmed Politics

by Suzanne Garment

About the author: *Suzanne Garment, a former* Wall Street Journal *columnist, is a resident scholar at the American Enterprise Institute in Washington, D.C.*

When you ask a public official what is responsible for today's surplus of scandal, the odds are that his first answer will be, "The press." And understandably so: Today's news media play an unprecedented role in our public life, and their power has shaped modern politics. "By the mid-eighties," writes Richard Clurman, press observer and former chief of correspondents for the Time-Life News Service, "the media had made themselves the cop on every beat." Yet the press did not muscle its way to the top of the current political heap against the opposition of all other forces on the public scene. Nor did the media impose values on American public life that were foreign to the interests and attitudes of everyone else who plays an active role in the political process. Instead, the rise of the press as a power in politics was simply one result of the general distaste for conventional political institutions that has made its mark on almost every aspect of our public life over the past 25 years. . . .

The Antagonistic Press

Observers are fairly clear that the general stance of the press is distinctly more antagonistic toward government and its officials than it was, say, 25 years ago. "When I was a young reporter," recalled *New York Times* writer Martin Tolchin, a 36-year veteran at the paper,

> we had assumptions about people in public life—that they had the interest of the public at heart, that they were honest and competent. It took a heck of a lot to overcome those assumptions. But today, some journalists have no assumptions and others have the opposite of the old assumptions. The old way, if you covered a politician, you were a friend and part of an entourage. Today, politicians know that journalists are *not* their friends—that there's no such thing as off the record, background, or anything of the sort.

One sign of the changed spirit is the recent growth in the number of press people who think of themselves as investigative journalists. The term refers less to specific techniques or modes of research than it does to an attitude: the determination to fight the established powers for the information whose exposure will bring about some malefactor's downfall. In labeling themselves investigative reporters or saying they are devoted to investigative journalism, reporters and news organizations signify that they have adopted the adversarial stance those words convey. Investigative reporters have traditionally been pictured, for good reason, as tenacious, often lonely fighters against the established powers in behalf of political and social justice. Nowadays, though, they are no longer so alone.

> *"Nearly 98 percent of the respondents said their organizations did at least some investigative reporting."*

In 1986 a survey aimed to find out from editors at the country's 500 biggest newspapers and top 200 TV stations whether they were doing more investigative reporting than they used to. The term was defined this way: "(1) it is a topic treated in an in-depth way, often using documents and records; (2) it reveals something significant that an agency or person wants to keep secret; (3) it largely is the result of a reporter's own work." Nearly 98 percent of the respondents said their organizations did at least some investigative reporting. Over half of them said they were doing more than they had done five years previously. More than 71 percent of the newspaper editors said the use of investigative reporting techniques had increased among beat reporters. Recent budget cuts by some types of news organizations have cut into the numbers of investigative and other reporters. But the figures are still well above what they were when today's investigative wave started.

Help for Reporters

The modern investigative reporter can get organized professional aid in learning how to practice his craft. The biggest advisory outfit is Investigative Reporters and Editors, Inc., based at the University of Missouri, with a membership of around 3,000. The IRE holds frequent conferences devoted mainly to helping members develop reportorial tools and techniques. Most of the articles in its newsletter dispense practical advice, a journalistic version of Heloise's household hints, with stories such as "Bankruptcy Court Fertile Snooping Ground" and "Investigating the Nuclear Power Plant." Readers learn what information corporations are required to file with the federal government, when it is legally permissible to search other people's garbage, and how to use the Freedom of Information Act to maximum effect.

Advice of this sort probably does not make much difference at the biggest metropolitan newspapers, but it almost certainly improves the technique of reporters elsewhere in the country. In recent years, the Cleveland *Plain Dealer*, the *San Jose Mercury News*, and the *St. Paul Pioneer Press Dispatch* have broken scandals concerning national politicians. Some of the most significant reporting on the savings and loan scandal came from papers in Michigan and Ohio. Paula Parkinson was brought to us by the Wilmington *News-Journal* and Donna Rice by the *Miami Herald*.

Veterans and Newcomers

One effect of this expansion is still more competition for the larger, more established news organizations. But there are other consequences as well, only partly accounted for by the simple pressures of competition. This country's great investigative journalists are a national treasure. Yet not long ago veteran investigative reporter Nick Kotz pointed to one of them when he commented on the recent changes in his field. "When I came to Washington in 1964, there was Jerry Landauer at the [*Wall Street*] *Journal*, Larry Stern and Morton Mintz at the *Washington Post*—damn few people doing the real, hard digging." Nowadays, Kotz continued, "There are so many *more* of them—or at least people who *call* themselves investigative reporters."

Kotz is not the only experienced journalist to have become uncomfortable about all the fresh troops "who *call* themselves investigative reporters." Another was star reporter Jerry Landauer, one of those mentioned by Kotz. Landauer worked at the *Journal* from 1963 until he died of a heart attack at the age of 49 in 1981.

If any reporter was ever "investigative," in the sense of being dedicated to uncovering malfeasance in American business and government it was Landauer. In 1971 he broke the story of how the dairy industry had shoveled large amounts of cash into the Nixon reelection fund in return for a hike in dairy price supports. In 1973 he revealed the story of bribe taking by then–vice president Spiro Agnew. In 1975 he exposed payoffs by U.S. corporations to corrupt government officials abroad.

Landauer was as guileful as any other first-rank reporter when it came to getting information. After his death, his friend Kenneth Bacon, also with the *Journal,* told about a news story that the two of them had covered, involving a payoff of nearly $500,000 by the Del Monte corporation through a business consultant to officials of the Guatemalan government. The two reporters had

> *"This country's great investigative journalists are a national treasure."*

the story from an anonymous tip but could not confirm it. So Landauer decided on a frontal assault and asked a Del Monte lawyer to meet the reporters for lunch at the Madison Hotel in Washington. Landauer's strategy, Bacon recalled, was very simple: "Since we knew almost nothing, we would pretend that we knew a lot and try to bluff the story out of him." At the Madison, said Bacon:

> I asked questions for hours and hours and the lawyer went through this very
> dull story. He finished with a great look of self-satisfaction and said, "You can

see there's absolutely nothing here to write about."

At which point Jerry went—slamming his hand on the table—"That's the most ridiculous thing I've ever heard! You mean you traveled 3,000 miles to tell us that? Look. Go back to San Francisco and talk to your clients who are paying you big money to come here and buy us lunch in the Madison Hotel and spend the whole day with us and tell them we need a few facts or we're just gonna have to say that your company paid $500,000 to a guy and you don't even know his name and you don't know what you got for it."

So the lawyer went back to San Francisco and came to Washington a week later and delivered a pretty full account of what had happened. Afterward, I said to Jerry, "How did you know he was going to come back with the facts?" And he said, "The harder you kick 'em, the faster they come back."

This basic technique was not what you would call overly polite or truthful. It is, however, immediately recognizable to many politicians who have been caught in an investigative reporter's sights.

Media Disinterest

Yet when the Koreagate influence-buying scandal broke in 1977, Landauer was not on the investigative train, and in an article for the *Journal* he explained why. More than two years before the scandal hit the headlines, he explained, a South Korean defector publicly charged that South Korea was in effect buying the favor of U.S. congressmen with campaign contributions. "The media," noted Landauer in his piece, "ignored him." But the Justice Department later began an investigation, the *Washington Post* reported on it in the fall of 1976, and the chase was on.

Press reports said that 22, then 90, then 115 congressmen were under investigation. The amount of money said to be involved mounted to $1 million a year. The scandal was said to be spreading—"scandals must always seem to be 'growing,' 'spreading,' or 'widening,' lest they appear stale," Landauer noted—to the Senate. Yet not a single senator was ever identified. When an indictment finally emerged, the case against sitting representatives involved less than $150,000 paid out over eight years, mostly in the form of legal contributions. Sources in the Justice Department and Leon Jaworski's congressional investigation staff said they were mystified as to where the hugely inflated numbers had come from.

> *"Landauer was as guileful as any other first-rank reporter when it came to getting information."*

Dangers of Scandal Journalism

Though some journalists did good reporting on the scandal, Landauer thought the way it grew demonstrated the dangers in the post-Watergate style of scandal journalism:

[I]n the capital these days a scandal isn't a scandal until important segments of the media "discover" it. Once perceived, a scandalous situation is likely to dominate the news, for no newspaper editor or television executive wants to miss another Watergate. Then, as more newspeople pounce on the story, competitive pressures can overshadow fair play, resulting in overstated coverage that may not end until another "scandal" comes along to divert the media's attention.

Shortly before he died, Landauer prepared a prospectus for a course on modern investigative reporting that he wanted to teach at Washington's left-leaning Institute for Policy Studies. The course would explore, he wrote,

several major themes: Is the press too ardent in the pursuit of scandal? Is there a proper concern for fairness and accuracy? Has the emphasis on investigative reporting generated perceptions of wrongdoing where none exists? And does the press needlessly contribute to disillusionment with government and other institutions of society?

That was the question Landauer left for his fellow reporters covering the Reagan administration, and it is the fundamental question that the disciples of investigative reporting must confront. For some time now, a debate has gone on about the ideological bias of the press. This bias clearly exists. But bias in the conventional liberal-versus-conservative sense may be less important in determining the scandal reporting we get today than the imperatives of the reporter's job as we have come to define it.

A Feeding Frenzy

When Speaker of the House Jim Wright emerged in the spring of 1989 as designated scandal target of the season, the counsel to the House ethics committee started releasing damaging information about him and journalists started gobbling it up and spewing it out. Some liberal opinion makers in the press were clearly uncomfortable about the way they were cooperating in bringing about Wright's political

"Scandals must always seem to be 'growing,' 'spreading,' or 'widening,' lest they appear stale."

demise, but the process did not stop. "All of us," said James T. Wooten of ABC News about himself and his colleagues in the press,

are trying unsuccessfully to avoid the appearance of a feeding frenzy. You hear them say, "Here come the sharks," but what the hell are we supposed to do except find people to answer our questions?

There is, indeed, often nothing else a reporter can do these days, for the aggressive, investigative, adversary style of journalism and the attitudes that go along with it have become the accepted measure of journalistic excellence. All good reporters, in this view, should mistrust official explanations, and reporters should occupy themselves by digging for things that established institutions do not want us to know. The central purpose of the journalistic craft, the argument continues, is to bring to citizens' attention the flaws in their institutions and leaders. If citizens learn more about nefarious political activities they will be better able to throw the bums out. Indeed, the basic reason for giving the press very broad protections and privileges in a democracy is that people need to know the bad news in order to perform their duties as citizens.

These principles can produce great acts of courage by individual journalists. The same principles can also provide a surefire recipe for increasing the amount of scandal put before the American citizenry. They do not necessarily constitute a bad way for the news media to function as a gadfly to government. But today's press is no gadfly; the nature of current politics has made the media more powerful than ever before in this century and sometimes more powerful than any other single institution, in determining how our public life will be perceived and conducted.

Under these circumstances when journalistic aloofness from political institutions edges toward nihilism, and reporters view every established leader or organization chiefly as a locus of possible crime, they can easily produce a steady scandal diet of the sort that will not do the job of encouraging citizens to be politically active and keep their public officials accountable. Instead, the constant scandal stories put forward by alienated news organizations can—and do—deter people from participating in politics at all. When this happens, the press stops helping people to be good citizens. And when it can no longer perform this function it loses the foundation of its own legitimacy.

Our modern journalism, teetering on this edge, is the lens through which we view and judge all the other actors in our scandal dramas.

The Media Should Not Sustain Rumors About Politicians

by Larry J. Sabato

About the author: *Larry J. Sabato is the author of* Feeding Frenzy: How Attack Journalism Has Transformed American Politics, *from which this viewpoint is excerpted.*

> *People may expect too much of journalism. Not only do they expect it to be entertaining, they expect it to be true.*

reporter and editor Lewis Lapham

Lapham is wrong. People have every right to expect the truth from the press, and most journalists fully accept their responsibility to report the news accurately. Despite deadline pressure, and even though the news is only the proverbial "rough first draft of history," newspeople by and large do a remarkably good job of delivering a reasonably reliable version of events. That is why the trend toward publishing and airing unverified rumors is so deeply disturbing, a throwback to the unbridled days of the early nineteenth century when journalists were little more than gossipmongers.

Rumors: Part of Politics

Granted, the reader's appetite for titillation has always motivated the press, and "half the people in the newsroom are here because they like to gossip and get paid for it," as the *Washington Post*'s Milton Coleman puts it. Then, too, rumors are part of the fabric of the political community, woven into the day-to-day contact reporters have with political consultants, activists, and officials. But the trafficking in innuendo has accelerated dramatically in recent years. A newsman for one of America's most prestigious publications recalled that in 1988 rumors were coming in so fast and furious "we had to separate them into categories of 'above the belt' and 'below the belt.'" When the telephone would ring at the desk of National Public Radio's Nina Totenberg, her colleague Cokie Roberts would tease, "Sex or drugs, Nina?" The sewer of hearsay has become the new mainstream of American politics for a long, sick season. Partly, the age of pervasive negative campaigning has created the conditions conducive to the spread of sleaze. Political consultants apply the knife of gossip with surgical skill, "getting a dozen people aggressively asking, 'have you heard the one about . . .' until enough chatter develops so that the press starts to think it's true," as Democratic political operative Michael McCurry describes it. But mainly, tattle is taking center stage in politics because everyone knows the press will print it, even without proof, if not on the front page then in "style" sections or gossip columns where lower standards sometimes prevail. And under the lowest-common-denominator rule, only one media outlet need give the story legitimacy before all can publish or broadcast it guilt-free.

> *"Partly, the age of pervasive negative campaigning has created the conditions conducive to the spread of sleaze."*

The on-the-record rumor mill is being fed by a growing belief among some journalists that even *unproved* facts, if widely accepted as true, can have a substantial effect on a campaign or public official, and are therefore reportable. "If you haven't been able to confirm the rumors, but the rumors won't die, that is a legitimate news story," insists one senior television journalist. Also supposedly appropriate for public consumption are allegations made by only indirectly connected but "credible" sources, whether evidence is on hand or not. Both guideposts represent a substantial and unwise lowering of the threshold for publishing and broadcasting information, which results in unwarranted damage being done to public figures and inaccurate reports reaching the public. It may sometimes seem to journalists that "everyone knows" the scuttlebutt, but that is only because a newsperson's universe of contacts is public affairs oriented. In truth, the circulation of any unpublished political rumor is usually restricted to a small circle of political elites—until the press makes it a general topic of conversation via newsprint and the airwaves. Consider the unfairness and injustice in these five recent examples.

The 1988 Presidential Campaign

• When Michael Dukakis's campaign sent out the "attack video" that torpedoed Joseph Biden's candidacy, Richard Gephardt at first received the blame. Private speculation about the identity of the perpetrator was unavoidable, but when the conventional wisdom fingered Gephardt and this conclusion seeped into print—as it did almost everywhere—the Missouri congressman's campaign for the Democratic presidential nomination was dealt a body blow. Gephardt's 1988 press secretary, Don Foley, offered this assessment:

> It did us a lot of damage. Up until that time Dick Gephardt was viewed by most people as someone who would not engage in dirty campaigning, and he

had a Boy Scout image. But this incident painted him as somebody who was a bit overanxious for the prize; in the eyes of a lot of people this took the shine off of the Gephardt aura.

Even when Dukakis's staff was revealed to be behind Biden's troubles, the tarnish seemed to stick to Gephardt's image.

• Not long after Biden's plagiarism became the focus of the nascent 1988 campaign, the Champaign, Illinois, *News-Gazette* published an article based purely on hearsay alleging that Jesse Jackson had left the University of Illinois in 1960 after plagiarizing an English term paper. The sole sources for the story were two college acquaintances of Jackson who told the newspaper they had heard about the incident from others. The Associated Press sent out a dispatch based on the *News-Gazette* account that was used by many major newspapers throughout the country. As it turned out, the professor who supposedly discovered Jackson's perfidy could not recall it, and the president of the University of Illinois certified that Jackson's academic record contained no notation of any disciplinary action for plagiarism.

Rumors at the State Level

• Texas's 1990 Republican gubernatorial candidate Clayton Williams was victimized by published suggestions that "honey hunts," a special Western kind of sexual frolic, had taken place on his ranch. Not a shred of evidence that any such hunt occurred was ever produced by the press or his opponents, but state newspapers printed the rumor on the pretext of his denial when he was asked about it by a *Houston Post* reporter. *Newsweek* followed up by headlining a "Periscope" item, "Rumors of a Honey Hunt," and helpfully recounted all variations of the canard:

> In one version of the story, it's a form of entertainment favored by Williams and his chums, who strip to their underwear at his ranch and shoot water pistols at nymphs dancing in the nude. Another version has Williams inviting prostitutes to tag along at deer hunts and cattle roundups. A third sends Williams to Africa on safari with hookers in tow.

• In a lengthy profile of Governor Gaston Caperton (D., W. Va.) and his marital and political troubles, the *Washington Post* strongly implied that Caperton might be a homosexual. Noting that the governor's divorce raised "questions about [his] personal life," the article surmised that Caperton "was able to deal with new rumors about his sexuality by letting it be known that he was seeing" a prominent Wheeling woman. While such rumors were apparently circulating in West Virginia, stoked mainly by Caperton's Republican opponents, close family and political associates of Caperton have convincingly insisted the homosexual characterization is untrue, and thus the

> *"Clayton Williams was victimized by published suggestions that 'honey hunts'. . . had taken place on his ranch."*

Post placed an unfair, additional burden on an unpopular, struggling governor. Incidentally Caperton has since wed the Wheeling woman, now West Virginia's first lady.

• *Westword*, a Denver weekly newspaper, published a cover story headlined "The Rumor About Romer" in June 1990. "Romer" was Colorado's Democratic governor Roy Romer, and the "rumor" was that he had maintained a longtime sexual relationship with his top female aide. Both individuals strenuously denied it, their anger all the more intense because *Westword* offered no proof—just numerous unnamed sources who "think" the two are "much more than friends and co-workers." *Westword*'s limited circulation might have contained the damage, but the *Denver Post* picked up the story, quoting *Westword*, of course.

> *"The rumor about George Bush's 'mistress' had a run longer than all but a handful of Broadway productions."*

These five incidents are not isolated examples, but part of a pattern every bit as convincing as the "character" continuums that capture the attention of the contemporary news media. Again and again, the same questionable practices noted in the above examples have arisen in national politics, affecting the careers of Jack Kemp, Gary Hart, Michael Dukakis, Dan Quayle, George Bush, John Tower, and Tom Foley. . . .

George Bush

The rumor about George Bush's "mistress" had a run longer than all but a handful of Broadway productions—and for the political cognoscenti, it was every bit as entertaining. However, the relatively harmless behind-the-scenes fun turned into yet another public morality play as the 1988 campaign unfolded.

The story began almost two full presidential cycles earlier. In late February of 1981, about a month after Bush had taken the oath of office as vice president, a Washington, D.C., woman thought she heard a police officer say that Bush had been shot. Not finding any news about the incident on television, she began calling news organizations to get the details. This innocent effort begat a rumor that took Washington newsrooms by storm, and spurred every journalist's best sources to call in the same tip—with all the repetitions seeming to most newspeople like confirmation. After embellishments that naturally developed in the hundreds of retellings, the rumor boiled down to this: Vice President George Bush had been nicked by a bullet as he left a woman's town house late one evening. The woman was his mistress and—here is where two separate versions developed—she was either a longtime member of his staff or the widow of a former Midwestern Republican congressman. Journalists for all the great newspapers and networks swarmed over a Capitol Hill residential neighborhood where the incident was alleged to have happened. Ellen Hume, then of the *Los Angeles Times*, was going door to door, trying to find anyone who knew anything about the "shooting," when she stumbled across Richard Roth of CBS doing the same thing. "We laughed and joined forces, but came up empty-handed," said Hume. The unfortunate woman who had first called the media was literally harassed by an invading army of journalists, none more obnoxious than a gumshoe from [*Washington Post* columnist] Jack Anderson's outfit who only left when the woman threatened to call the police. Both of the alleged mistresses were interviewed, too; both adamantly denied the specific incident and the general suggestion.

Gradually, it became apparent that the rumor was not true; an angry George Bush even had the FBI interview him about it so that he could get his denial on the official record. . . .

The Alleged Mistress

Ann Devroy (then of Gannett News Service and now with the *Washington Post*) spent several months in late 1981 and early 1982 examining Bush's vice presidential operation—and especially the role his alleged mistress played in it. The woman in question had worked for Bush for many years, and after Devroy interviewed three dozen close associates of Bush during various stages of his career, a less-than-flattering picture emerged of her. According to Devroy, "She was said to have fits of temper and screaming that totally disrupted the staff, to limit access to Bush unfairly, and to argue with everyone. And people kept hinting to me that there was a sexual relationship here." But when Devroy confronted the woman with her coworkers' suspicions, "She cried and screamed and expressed outrage." So Devroy looked elsewhere for proof, and after many weeks reached a conclusion: "I found absolutely no evidence of anything going on. After spending more time on this topic than any reporter I know of, I just came to disbelieve the rumor." Several other meticulous reporters like Devroy also investigated the situation, and reached the same conclusion. One journalist managed to find an airline pilot who had once been engaged to Bush's aide, but broke it off "because of his *suspicions* that she was having an affair with a married man whom he'd always *believed* to be George Bush." This was not exactly the kind of evidence that would stand up in divorce court.

> *"Even when the media's front door is shut, gossip can become legitimate news through the back door."*

The Rumor Persists

Of course, the reporters who disproved the rumor to their satisfaction never published their findings, so all the others continued to believe the gossip, fueled from time to time by the reports of a Bush staff shake-up in which the alleged mistress was involved or a series of mysterious Bush "disappearances" during 1978 and 1979 when Bush would tell his aides he was flying off to Washington for clandestine meetings with fellow former Central Intelligence Agency directors—meetings which all the other spymasters say were never held. Again, the "mistress" rumor was never mentioned in these stories, but those in the know read between the lines for what they believed was the hidden subtext.

The rumor having been sustained in Bush lore for seven years, its surfacing in the 1988 campaign seemed preordained. And Bush's Republican primary opponents were not about to leave it for the Democrats to mine. Both the Bob Dole and Kemp campaigns were involved in spreading the gossip, and after Gary Hart's debacle [Hart abandoned the campaign after allegations of adultery with Donna Rice], their efforts to get a major news organization to break the story went into high gear. Many broadcast network reporters and editors recalled a flurry of contacts in May and June of 1987 utilizing the familiar pressure tactic that "everybody else" was close to breaking the story. ABC News had assigned a half dozen personnel to try to divine the truth or falsity of the rumor, and they had come up with the same evidence as their predecessors at other media outlets: none. . . .

Bordering on Garbage

One more campaign installment for the Bush mistress rumor remained in 1988. While this additional airing, like its predecessors, was not damaging to Bush, it demonstrated that even when the media's front door is shut, gossip can become legitimate news through the back door. In mid-October, when thousands of reporters crowded into Los Angeles for the final Bush-Dukakis debate, the *L.A. Weekly*, a local left-wing newspaper, published a front-page story discreetly entitled, "George Bush: Loverboy." Its author Richard Ryan regurgitated all the old tales about Bush and his staff aide, adding generous scoops of speculation and prurient interpretation. Bush was "said" by anonymous sources to "have had a number of affairs over the years"; not a scintilla of proof was offered for what Ryan himself called "common gossip." Hal Bruno [of ABC News] dismissed the piece by noting, "When we saw it, all of us laughed; this was less than what we had thrown away a

> *"[John] Tower himself . . . called his confirmation defeat an 'exercise in character assassination.'"*

year and a half earlier." CNN's Frank Sesno, who was accompanying Bush when the *L.A. Weekly* edition was distributed to the press, remembered, "Not a single member of the [press] pool questioned Bush about it because it was such total garbage." Unfortunately, two British tabloids, the *Evening Standard* and *Today*, as well as the New York *Daily News*, picked up the *L.A. Weekly*'s trash, though no responsible media outlet did so. But on Wednesday, October 19, an event occurred that could not be ignored. A rumor that the *Washington Post* was going to publish an exposé on Bush's mistress ripped through Wall Street, triggering a forty-three-point drop in the Dow Jones average. To this day, no one knows exactly how the rumor was introduced to the financial district. . . .

John Tower

Something truly extraordinary was at work in the U.S. Senate vote that sent John Tower down to defeat in March 1989—the first time ever that any new president had been denied one of his cabinet choices or that a former senator had been rejected for a cabinet post by his ex-colleagues. It may well have been that Tower was not a good choice for secretary of defense, that problems in his personal and professional life made him unfit to be near the top of the military chain of command. But one conclusion from an examination of the Tower affair is inescapable: The former Texas legislator was a victim of unfounded rumor and out-of-control press behavior that was at least as scandalous as his alleged offenses.

No one will be surprised that Tower himself, before his April 1991 death in a plane crash, called his confirmation defeat an "exercise in character assassination." Nor will eyebrows be raised when Tower's one-time press spokesman, Dan Howard, criticizes the press for letting their "standards slip in the pressure-cooker environment of a hot story." But one of Tower's chief accusers, conservative leader Paul Weyrich, whose testimony about Tower's alleged alcohol abuse and womanizing opened the floodgates to disparaging charges about the nominee, also is sharply critical of the media coverage:

> *"Congressman Thomas S. Foley of Washington was the victim of a smear at his moment of greatest political triumph."*

> Even though I wanted to see John Tower defeated, the press was very unfair to him. The man was not given a fair shake. While I approved of the outcome, I had the feeling you might get in watching your mother-in-law drive off the bridge in your new Cadillac.

Even more arresting is the self-criticism journalists direct at their own profession's handling of Tower. In retrospect, many newspeople believe the reporting became caught up in a frenzy fervor; competitive news organizations matched their rivals' unsubstantiated allegations tit for tat, whipping up public sentiment that played into the hands of the partisans conducting a rumor-fed lynching. "Much of the reporting about Tower was unconscionable," declared NBC's Tom Brokaw. "Everything became fair game, including the airing of very damaging allegations without documentation or confirmation."

The Media's Misdeeds

Tower was dismantled piece by piece beginning almost from the moment his confirmation hearings opened on January 25 and continuing over six agonizing weeks until the Senate vote rejecting him on March 9. Many arguably legitimate questions were raised about Tower's indiscreet private behavior and possible public conflicts of interest in his dealings with the defense industry. . . .

But John Tower's sins cannot excuse the media's misdeeds. As ABC's Pentagon correspondent Bob Zelnick observes, "Most of the speculation done on his private life was uncalled for, and it never passed the threshold of relevancy that would have made it a fit subject to explore." The last point is debatable. Alcohol use and abuse is always a legitimate concern about someone in the military chain of command; indiscreet behavior can be dangerously compromising in any top official; and womanizing is highly inappropriate for a potential Defense Department chief who serves as a role model for the men and women of the armed forces. The real threshold that much of the printed and broadcast information about John Tower failed to pass was not relevancy but the most important standard of all: proof. This glaring inadequacy was the true source of the press's unfairness during the Tower affair.

Tom Foley

The smear is as old as politics, a time-dishonored technique designed to destroy an opponent by slander. Ironically, Congressman Thomas S. Foley of Washington was the victim of a smear at his moment of greatest political triumph, the ascension to the Speakership of the U.S. House of Representatives on June 6, 1989. An unholy alliance of Foley's own Democratic partisans and Republican party opponents orchestrated the conniving behind Foley's calumniation, with the press as an unwitting coconspirator.

As Speaker Jim Wright struggled under the weight of scandal in the spring of 1989, the eyes of Congress and the press increasingly turned to Wright's next in command and likely successor, Majority Leader Foley. Some of Wright's closest allies sought a last-ditch rescue of their Speaker by use of the innuendo that Foley was homosexual. Like hundreds of other items of gossip, this completely unsubstantiated rumor had wafted through the halls of Congress for years, and a few journalists had picked up on it from time to time. But now a few senior Democratic congressmen were spreading the rumor. As Steve Roberts [of *U.S. News & World Report*] explained it, "Wright's more devious supporters were creating a backfire of doubt about Foley as a way of slowing the momentum to get rid of Wright." The "documentation" used by the Wright backers was an FBI report on an apparently deranged individual who had made threats against Foley and claimed past homosexual contact with the Speaker-to-be. This report was filed in the office of the House sergeant at arms, where it was available to Wright's backers. Some concerned senior Democrats, including House Ways and Means Committee Chairman Dan Rostenkowski (D., Ill.), confronted Foley directly about the allegation, and Foley adamantly denied it.

Continued Gossip

Thus the Democratic rumor channel dried up, but the gossip continued to flow from two other sources. The Republican party was naturally delighted to see the Democrats in disarray, and wanted to be helpful in fostering additional chaos in the opposition party. Among the many Republicans passing along the rumor was an aide to House GOP [Grand Old Party] Whip Newt Gingrich of Georgia. This staffer was particularly aggressive in her rumormongering, and she attempted to play one media outlet off against the other in the traditional game of "Beat Your Competitor" (that is, "The *Washington Post* has this already so you'd better hurry up and get it into print"). Less intentionally, some in the news media were also doing their part to keep the rumor alive. In mid-May Rowland Evans and Robert Novak quoted a

> *"Fred Barnes of the* **New Republic** *referred to a 'rumor about sexual misconduct by Foley.'"*

Democratic party insider's small-circulation newsletter in their large-circulation column about the "alleged homosexuality of one Democrat who might move up the succession ladder." Fred Barnes of the *New Republic* referred to a "rumor about sexual misconduct by Foley." ("I wish now I hadn't put that sentence in," concedes Barnes.) CBS News was hot on the trail of the Foley rumor as well. Phil Jones, the network's widely respected Capitol Hill correspondent, worked for weeks to nail down a purported Foley homosexual liaison with a man who by May 1989 was a prisoner at Lorton reformatory (just outside the District of Columbia in suburban Virginia). . . .

The most explicit press airing of the Foley rumor came in a column by the New York *Daily News*'s Lars-Erik Nelson on June 5. His intentions were good—an exposé of the Gingrich aide's rumormongering. But in so doing, Nelson revealed some of the heretofore unpublished details of the charges (such as the Lorton inmate's allegation). "In the process of making references to the rumor, some journalists spread gossip to millions that previously had the attention of about 2,000 people," observed the *Washington Post*'s media critic, Eleanor Randolph.

The press was primed, and the public stage set, for a grand denouement. The Republican National Committee's communications director, Mark Goodin, obliged by providing the plot's finale. Goodin circulated a four-page memo addressed to Republican leaders on Capitol Hill that was headlined: "Tom Foley: Out of the Liberal Closet." The homosexual allusion was further enhanced by a comparison of Foley's voting record with that of Massachusetts's avowedly gay congressman Barney Frank. The memo was leaked from the Hill to several reporters, and its contents were publicly divulged on the very day Foley ascended to the Speakership. In most newspapers across America, the unproven rumor shared nearly equal billing with Foley's election, and Foley felt compelled to declare on national television, "I am, of course, not a homosexual."

Media Coverage of the President's Character Is Counterproductive

by Jon Katz

About the author: *Jon Katz writes a media column for the weekly magazine New York.*

Think of it as a contemporary variation on an enduring American scene: *Suddenly, the door to an office bursts open. A shouting throng of guys in stenciled windbreakers rushes inside, yelling for everybody to get down. The men start grabbing folders and yanking the cabinets open. The people inside scream, hit the floor, and are dragged out in handcuffs.*

The man—or maybe it's a woman—behind the desk stares at the intruders in shock. "Who are you, FBI? SEC [Securities and Exchange Commission]?"

"No, governor," the cadre leader spits out as his troops start snapping photos. "It's much more serious than that. Those guys need a warrant to come in here. We're the media."

It's an interesting question: What *is* the difference between a Washington reporter and a G-man?

Journalistic Disdain

In modern American journalism, being arrogant and disliked has somehow mutated into a virtue. While politicians are supposed to reflect the people's will, journalists are trained to ignore it. The people's business can wait while campaigns, leaders, and the business of governing itself become paralyzed by journalists' presumptions about their own self-important role. Who among them cares that nobody likes what they're doing? Are editors and reporters worried that Americans think issues like violence and health care are being pushed aside so that journalists can play cop? Today's journalistic ethic says, "They're not supposed to like us—only read and watch us, because we know their interests better than they do. And the more they hate us, the more that proves we are righteous."

And they sure *don't* like us. Sixty-seven percent of people answering a Los Angeles *Times* poll in 1993 agreed with this statement: "The news media give more coverage to stories that support their own point of view than to those that don't." Other news-organization polls—along with those conducted by outfits like Harris, Gallup, and Yankelovich—all show declining respect for journalism and rising pique over its greater intrusions into government and public life. And much of the American media have gotten out of the habit of listening to the people who read and watch them, considering that pandering. Readers and viewers are presumed too dumb to know what's good for them—their brains and judgment rotted by *Inside Edition*, Oprah, and Beavis and Butt-head, all stunningly successful programs that listen very closely to what *their* consumers think. Whitewater has become a prime example of how journalism relentlessly alienates itself from its own consumers.

What Became of Real Investigative Reporting?

If the discovery that our new president and his spouse were up to their necks in speculative land hustles while spouting pious populist aphorisms is unnerving, here's something even scarier: The line between journalism and law enforcement is disappearing. Of course the media should do some investigating, especially when prosecutors and police fail to do their jobs. There were 1,800 reporters accredited to cover the Reagan White House (as compared with six who covered F.D.R.'s [Franklin Delano Roosevelt] White House during World War II)—and it would have been swell if one had discovered that Oliver North was running his own war out of the basement instead of having a Beirut weekly break the story. Crusading journalists such as hell-raising Thomas Paine; Nellie Bly, who got herself committed in order to witness conditions inside a lunatic asylum; and Randy Shilts, who dropped the anesthetizing journalistic pose of objectivity to portray the story of AIDS in America, have always transcended mere reporting to expose indifference, corruption, injustice.

> *"Campaigns, leaders, and the business of governing itself become paralyzed by journalists' presumptions about their own self-important role."*

But real investigative reporting has almost vanished from mainstream journalism, while variously disingenuous and Cotton Mather-ish obsessions with character and morality have become part of its central ideology. These days, nothing makes journalistic blood boil more than impropriety or its appearance—not bodies piling up in municipal emergency rooms or people living in the streets. It seems that there is no bigger story than the press and its journalistic notions of self-importance. "Well, you have to understand that they don't give awards or make movies about reporters who cover municipal government well," says a City Hall reporter for New York *Newsday*.

What's taken for investigative reporting today is actually closer to inquisition by mob, and journalism by leak and humiliation. Since they have no training in police-style investigation and there are no statutes restricting the scope of their inquiries, reporters are free to pursue or explore any behavior their editors or producers deem immoral or improper or vaguely scummy. No line of questioning is off-limits. After 200 years in which police abuses have been steadily lessened and state intrusions into individuals' moral and sexual lives beaten back, journalists are scrambling to replace the Morals Squads, an irony brought home vividly during the 1992 campaign, when reporters joined forces with Gennifer Flowers [who alleged that she and Bill Clinton had a lengthy affair] to wound and nearly derail Clinton.

> *"Whitewater is primarily a production of the New York* Times, *with crucial aid and comfort provided by . . . the* Wall Street Journal *editorial page."*

Whitewater

Although the details of Whitewater are profoundly confusing, the implications raised by the press are clear enough: WHITEWATER: ANGUISH INSIDE THE WHITE HOUSE ran a line at the top of March 28's [1994] *Newsweek*. And DEEP WATER said the cover line on *Time*: HOW THE PRESIDENT'S MEN TRIED TO HINDER THE WHITEWATER INVESTIGATION. That over an ominous black-and-white photo of a president looking as deep in crisis as anyone ever has. If it's on the cover of *Time*, it's the most important story in the world, right? But is it?

We all know the drill by now. Any other agenda gets shoved aside while journalists scrutinize every meeting, conversation, log, and document. While the bloated Washington press corps is now in full pursuit, generating fire storms of heat but pinpoints of light, Whitewater is primarily a production of the New York *Times*, with crucial aid and comfort provided by the pit bulls of the *Wall Street Journal* editorial page.

First reported by Jeff Gerth of the *Times* Washington bureau in 1992, Whitewater has also endured because of the attention paid it by *Times* Washington columnist William Safire, the James Jesus Angleton of capital intrigue. Safire has written darkly of Whitewater ever since the Vincent Foster [deputy White House counsel] suicide, but on March 28, 1994, he broke new ground in insider Washington journalism, boring directly into Hillary Rodham Clinton's head to produce a column. (Didn't the *Times* used to have armies of imperious editors who didn't like making things up?) Here is Safire imagining Hillary's thinking on Whitewater: "Bill struck the perfect note in his prime-time press conference. No more fingers-on-the-chest, 'Who, me guilty?' and no more 'no, no, no, no' pounding on the lectern. Just the statesman who won't be distracted. Sometimes he's just marvelous. . . . I can't do that; I know too much. For a few more weeks, I can give interviews to the gentler journalists but sooner or later somebody's going to hit me with a murder drill."

A murder drill? Can somebody please save us from our best journalists?

"You wouldn't believe the tenor of the Whitewater story-planning meetings," says a *Times* editor who has attended several. "I think I'm working for the Justice Department. Everybody's looking for the big break. There's a lot of deployment and memos and legal talk, but not much on the conceptual nature of the coverage, if you know what I mean."

We know what he means. "I don't know what it is," says a Washington *Post* political reporter, "but the more education journalists have, the more seriously they seem to take themselves."

All of this makes one think that maybe Watergate wasn't such a journalistic high-water mark after all. Maybe the most salient lesson of our great modern presidential scandal isn't that the media should bring down a president but that journalists *could*—and get rich, famous, and much more powerful in the process.

Ignoring Issues

As we drown in suggestions of presidential impropriety, Americans might want to contemplate the issues that aren't being talked about. This isn't just a panel-discussion difference over journalistic philosophy. When the pack are swarming on one thing, it means that they are ignoring others. A case in point: Even though it was nowhere near the front page, the *Times* broke a huge story in April 1994, reporting on a Clinton-administration initiative: a plan to respond to the epidemic of teenage pregnancies by creating a system that would send a million adults into 1,000 mostly poor inner-city schools to "mentor" urban kids. Most everyone has heard of Whitewater—but few have heard about this communitarian scheme or had a chance to debate its merits.

> *"As we drown in suggestions of presidential impropriety, Americans might want to contemplate the issues that aren't being talked about."*

The fact is, journalists, preoccupied as they are by the daily scramble of deadlines and stories, may be the least equipped people in public life to spend so much time delineating and sorting through complex notions of morality, sexual propriety, even questions of character. Theologians, academics, and philosophers have spent centuries defining morality, ethics, and character. There's nothing about journalists that suggests these questions would be better left to them.

Chapter 4

Should Legal Measures
Address Ethics in Politics?

Chapter Preface

In 1978, in the aftermath of the Watergate scandal, Congress created the independent Office of Special Counsel. Through this office, independent prosecutors (also known as special prosecutors) investigate and, if necessary, prosecute high-ranking executive-branch officials suspected of violating the law.

Politicians and others advocate ethical conduct in government, but they disagree about whether the independent prosecutor statute effectively serves that purpose. According to critics, special prosecutor investigations do more to smear government officials than to probe unethical behavior. Former U.S. Supreme Court nominee Robert H. Bork writes, "The independent counsel damages lives and reputations in ways that few regular prosecutors ever could or would." Bork argues that because they are given wide latitude in their investigations, prosecutors frequently and unjustly malign officials without levying charges against them.

In defense of the independent prosecutor system, proponents contend that appointing a prosecutor without official ties to the executive branch is the proper way to investigate suspected wrongdoing. According to former special prosecutor James C. McKay, "The independent-counsel statute serve[s] a useful purpose and . . . eliminate[s] institutional conflicts of interest." McKay adds that the public more readily accepts independent prosecutors' decisions than judgments made by Department of Justice officials.

The independent prosecutor statute is one of the legal measures aimed at promoting ethics in politics that are examined in this chapter.

Campaign Finance Reform Should Address Congressmembers' Improper Spending

by Dwight Morris and Murielle E. Gamache

About the authors: *Dwight Morris is an editor for special investigations at the* Los Angeles Times *bureau in Washington, D.C. Murielle E. Gamache is a senior editorial researcher at the bureau.*

While most members of Congress say they want [campaign finance] "reform," the definitions of that term differ so vastly that any meaningful reform is unlikely. . . .

No reform that allows candidates to spend campaign money on luxury automobiles and other items that do little more than enhance their personal lifestyles can be called reform. Campaign spending should be limited to campaigns. If members of Congress are serious about campaign finance reform, then Rep. William L. Clay (D-Mo.) should not be able to tap his campaign to pay the $799 monthly lease and repair bills on a car he drives in Washington, D.C. He should be forbidden from using campaign money to buy season tickets to Washington Redskins games or pay for travel to New Jersey for meetings with the Board of Benedict College and with the United Negro College Fund. He most certainly should not be allowed to use campaign funds to pay for his $310 dues at the Robin Hood Swim Club in Silver Spring, Maryland. If he wants to attend the Congressional Black Caucus Weekend retreats, his campaign should not pick up the tab, nor should it pay for expenses incurred on trips to Jamaica, New York, for meetings of the Clay Scholarship Board and for a reception for former Rep. William H. Gray III.

If Congress is serious about reducing the cost of campaigns, as opposed to the cost of politics, then Rep. Barbara-Rose Collins (D-Mich.) should not be able to spend nearly $9,000 over two election cycles on clothes and image consulta-tions. [Republican New York senator] Alfonse D'Amato should not be able to tap his campaign treasury for $156,729 to lease and maintain two luxury auto-mobiles, one of which is used by the senator in Washington, D.C., not in New York. Nor should D'Amato be able to spend campaign funds to cover a $4,439 harvest day celebration of New York agricultural products to which senators and their staffs are invited. Rep. Henry A. Waxman (D-Calif.) should never again be permitted to spend $4,500 of his campaign treasury to help defray the cost of a trip that he and his wife take to Israel or any other foreign destination.

Under anything that would pass for real reform, Rep. Louis Stokes (D-Ohio) would not be allowed to spend $4,111 on a reception at the House [of Represen-tatives] restaurant for attendees of the National Baptist Convention, nor would he be allowed to tap his campaign treasury to cover the cost of his family's ac-commodations at Walt Disney World Resorts, as he did in April 1992, or to cover the $3,199 bill at the Washington Hilton and Towers, where he and his family stayed during a Congressional Black Caucus annual weekend bash. Sen. Bob Graham (D-Fla.) would not be able to spend $3,905 of his campaign funds on Super Bowl tickets given to his friends, nor would he be allowed to spend $4,156 on gifts, including boxes of pecans and "Florida ties" handed out to fel-low senators and employees of the congressional barbershop and shoe-shine stand. Challenger Allan L. Keyes (R-Md.) would not be permitted to pay himself an $8,500 monthly salary from campaign funds should he decide to run again, a practice that brought him a $49,614 income during his challenge to Democratic Sen. Barbara A. Mikulski. Real reform would forbid the lavish, lifestyle enhanc-ing expenditures of Senate hopeful Carol Moseley-Braun, who dropped $22,445 of her campaign funds during the four-day Democratic National Convention in New York. True reform would provide for a careful review of D'Amato's $35,252 tab at Gandel's Gourmet and the 220 meals of $200 or less con-sumed by Sen. Daniel K. Inouye (D-Hawaii) in the Washington, D.C., metropolitan area.

> *"Senate hopeful Carol Moseley-Braun . . . dropped $22,445 of her campaign funds during the four-day Democratic National Convention in New York."*

Real reform would ban contribu-tions such as the $85,198 Rep. Paul E. Gillmor (R-Ohio) funneled from his own campaign treasury into that of his wife Karen, who waged a successful campaign for the state senate. It would prohibit Inouye from tapping his campaign treasury for a $150,000 donation to the Hawaii Education Foundation, an organization he founded to provide scholar-ships to Hawaiian high school students. While it may be a worthy cause, Inouye's foundation has nothing to do with campaigning. The $94,319 television campaign spearheaded by Rep. David E. Bonior (D-Mich.) on behalf of a proposed ballot initiative to give middle income homeowners a $500 property tax cut also had nothing to do with the 1992 campaign. The initiative was sponsored by the Michigan Homeowners Tax Break Committee, which Bonior cochaired.

When members find themselves in need of a lawyer to defend them against ethical and criminal charges, they should not be able to tap their funds to pay for legal counsel. Such expenses certainly should not be included in the list of exemptions from any spending limits that are imposed. Eliminating these expenditures would

"Random audits might have discouraged some campaigns from spending money in questionable ways."

do far more to reduce the cost of campaigns than any of the spending limits currently under discussion.

Empower the Federal Election Commission

No reform will be useful unless the Federal Election Commission (FEC) is given the power to act. Its current six-member structure, which mandates that the commission have three Republican and three Democratic members, was from the beginning an invitation to failure. While Congress seems unlikely to create an agency that truly has watchdog authority over campaign practices, that is ultimately the only path to true reform.

Rather than cutting the FEC's budget, as both President Bill Clinton and members of Congress have proposed, the agency's budget should be increased. No election law is worth anything if it is not enforced. At present, the FEC's budget does not allow them to pursue all the cases that we have routinely brought to their attention.

Along with that increased budget, Congress should also give the FEC authority to conduct random audits of campaigns. The FEC should invest some of that larger budget in additional staff auditors. Following the 1992 campaign, FEC staff analysts identified forty-six campaigns that deserved an audit according to the agency's formula developed to score accounting problems. Citing insufficient staff, the FEC launched audits of only eight campaigns with the most egregious problems, including Moseley-Braun's.

Pleading Guilt

Random audits might have discouraged some campaigns from spending money in questionable ways. A random audit of the 1989 and 1990 campaign books of Sen. Charles S. Robb (D-Va.) most certainly would have raised questions about purposefully misleading entries made by David K. McCloud, Robb's then-chief of staff.

In May 1992 McCloud plead guilty to authorizing the use of campaign funds to purchase an illegal audiotape of a conversation between Virginia Gov. Douglas Wilder and a supporter. The $2,375 bill from the law firm of Hofheimer, Nusbaum, McPhaul, and Samuels was originally rejected by the campaign because

McCloud "could not pay the bill as submitted." The law firm then folded the charge into a $4,790 bill for "research services." McCloud also admitted to recording as fund-raising costs a $500 payment that was actually used to pay the travel expenses of an aide who went to Boston to meet with a woman who claimed she had had an affair with Robb while he was governor.

Random audits would also have uncovered that Rep. Carroll Hubbard, Jr. (D-Ky.) diverted $50,000 in campaign funds to personal use. This began in 1990 when he ordered his staffers not to report to the FEC campaign payments to him totaling $5,500. Such diversions were carried on throughout much of the 1992 cycle. He used the money to pay his home heating bills, school tuition for his daughter, credit card bills, and his ex-wife's cable television bills, among other things. He used his campaign assets as collateral to obtain a $15,000 personal loan, another violation of federal law. Hubbard routinely demanded that congressional staffers campaign for him and his current wife— who also sought a House seat in Kentucky—while on the government payroll. Hubbard's foibles accidentally came to light as a result of the investigation into the House banking scandal. In April 1994 Hubbard plead guilty to federal charges of conspiring to defraud the FEC, stealing government property, and obstructing justice.

> *"Artful dodges in the name of reform will only serve to deepen the public's distrust of politicians and the government they represent."*

Failing to Itemize

The FEC should more carefully scrutinize those who routinely fail to itemize thousands of dollars in expenses. While it is possible that the campaign of Rep. Mary Rose Oakar (D-Ohio) spent $121,630 in two years on items that cost less than $200, the fact that this represented 10 percent of her total spending should raise questions. Rep. John P. Murtha (D-Pa.) should not have been permitted to list only the vendors on an $8,139 Visa bill without stating what he bought from each vendor or how much each item cost. . . .

Reform is possible, and in a system increasingly characterized by voter cynicism, it is absolutely crucial that *meaningful* reforms be instituted. If, as [Oklahoma representative] Mike Synar put it, "the American public made a bold statement about gridlock and change in Washington" in 1992, then artful dodges in the name of reform will only serve to deepen the public's distrust of politicians and the government they represent.

"Soft Money" Campaign Contributions Require Stronger Regulation

by Anthony Corrado

About the author: *Anthony Corrado is an assistant professor of government at Colby College in Waterville, Maine. He served as presidential campaign coordinator for Nebraska senator Bob Kerrey in 1992.*

No reform of the campaign finance system can be considered successful if it fails to address the problems created by the rise of soft money [individual and group campaign contributions in any amount that are given to political parties' national committees for nonfederal election use only] in general election campaigns. Soft money has been the focal point of most of the criticisms leveled against the FECA [Federal Election Campaign Act] in recent years and many observers have advocated an outright ban on this source of funding. It is important to note, however, that soft money has certain merits in addition to its problems. Most importantly, it permits party organizations to participate in national electoral campaigns. Future reform in this area should therefore not eliminate soft money altogether, but instead prevent the abuses that have occurred in the past while retaining some means for national party organizations to play a role in presidential elections. That is, proposals for reform should balance the need to strengthen the role of parties in the political system with the need to provide full disclosure and protect against any possible undue influence on the part of large donors.

Full Disclosure

The first step that must be taken in order to improve the present system is to ensure that all soft money transactions are subject to full disclosure. The FEC [Federal Election Commission] now requires national party committees to report all receipts and disbursements made from party accounts, whether or not

Excerpted from Anthony Corrado, *Paying for Presidents: Public Financing in National Elections* (New York: Twentieth Century Fund, 1993); © 1993 by the Twentieth Century Fund, Inc. Reprinted by permission of the publisher.

they are connected to federal election activity. The Commission also requires that contributions and allocations from nonfederal funds be disclosed. These changes constitute an important first step in addressing the issues raised by soft money financing. Significant sums of money, however, remain hidden from public view. The law needs to be strengthened to ensure that a complete accounting of party activity is made available to the public.

Federal law should also require a detailed accounting of all soft money transactions. Besides reporting the amount and source of each donation and the accounts into which it was deposited, the committees should also disclose the details of any transfers made between accounts. The disclosure reports filed in 1992 under the FEC regulations show hundreds of thousands of dollars at a time being shifted around with the only description noted as "interfund transfer." Such scant information makes it impossible to trace the flow of nonfederal funds in the political system. Any transfers made between party accounts should include a specific itemization of the reason for the transfer. While these provisions will increase the reporting burden imposed on national party organizations, they are needed to provide a clear understanding of the flow of nonfederal funds at the federal level and to prevent any inappropriate commingling of nonfederal and federal monies.

State and Local Committees

Another way to improve disclosure is to require state and local committees to report the amounts and purposes of any contributions and disbursements made from accounts maintained by state party organizations. Under the current rules, national committees are required to report the amounts transferred to state and local party organs, and these committees report monies raised and spent in support of federal candidates. Other sums raised by state and local committees can only be determined, at best, by reviewing state disclosure records. Given the efficacy of these laws, the use of these funds essentially remains a mystery. While it is important to respect state authority and the principle of federalism, federal law could require state and local committees to disclose all disbursements for such activities as voter registration drives, voter identification and mobilization programs, polling, and generic advertising, since these

> *"Generally, reform should follow a path designed to turn soft money into hard money."*

efforts may influence federal elections. This would provide more knowledge of the role of soft money in national elections and of the extent to which nonfederal funds are used to assist federal candidates.

The second step needed to clean up soft money is to place limits on the sources and size of contributions to national party accounts. Generally, reform should follow a path designed to turn soft money into hard money; that is, to bring contributions for nonfederal or grass-roots activity into the purview of federal regulation and limit these donations. Most importantly, federal law should ban any contributions made by corporations or drawn from labor union treasury funds. These two sources of contributions have long been prohibited in federal campaigns and, even though the funds are not directly given to candidates, should be banned as a vehicle for backdoor financing. Prohibiting contributions from these sources is in keeping with the original spirit of the earliest federal campaign finance laws and will help to diminish popular perceptions of the role of special interests in national campaigns.

> *"Federal reform is not enough. Reform is also needed at the state level."*

Limiting Individual Donations

Individual contributions to nonfederal accounts should also be limited. In this regard, one proposal worth consideration is an idea suggested by the Clinton administration, which calls for the creation of a new contribution category—donations for grass-roots political activities. Under current law, an individual is allowed to give a total of $25,000 to federal candidates and parties each year, or $50,000 for each two-year election cycle. The maximum amount an individual can give to a candidate is $1,000 per election and, to a party, $20,000 a year. The administration's proposal would increase the two-year maximum to $60,000. Within that limit, an individual can donate up to $25,000 to candidates, $20,000 to the national party committees, and up to $20,000 to a party for grass-roots political activities in the states. The proposal thus limits the amount an individual can give for the types of activities exempted under the FECA's soft money provisions. Because the total amount represented in the three categories exceeds the maximum amount an individual may contribute, donors will have to choose how to distribute their funds among these broad purposes and establish their own priorities.

The merits of this plan are that it limits the size and sources of contributions, while allowing the national committees to maintain a role in the financing of national elections. An individual would be allowed to give no more than $40,000 to a national party committee for the financing of grass-roots or nonfederal activities in each election cycle. The plan thus eliminates the large, unrestricted soft money gifts that have raised so much concern in recent elections. The national committee would also no longer be able to accept huge corporate gifts or labor union donations. At the same time, the contribution level is set high enough so that parties will be able to raise sufficient funds to finance voter outreach programs, provide limited services to party subsidiaries and candidates, and make contributions to those seeking office at the state and local level. While some may question the particulars of this approach, the basic notion meets the broad criteria that should ground any future reform: it preserves a meaningful role for party organizations in national elections and eliminates large donations from wealthy interests.

The major shortcoming of this proposal is its failure to prevent wealthy interests from making large soft money contributions. Since state laws would still allow such donations, contributors could still give large sums for grass-roots activities by making these contributions directly to the state parties. This possibility highlights the problem of relying on federal statutes to regulate activity in a party system grounded on the principle of federalism. In order to eliminate the role of large contributors from the political system, federal reform is not enough. Reform is also needed at the state level, especially in those states that still allow unlimited political donations and contributions from corporations and labor unions.

New State Codes Are Needed

As the Center for Responsive Politics has suggested, there is a need for uniform campaign finance codes at the state level, similar to the Uniform Commercial Code that was established some years ago to standardize state approaches to regulating commercial transactions. Toward this end, the Council on Governmental Ethics Laws has drafted a model campaign finance statute for use as a guide to help states frame new legislation. While state legislatures are making progress in this area (in 1991 alone ten states passed new laws establishing or reducing campaign contribution limits), more needs to be done before these fat cat contributions are cleansed from the political system.

As long as state laws allow unlimited corporate and individual gifts, national party staff or campaign personnel could conceivably circumvent any federally imposed limits on soft money by soliciting large gifts that would violate federal law and directing them to state committees. For example, national party fundraisers could ask wealthy contributors to send a contribution of $100,000 or more directly to a particular state party account without the donation ever being deposited in a national party's bank account. To minimize this possibility, federal regulations should ban the solicitation of such gifts. Congress should adopt provisions similar to those that have been drafted for independent expenditures, which would prohibit any federal candidate, campaign staff member, party staff member, fundraiser, or other agent from soliciting, commanding, influencing, or controlling contributions made directly to state parties. In addition, Congress should establish a provision similar to that contained in Senate bill S. 3, which was adopted by the Senate in 1993 and prohibits any federal candidate or office-holder from raising or spending any funds in connection with a federal, state, or local election, including funds for registration and get-out-the-vote drives and generic advertising, unless the funds are raised in accordance with federal law.

> *"A ceiling on grass-roots spending would guard against excessive spending in a particular state."*

Grass-Roots Activities

Another provision of S. 3 that should be incorporated into federal regulations is a limitation on the amount a party may spend on exempted grass-roots activities. Instead of the unrestricted spending allowed under current law, the bill establishes a limit of four cents times the voting age population of a state on all spending by state and local party committees in connection with a presidential general election campaign. This new coordinated expenditure allowance, which is imposed on all expenditures other than generic television advertising, would supplement the current limit on national party coordinated spending. Had this provision been in place for the 1992 election cycle, it would have restricted soft money expenditures, excluding television advertising, to a total of $20.6 million per party.

A ceiling on grass-roots spending would guard against excessive spending in a particular state and encourage national party committees to distribute grass-roots funds more evenly among the states. It would also force state and local party committees within a state to work together more closely to plan spending strategies and establish financial priorities. So, despite limiting party spending to a certain extent, this reform will not only provide party organizations with the funds needed to conduct extensive voter registration and turnout drives, but will also serve to enhance the role of the national committees as financial brokers and active participants in the development of general election strategies. This change may also help to broaden participation in the planning and implementation of such programs, and encourage stronger working relationships between national and state party organizations.

Congress Needs Improved Ethics Committees

by Dennis F. Thompson

About the author: *Dennis F. Thompson, a former Brookings Institution scholar, is a professor of political philosophy and the director of Programs in Ethics and the Professions at Harvard University's John F. Kennedy School of Government in Cambridge, Massachusetts.*

Although both elections and courts serve as important tribunals for the enforcement of the standards of conduct for legislators, neither can substitute for Congress itself. Ethics committees are here to stay, and Congress must look for ways to make their procedures better fulfill the principles of legislative ethics. The most important reform would establish a new outside commission, as described later in this viewpoint. But even without this commission, a number of changes could improve the way the committees conduct their business. Even with such a commission, the other changes could help the committees do their job better. In either case the committees would still play a major role in enforcing ethics standards because Congress retains final authority for imposing ethics sanctions on its own members. To recognize the deficiencies of self-discipline is not to call for the abolition of the ethics committees.

Partisanship Concerns

Partisanship is the first fear that comes to members' minds when the independence of the ethics process is challenged. The Senate created a strictly bipartisan committee in 1964, partly in response to the partisan disputes over the investigation of Bobby Baker, the secretary of the majority, who was later convicted of criminal charges involving the misuse of his office and campaign contributions. The House followed suit in 1967 after the controversial case of Adam Clayton Powell, who was "excluded" by the House but was later reinstated by the Supreme Court. To avoid partisanship, the ethics committees have an equal number of members from each party, the only congressional committees to have such balanced representation. The members chosen for service are generally known as moderates and are usually less partisan than their colleagues. Members rarely volunteer for service on these committees.

The public decisions that the committees have reached generally do not seem to be partisan. The final votes are almost always unanimous and dissenting opinions are rare. The committees have imposed sanctions on more Democrats than Republicans from 1980 to 1995, even though the Democrats controlled Congress during most of this period. On average Democrats made up two-thirds of Congress but four-fifths of the total of members who received sanctions. There is no reason to believe that Democrats are more corrupt than their higher rate of sanction implies. Rather, it appears that the offenses they are more likely to commit are those most likely to receive more severe sanctions. Democrats are more often charged with bribery and related offenses; Republicans are more often accused of conflicts of interest. . . .

Committee Reports

The committees have the power to convene executive sessions at any time. In the House the committee is required to make public only a brief statement of an alleged violation and any written response from the accused member once a formal inquiry has begun. In the Senate the reports of staff and special counsel are treated as confidential. The special counsel's report in the Keating Five case [of U.S. senators charged with accepting illegal contributions from savings and loan operator Charles Keating] became public only because one of the committee members made it part of his own report. Some other members even brought charges against him for leaking a confidential document. When the committees do issue public reports, they are often too brief to be informative. From reading only the Senate committee's report on the Alfonse D'Amato case, even well-informed readers would have difficulty in discovering what conduct led to [bribery and improper influence] charges, let alone why the committee thought the conduct did not violate any standards. Although critics later raised questions about D'Amato's testimony, the committee never released the transcripts of the hearings.

> *"The ethics committees should be required to make public the content of all complaints and their disposition."*

Some of this secrecy is understandable. It not only protects the rights of members and witnesses, it also encourages citizens to bring forward complaints and enables committees to investigate them effectively and objectively. If a semi-independent commission took over the early phases of the process, perhaps confidentiality would be more acceptable. But in conjunction with the problem of members judging members, secrecy undermines public confidence. It tilts the balance too far against accountability.

If the present structure of the ethics process is not changed, the ethics committees should be required to make public the content of all complaints and their disposition. If the complaint is dismissed, reasons should be given. Committees should issue a full report at the end of any investigation and at the conclusion of any adjudication. If a special counsel is appointed at any stage, he or she should be required to prepare a report, which should also be made public at an appropriate time. The need for accountability and public confidence outweighs any increased burden of work and any risk of harm from leaked reports. Furthermore, if citizens knew that a full report would be made public at some stage, they could more easily accept the fact that some of the proceedings would be kept confidential in the earlier stages. . . .

> *"The range of sanctions available to the ethics committees and the chamber as a whole is limited."*

Disciplinary Power

The ultimate instrument of accountability inside Congress is the power to discipline members; yet the range of sanctions available to the ethics committees and the chamber as a whole is limited. Because expulsion is rarely used, public criticism ranging from censure to reproval is the principal mode of discipline. (In recent years, fines have occasionally been imposed, as in the David Durenberger case.) In the Senate the absence of fixed terminology of criticism has led the attorneys of accused members, evidently armed with thesauruses, to negotiate for the mildest possible language. Senators Herman Talmadge and Durenberger preferred to be "denounced" rather than "censured," and the ethics committee complied. The proliferation of terms—confusing to members as well as to the public—has probably contributed to suspicions about the fairness and openness of the process.

The Senate Ethics Study Commission's recommendation to simplify the schema of sanctions (bringing it closer to the one used by the House) could help alleviate the problem. Committees themselves should take more responsibility to clarify the meaning of the sanction in each case they decide. In addition to specifying the level of severity and the rule or standard that was violated, a formal judgment by a committee could describe the kind of injury to individuals and the kind of damage to the institution at stake.

Measures could also be taken to give the committee (or at least the chamber as a whole) more authority over what can be one of the most potent sanctions: the loss of positions of power within Congress (chairmanships, ranking memberships, and seniority). At present the Senate committee can only recommend these sanctions to party conferences, which have never imposed any such discipline. In the House since 1980 the Democratic Caucus has required members who are indicted in the criminal process to step down from chairmanships. Republicans have been more reluctant to discipline members under such circumstances. The party refused to remove Joseph McDade from his position as ranking member of the Appropriations Committee long after he had been indicted in 1992 on charges of bribery. Because party organizations in Congress have not acted as vigorously as they should, prohibitions should become part of the chambers' rules, and ethics committees should be given the authority to impose these sanctions. The positions from which members would be removed are properly considered offices of the institution, not the private property of the parties or individual members. All citizens and therefore all members have a legitimate interest in making sure that those who hold these positions live up to the ethical standards of the institution.

The Need for Ethics Commissions

No matter how much the ethics committees are strengthened and their procedures improved, the institutional conflict of interest inherent in members judging members remains. Most other professions and most other institutions have come to appreciate that self-regulation of ethics is not adequate and have accepted at least a modest measure of outside discipline. Congress should do the same.

Proposals to establish an independent body that would supplement and partially replace the functions of the ethics committees are not popular in Congress. In 1994 the Senate Ethics Study Commission considered and rejected all proposals that would involve outsiders in the process. Nevertheless, support for them is growing. Members in both houses have introduced resolutions—at last count, five—that would establish some version of an independent body. Many state legislatures have set up independent ethics commissions, many of which regulate conduct of legislators as well as campaign practices and lobbyists. Some city councils have created similar commissions.

The advantages of delegating some authority to a relatively independent body should be clear. . . . An outside body would be likely to reach more objective, independent judgments. It could more credibly protect members' rights and enforce institutional obligations without regard to political or personal loyalties. It would provide more effective accountability and help restore the confidence of the public in the ethics process. An additional advantage that should appeal to all members: an outside body would reduce the time that any member would have to spend on the chores of ethics regulation.

> *"The institutional conflict of interest inherent in members judging members remains."*

The need for an outside body is especially important in cases of institutional corruption. Here the institutional conflict of interest is at its most severe. When members judge other members for conduct that is part of the job they all do together, the perspectives of the judge and the judged converge most closely. The conduct at issue cannot be separated from the norms and practices of the institution, and the judgment in the case implicates all who are governed by those norms and practices. The political fate of the judges and the judged is also joined together. Even if they are of different parties, they face similar political pressures. Especially when the institution is implicated in the corruption, some of those who judge the corruption should come from outside the institution.

There are many different ways of involving nonmembers in the process, and some are more likely than others to achieve the needed improvements. In general, the better methods keep the roles of the members and nonmembers separate. Any such reform should also be consistent with a two-step process of investigation and adjudication and with the principles of legislative ethics. Here is one version of an enforcement process that meets these criteria.

A Model for Ethics Commissions

Two bodies in each chamber would be responsible for enforcing standards of ethics in Congress: an ethics committee resembling the present body and a semi-independent ethics commission. (A possible variation would establish a single commission for both chambers.) The commissions would investigate charges against members to determine whether there is substantial, credible evidence that a violation of the chamber's ethics rules has occurred. The proceedings of the commissions would not normally be public, but they would publicly report their findings to their respective ethics committees. The commissions' membership, budget, and the standards they enforce would all be under the control of their ethics committee or each chamber as a whole.

Each commission would consist of seven distinguished citizens with a knowledge of legislative ethics and congressional practice. Three would

> *"The conduct at issue cannot be separated from the norms and practices of the institution."*

be appointed by the majority leader or Speaker and three by the minority leader of each chamber. The seventh, who would serve as chair, would be chosen by the other six from a list of three proposed by the ethics committee of the relevant chamber (with a random procedure for breaking ties). Commission members would serve six-year, staggered terms. No sitting members, family or business associates of members, lobbyists, or others with close current connections to Congress could serve.

The number of former members who might serve should be limited, perhaps to a maximum of two, although few former members would be likely to meet criteria set out above and also be willing to serve. No more than one or two former members would probably be needed to make sure that the commissions are adequately informed about the customs and practices of congressional life. More would be likely to dominate the process, as professionals typically do on ethics committees and disciplinary boards that include lay representation. Further, it is important to keep this part of the process as independent as possible, primarily to inspire public confidence. Also, the more independent the commissions are, the more acceptable the confidentiality of the proceedings is likely to be. With relatively independent commissions, confidentiality could be consistent with accountability and promote fairness and independence at the same time.

In addition to investigating cases, the commissions could also take over the advisory and educational functions now exercised by the ethics committees. They could also oversee the audit of the financial disclosure reports. The staffs of the commissions would operate more like a congressional service such as the Congressional Budget Office. The aim would be to develop a professional staff as independent as possible from the partisan divisions and collegial pressures of the Senate and House. The commissions would also be well placed to review not only individual conduct but also institutional practices and make recommendations for institutional reforms.

The Role of the Ethics Committees

Under this proposal the composition of the ethics committees would not necessarily change, but their functions would be significantly modified. They would hear and decide cases only after the commission had found credible evidence of a violation. They would then make a final judgment or a recommendation to the full chamber. If the work of the commission and its report were as thorough and fair as it should be, a committee's task would be much simpler than it is now. Many cases could probably be settled without any hearings, and in those that could not, the hearings would probably be much shorter.

It is true that in cases in which a committee disagreed with a commission's finding, the committee could feel forced to conduct extensive hearings itself. But these hearings would not likely be any longer than those in the present system or those in any of the other proposed systems, and on this plan they would be less frequent. The committees would still have the final authority on any changes in the standards, although the recommendations could come from the commissions and their staffs.

> *"The more independent the commissions are, the more acceptable the confidentiality of the proceedings is likely to be."*

Simplifying the tasks of the ethics committees in this way would make many of the questions that critics have raised about the present system less urgent. There would be no need to expand the number of members. More senior members might be persuaded to serve. Rotating terms (which reduce continuity) would be less necessary. There would be no problems about the status of nonmembers on a congressional committee. Other tensions in the present system, such as the conflict between confidentiality and accountability, would also be reduced.

The Federal Election Commission Should Be Overhauled

by Brooks Jackson

About the author: *Brooks Jackson is a correspondent for the Cable News Network (CNN) and is a former investigative reporter for the* Wall Street Journal.

True [campaign finance] reform will require a program endorsed by the best and most influential people in both parties, one potent enough to return power to voters and to cure the paralyzing money fever that grips Congress. To arouse the interest of a skeptical public, it needs to be as progressive and bold as the tax-reform bill of 1986. To work, it will require much stronger enforcement than the Federal Election Commission [FEC, an independent agency that administers and enforces campaign finance laws] has provided. . . .

A rejuvenated Federal Election Commission would begin strict enforcement of fewer and simpler regulations, including total disclosure of all hidden sources of party money. . . .

Designed to Fail

The Federal Election Commission doesn't do its job, and so any serious reform plan must overhaul it or replace it.

Congress designed the commission to fail, building in the propensity for partisan deadlocks, insisting on the appointment of pliant commissioners and creating a morass of procedural defenses for suspected wrongdoers. Enforcement is so weak that political professionals often calculate that the benefits of taking money in violation of the rules far outweigh the slim risk of being caught and fined. "People take the attitude that the commission is never going to get four votes, and so they can do anything they want," says Daniel Swillinger, a lawyer who once was an assistant general counsel at the FEC.

The commission needs a strong chairman. Unlike that of most other regulatory agencies, the FEC's leadership is largely ceremonial and rotates among its six members. Each serves a year at a time, presiding at meetings and signing documents, but lacks real authority over staff or exerts more than a trivial influence on the agenda. In all important matters, each commissioner has an equal say, making drift and deadlock inevitable.

A reform plan should give the chairman a multi-year term and authority to hire and fire staff, to authorize routine inquiries into alleged violations, and to issue warning letters or citations for the minor violations that make up the bulk of enforcement cases. The other commission members should vote only to set policies, to authorize subpoenas in the most serious investigations, and to act as a court of appeal.

Commission procedures also need streamlining; it currently requires several months and cumbersome legal analysis before the commission can extract a fine for a tardy disclosure report. For such common offenses, the equivalent of a traffic ticket would do. The laws need simplifying. The unenforceable state-by-state spending limits for presidential candidates, for example, should be abolished. The FEC also should hire a cadre of trained investigators skilled in following the paper trails that money leaves. Presently its lawyers take a passive role, mainly evaluating statements sent in by complainants and accused violators. The commission also needs a secure budget that can't be held hostage by members of Congress who are displeased when their own campaign violations are uncovered. It should have what California's election-law agency has—a yearly, inflation-adjusted budget that the legislature can increase, but cannot legally cut.

A New Panel

Ideally, the present commissioners should be removed and a new, five-member panel installed. The current members [as of 1990], with one or two exceptions, are too closely identified with the PACs [political action committees], parties and incumbent lawmakers they are supposed to be regulating. A new slate of commissioners would allow a fresh start and help restore public trust. Reducing the size to five would also get rid of the built-in tendency for the commission to deadlock. The structural bias should be in favor of enforcement, not against.

> *"The FEC also should hire a cadre of trained investigators skilled in following the paper trails that money leaves."*

Without safeguards, a strong chairman might abuse his or her position for partisan advantage. That danger can be reduced by requiring that the chairman be chosen from outside the president's political party, subject of course to confirmation by Congress. Presidents have gladly appointed partisan hacks from among the ranks of their own party, but when looking outside they would be more likely to search for a statesman, perhaps a retiring senator, governor or university president. In addition, Congress should require that at least one of the five commissioners should be a "public" member, not strongly affiliated with either major party. The "public" member would then become the tiebreaker if the two Democrats and two Republicans vote along partisan lines.

Seeking Justice

Nothing, of course, can guarantee perfect justice. A president might still install an overzealous, partisan chairman who could attempt to persecute political enemies. But the commission's ultimate power would still be to sue an alleged violator in federal court, where anyone unfairly accused would have all the safeguards available to any defendant.

The greatest danger is one that exists today, that the FEC would ignore abuses. Therefore, the law ought to be changed to make it easier for victims of serious violations to take their own grievances to court if the commission refuses to act. Currently, the FEC has exclusive jurisdiction, so victims have nowhere else to go for help.

> *"The law ought to be changed to make it easier for victims of serious violations to take their own grievances to court."*

Structural changes alone aren't enough. The FEC's institutional culture has decayed, and a new spirit must be instilled. Commissioners spend their time haggling over legal technicalities, drafting ever more permissive interpretations of increasingly complicated rules and maneuvering for partisan advantage. They see their constituency as the members of Congress and the parties, not the voting public.

The commission's performance has been so poor, and its friends are so few, that an overhaul might be the easiest of all reforms to get through Congress.

Congress Should Eliminate Its Special Privileges

by The Heritage Foundation

About the author: *The Heritage Foundation is a conservative public policy research institute in Washington, D.C., that advocates free-market economics and limited government.*

Members of Congress continue to enjoy numerous unjustifiable perks, despite the strides made by the new congressional majority [of Republicans in 1995] against waste and big spending on Capitol Hill. Eliminating seven special benefits still enjoyed by Members of Congress is the objective of the Citizen Congress Act, which was introduced in the House in November 1995.

Republicans Mark Sanford (SC) and Wayne Allard (CO) introduced the bill, which they view as furthering reforms, such as reduced congressional spending and staffing and the application of private-sector laws to Congress, already achieved by the 104th Congress. The bill would reform congressional pay, pensions, health care, travel, and mailing practices. It is being backed vigorously by term limits supporters, who see it as a useful and immediately achievable step toward making Congress more directly responsive to American citizens.

Seven Perks

• *The congressional pension system.* The Citizen Congress Act would abolish the congressional pension system, replacing it with arrangements by which Members of Congress would allocate part of their existing pay for retirement savings. Benefits accrued by Members as of the date of enactment of the bill would be grandfathered.

The existing congressional pension system provides benefits significantly in excess of those provided by most private-sector retirement plans. Congressional benefits even exceed those of most other federal employees, since Congress treats itself in the same fashion as high-risk occupations such as police and firefighters are treated.

The Heritage Foundation, "Ending the Seven Pillars of Perkdom: The Citizen Congress Act," *Reforming Congress*, no. 27, October 1995. Reprinted with permission.

The generous pensions not only burden taxpayers, but also promote political careerism by providing a huge incentive for lawmakers to extend their tenure. Over 250 Members of the 103rd Congress could become "pension million-aires," receiving pension income after retirement in excess of $1 million. For example, former Speaker of the House Tom Foley receives nearly $124,000 per year, with annual adjustments for inflation, since being kicked out of office by the voters in his district.

The House and Senate included provisions in the 1995 budget reconciliation legislation to bring congressional pensions in line with those of other government employees, but under the term limits philosophy, there is no reason for Congress-men to enjoy taxpayer-funded pensions at all. If Congress is not a career, then making allowances for personal retirement saving should be sufficient.

Free Mail

• *Free ("franked") mass mail.* Franked mail allows Congressmen to blanket their districts with self-serving propaganda at taxpayer expense. The vast ma-jority of mail (over 90 percent by some estimates) is sent at congressional ini-tiative, with only a small fraction devoted to responses to constituent inquiries and requests. Beyond the waste of money, taxpayer-funded mail contributes significantly to high incumbent reelection rates. The franking allowance—more than the total campaign budgets of many congressional challengers—amounts to taxpayer financing of campaigns, but for incumbents only.

> *"There is no reason for Congressmen to enjoy taxpayer-funded pensions at all."*

As with congressional pensions, the House took significant steps in 1995 to reduce franking allowances. There is, however, no justification for franked mass mailings, and the practice could be abolished. The result would be lower government spending and fairer elections.

• *Automatic pay raises for Congressmen.* Current law provides Congressmen with automatic pay raises, tied to the consumer price index, each year with no vote required. The Citizen Congress Act would abolish automatic raises and re-quire Members of Congress to go on the record if they want to increase their pay. Lawmakers' salaries already exceed $11,000 a month, and few (if any) other workers receive automatic pay hikes every year regardless of perfor-mance, profits, or other factors. While the appropriate level of pay for Con-gressmen is debatable (many believe it is already far too high), it is impossible to see why Congress should receive pay raises without even voting on (and therefore taking responsibility for) the increases.

Health Care

• *Free medical and dental care at military hospitals.* Unlike other citizens, Members of Congress can receive free medical or dental attention at military hospitals. Since Congressmen are eligible for the same generous health benefits as other federal employees, there is no reason for them to receive free care at military medical facilities. Beyond the unjustifiable special treatment, congressional patients only displace military personnel and veterans for whom military hospitals are intended. The Citizen Congress Act would end the free military care perk for Congressmen (unless the Member is a veteran).

> *"Ending unnecessary spending and indulgence in perquisites would bring Congress closer to the daily experiences of average citizens."*

• *Special parking privileges at Washington-area airports.* Members of Congress park for free in choice spaces at Washington's National and Dulles airports. There is no reason why Congressmen cannot get a ride, take a cab, or pay for parking (out of their official office budgets when appropriate) just as other busy travelers do. Defenders of the parking privilege argue that cab fares and parking fees could cost more than the special lots do now. While that is unlikely, the real point of the Citizen Congress Act's free parking repeal is to eliminate a special privilege that tends to place Members of Congress on a plane above other citizens.

• *Personal use of frequent flier mileage accrued on official business.* The Citizen Congress Act would prohibit personal use of frequent flier mileage accumulated through official congressional travel. Executive branch employees are required to return frequent flier credits to their agencies, which make arrangements to apply them to official government travel. Allowing Members of Congress to enjoy personal use of frequent flier miles amounts to tax-subsidized vacations. The Senate already has abolished this perk, and the House should follow suit.

• *Travel on military aircraft.* Travel on military aircraft is another expensive and unnecessary privilege for Members of Congress. Unless military travel is proven less expensive and the cost is reported at the time of the trip, or unless there are no commercial flights to a destination, travel on military aircraft would be prohibited under this bill.

Ending Careerism

Though Congress failed in 1995 to pass term limits, the Citizen Congress Act would go a long way toward ending the career mentality in Congress. Ending unnecessary spending and indulgence in perquisites would bring Congress closer to the daily experiences of average citizens. The new proposal also would make elections more competitive by eliminating the incumbents' advantage of taxpayer-funded franked mail. Just as important, these seven proposals would help restore some of the trust in government that many Americans have lost.

Campaign Finance and Lobbying Reform Would Not Improve Ethics

by Michael DeBow

About the author: *Michael DeBow is a law professor at Samford University's Cumberland Law School in Birmingham, Alabama.*

The reform of campaign finance and lobbying is a perennial subject for Americans, particularly those of the "good government" persuasion. The reformers' conventional wisdom on these issues laments the fact that American politicians solicit, and receive, large amounts of campaign contributions from individuals and organizations with vital interests at stake in the political arena. In the conventional wisdom, money is the root of almost all political evil. Most importantly, bad public policies are supported by Congressmen as a payback to their contributors. This baleful result is traced particularly to the activities of political action committees, or PACs.

Reformers' Delusion

The reformers apparently think that, without the "corrupting" influence of campaign contributions and other lobbying efforts, Congress would make "better" decisions. This position is, in turn, based on an assumption that there is a correct answer to any given public policy question, and that this answer would be rather easily identified and implemented by a Congress freed of the corrupting influences of money and, thereby, acting "responsibly."

This is a delusion.

In virtually every instance, there is no "correct" answer to a public policy question waiting to be discovered by well-meaning officeholders. Exceptions to this rule may well exist in times of war and other national emergencies, but in peacetime there are no clear "answers" to most of the questions that government is increasingly called upon to answer.

Michael DeBow, "Reforming Politics in the Age of Leviathan: A Skeptical View," *Freeman*, October 1995. Original endnotes have been omitted.

To see that this is so, consider the related issues of government spending and taxing. While 90 percent or more of Americans might "agree" that the deficit should be lowered—or at least not increased—they will not agree on how such a state of affairs is to be reached. Should the rate of increase in Social Security benefits be reduced? Should appropriations to Aid to Families with Dependent Children, or National Public Radio, or farm price supports be cut—and if so, by how much? To state the problem is to answer it; there is no "answer." The political process will, of course, generate some sort of answer, but there is absolutely no reason to believe that any answer adopted by Congress is "the" answer.

Big Government Is the Problem

In seeking to change campaign finance and lobbying methods, reformers are focusing on a symptom of the problem—spending to influence government decisionmaking—rather than on the real problem—the vast size and scope of American government.

For roughly the last 60 years, the size and scope of the national government have steadily increased, along with tax rates and the reach of government regulation into many areas of our lives. As a result, the idea that there are, or should be, any limits on the powers of the government has largely passed from the contemporary scene. This is particularly true with respect to the federal government and to the regulation of economic activity. Not only do we not have a national government of enumerated powers as envisioned by the Founders, we have a national government of such unlimited scope that it would be very difficult to agree on an enumeration of powers that it does *not* have.

Do you doubt it? Reflect on the fact that in the debate over health care, *no* serious attention was paid to the question whether the federal government has the authority to regulate this area of our lives. Instead, arguments focused on whether such regulation would lead to beneficial results.

In short, Americans have, consciously or unconsciously, rejected the concept of limited government. In its place, we now have Leviathan [a very powerful central government]. The growth of Leviathan triggered a parallel growth in the efforts of private interests to extract favorable treatment from the government.

"Reformers are focusing on a symptom of the problem— spending to influence government decisionmaking."

Given the size of government and the virtually unlimited scope of its powers, private interests—businesses, unions, ideological groups, retirees, and so on and on—face tremendous incentives to become active in the political sphere in order to pursue governmentally conferred benefits and to oppose like efforts put forth by others. From society's viewpoint, all this activity is a waste of resources.

Moreover, the problem of private interest capture of government power is only one problem aggravated by the growth of government power. The other major problem is that massive government power is subject to massive mistakes and miscalculations even in the absence of private-interest manipulation or, indeed, in the absence of any corruption at all. Platonic Guardians can make mistakes, too, and given all that we ask them to do today, we'd be better off with a smaller government than with our current government even if it were staffed with public-spirited experts.

In short, any attempt to reform politics that does not include a serious effort at downsizing government is doomed to impotence.

Reform Is Not Likely to Help

If you accept my argument thus far, you may still think campaign finance and lobbying reform could do no harm—even if it is likely to have little or no positive effect, given the size and scope of government. Shouldn't we at least try to reform politics, even if we recognize that the real source of our problems is the virtually unlimited scope of government power?

Maybe not. There are several good reasons to reject the view that increased regulation of campaign spending and fundraising and interest-group lobbying would improve the political process.

First, attempting to limit the effectiveness of political interest groups by regulating campaign finance and lobbying would raise severe First Amendment questions. Bluntly put, the First Amendment was designed to protect the kinds of activities that the

> *"There are several good reasons to reject the view that increased regulation of campaign spending . . . would improve the political process."*

good-government crowd seeks to curtail. Given the current state of First Amendment case law, any serious attempt to regulate in these areas may very well be struck down by the courts.

Professor Lillian BeVier of the University of Virginia Law School has argued that First Amendment protection of this kind of "speech" is in fact in the broad public interest.

> "Special interest" groups, and political action committees that they form, are a means of overcoming the collective action problems that [the rational ignorance of most voters] engenders. Because they serve this function, special interest groups may arguably be regarded as benign if not indispensable players in the democratic process. With respect at least to their own particular interests, such groups have the significant potential effectively to monitor legislative behavior and thus to reduce legislative shirking. They convey information to otherwise uninformed and powerless group members about legislative activity and in turn funnel information from the group back to the legislature. Under this view, special interest groups deserve the protection of the First Amendment's freedom of association because of the indispensable role they play in monitoring elected officials.

Put another way, there is simply too much at stake for politics to be conducted without efforts by "outsiders" (that is, the governed) to influence the process, and it is a good thing that the First Amendment case law recognizes this fact.

First Amendment Concern

Second, interest groups, according to Steven D. Levitt, "have a number of close substitutes to direct contributions—lobbying, voter mobilization efforts, 'soft money' donations, and so on." Any attempt to regulate independent efforts to advance a particular candidate or espouse a particular viewpoint on a contested issue would be even more vulnerable to First Amendment attack than limits on direct campaign contributions. Thus, interest groups would likely be able to live with and work around, at least to some extent, any new restrictions that did survive First Amendment scrutiny.

Third, it stands to reason that from time to time interest groups will inadvertently represent the interests of most of the general public even as they represent their own private interests. For example, the interest groups that fought the Clinton Administration's health-care proposals represented the interests of the general public at the same time they represented their own private interests. When President Clinton proclaimed that it was his health-care reform against the special interests, most Americans should have cheered for the special interests—which prevailed, in the end. With a government as powerful and intrusive as ours, we should not be too quick to blunt the effectiveness of interest groups who will oppose further accretions of government power. Since almost any given interest group may, on a particular issue, oppose the expansion of government, this point covers a lot of territory.

> *"Government's authority is so great that there will be competition, legal and illegal, for influence over it."*

Fourth, if current efforts at campaign finance and lobbying reform succeed and have a real effect on the ability of interest groups to influence politicians via legal campaign contributions and so on, this would likely increase the amount of under-the-table bribes and payoffs to politicians. Simply put, "meaningful" reform would shift a portion of the market for influence underground. This is simply a result of the fact that government's authority is so great that there will be competition, legal and illegal, for influence over it.

Challenging Conventional Wisdom

Finally, the conventional wisdom about campaign spending/fundraising may very well be wrong. For example, the line of causation in campaign contributions is often cloudy. Does Interest Group X contribute to Congressman Y because he agrees with them, or does Y agree with them only (largely?) to gain their contributions? Moreover, recent research presents a strong challenge to the conventional wisdom on campaign finance reform. This research brings into doubt the reformers' claims that (1) the incumbents' financial edge over challengers is critically important, and (2) PAC contributions have a substantial effect on the political system. As Harvard economist Steven Levitt put it, "The substantial amount of energy devoted to the topic by the public, the media, and politicians might be more productively channeled towards other issues." While this research will be subjected to further testing and debate, it currently stands as an important reason to hold off on any major attempt to rewrite campaign finance law, at least pending the outcome of further research.

In summary, any effort to reform the practice of seeking political influence without first reducing the size and power of government is not likely to have a significant positive effect, and may well infringe the First Amendment and other widely held values.

Congressional Ethics Committees Should Be Abolished

by David Grann

About the author: *David Grann is the executive editor of the* Hill, *a weekly newspaper published in Washington, D.C.*

The trial of the century [of accused murderer O.J. Simpson] in Los Angeles overshadowed its political equivalent in Washington: the forced resignation of Sen. Bob Packwood. The Oregonian lothario exited Congress quietly on October 1, 1995. There were no crowds or cameras, no white vans, but there was a delicious double irony at work. Though Simpson got away with murder, the judicial system worked—a jury of his peers found him not guilty. Packwood, on the other hand, got what he deserved, even as the congressional ethics process that nailed him revealed itself as an abject failure.

A Mockery

It took the Ethics Committee nearly three years to investigate the allegations of sexual and official misconduct, longer than even the O.J. trial. Those who celebrated Packwood's demise ignored the Senate Ethics Committee's brazen conduct. Seventeen of the 18 charges of sexual misconduct leveled against Packwood went beyond any legal statute of limitations; one allegation dated back to 1969. And the committee, showing little judicial restraint, equated kissing a hotel clerk with pinning a staffer against the wall.

"The Ethics Committee's performance . . . strongly vindicates the ability of the Senate to police its own," said its chairman, Mitch McConnell. He was wrong.

"The committee made a mockery of the process," says Stanley Brand, a former Democratic general counsel to the House [of Representatives]. He's right.

As chairman of the Finance Committee, Packwood ruled over people who would eventually judge him. A longtime moderate, he endorsed radical welfare-

David Grann, "Kill the Ethics Committees," *Weekly Standard*, November 20, 1995. Reprinted with permission.

reform proposals in order to curry favor with Majority Leader Bob Dole. No wonder Sen. Howell Heflin, a former Ethics chairman, concluded after the case: "It is simply too hard for members . . . to effectively judge one another."

No Consistency

But the best case against the current ethics process is that there is no consistency to it. Packwood gets the boot while Rep. Gerry Studds, who had sex with an adolescent page, gets his wrist slapped. Worse, the committee's probes create systemic corruption. McConnell must barter with Packwood on legislation if he is to effectively represent his constituents, while Packwood's best friend, Sen. Daniel Patrick Moynihan, must vote on Packwood's fate; not surprisingly, he was the only Democrat to oppose open hearings.

> *"The [Republican] party must . . . abolish the two ethics committees. It must let the courts convict and the voters vanquish."*

Heflin suggests turning over the process to an outside committee of former members. But if the GOP [Grand Old Party] truly wants a revolution in Congress, the party must go one step further—and abolish the two ethics committees. It must let the courts convict and the voters vanquish.

Some, like the dignified Sen. Richard Lugar, have suggested as much. They have James Madison on their side, who wrote two centuries ago in the *Federalist Papers*: "No man is allowed to be a judge in his own cause, because his interest would certainly bias his judgment. . . . With equal, nay with greater reason, a body of men are unfit to be both judges and parties at the same time."

Even those who sympathize with this position usually recoil from its political implications. Why give one's opponents such campaign fodder? Why take on Washington's powerful advocacy groups?

The answer to both questions is simple: ethics.

Checks on Misconduct

Members of Congress should be treated like everybody else. If they commit bribery or sexual harassment, they can and should be prosecuted in a court of law. If they lower the standards of the institution with dubious, but legal, behavior, they should be exposed by the press and penalized by the public. Since Watergate, public officials receive more media and public scrutiny than any profession; they also face stricter laws.

When the Select Committee on Ethics was formed in 1964, Brand notes, there was no Federal Election Campaign Act, no Ethics in Government Act, no code of conduct for members, and no special section at the Justice Department to target public officials. Now, the ethics process largely duplicates these functions. Meanwhile, corrupt officials can be expelled by a simple majority of their clients—the voters.

These checks work better than most people think. In 1994, voters booted Rep. Dan Rostenkowski after the press revealed his financial wrongdoing; the courts continue to prosecute him. And in 1995, without a word from the Ethics Committee, Rep. Mel Reynolds got thrown in the slammer for statutory rape.

The real obstacle to such reform is persuading the American people that Congress won't be lowering the threshold of justice if it moves toward abolishing the committees. Hard, but not impossible. As it stands, the Ethics Committee increases public cynicism rather than diminishes it.

With its myriad secrecy oaths and arcane processes, the committee constrains the press and provides artificial cover for members. It placates, without purging. It wastes taxpayers thousands of dollars. And it distracts the majority of decent members from doing their primary job: legislating.

While turning the Ethics Committee over to an outside panel of retired members tries to address this question, there is only one difference between current and retired lawmakers: The former are accountable to the public, while the latter are accountable only to themselves. And an outside panel, even one composed of judges, poses the same danger of vigilantism as an independent prosecutor.

Politicized Prosecutions

Of course, abolishing the Ethics Committee will not solve every problem. Some crimes will inevitably slip through the cracks (though probably fewer than now). And President Bill Clinton or his successor might just unleash the Justice Department on Newt Gingrich or whatever congressional pol is getting in his way. But the press and independent watchdog groups have generally prevented such witch hunts. And juries—not to mention the voters—stand in the way of politicized prosecutions.

For those who claim the Packwood case obviates the need for change, they should reexamine the evidence. The GOP turned on Packwood not out of a sense of justice but because Packwood turned on them. After Republicans walked the plank on his behalf, voting against open hearings in spite of public opinion, he threatened to derail the GOP revolution with just such proceedings.

> *"As it stands, the Ethics Committee increases public cynicism rather than diminishes it."*

To rise out of this ethical morass, Congress should let prosecutors prosecute, the press sniff out scandals, and the voters render a verdict.

While some say this would violate the Constitution, which requires Congress to police its own, just the opposite is true. Such a system would allow Congress to finally fulfill its obligations.

Justice was served in the Packwood case. Next time, it's unlikely we'll be so lucky.

Appearance Rules and Standards Have Harmed Government

by Peter W. Morgan

About the author: *Peter W. Morgan is a partner at the law firm of Dickstein, Shapiro, and Morin in Washington, D.C.*

If our experience with the long list of ethics investigations over the past two decades teaches anything, it teaches that while the post-Watergate ethics reforms have yielded substantial benefits, they have also exacted significant costs. Much of the discussion of these costs has focused upon the mistreatment of officials in individual cases or, more generally, the extent to which we may be discouraging qualified persons from entering public service. Less attention has been paid to some of the adverse effects these reforms have had on the way government operates. The following discussion considers a few of these effects. By way of background, the discussion first briefly reviews the post-Watergate institutionalization of ethics programs and the ensuing rise of appearance regulations.

The Focus on Appearances

When the Senate Committee on Government Operations convened hearings on post-Watergate reform legislation in 1975, there was considerable discussion of the need for institutional reforms and greater attention to the appearance of integrity in government. One Justice Department witness opined that, "in the shadow of Watergate," "the appearance of justice" was "almost as important" as justice itself. The resulting legislation, the Ethics in Government Act of 1978, addressed these concerns by establishing both the special prosecutor's office (today, the Office of Independent Counsel) and the Office of Government Ethics [OGE], by requiring extensive financial disclosures by executive- and judicial-branch officials, and by implementing elaborate "revolving door" restrictions.

This institutionalization of federal ethics programs, and the concomitant empha-

Peter Morgan, "Broader Costs of the New Prosecutorial Ethics," *Journal of Law & Politics*, vol. 11, Summer 1995. Reprinted with permission.

sis upon "appearance" rules, has contributed to the promulgation of wide-ranging ethics rules and regulations by OGE, by other federal agencies and departments, by the Senate itself, and—in a sort of "trickle down" effect—by state and local governments as well. These reforms both expanded the menu of ethical rules—especially "appearance" rules—one could be said to violate, and created new investigative bodies before which one's political opponents could level charges of ethical misconduct.

> *"One legacy of the post-Watergate reforms has been an excessive focus on appearances, and too little on substance."*

Appearances *are* important, and the failure to appreciate how one's conduct might appear to others is incompatible with the classic virtue of *prudentia*. But one legacy of the post-Watergate reforms has been an excessive focus on appearances, and too little on substance. As alluded to above, this preoccupation has unfairly tarnished the reputation of a number of government officials in individual cases, by allowing unscrupulous individuals and groups to use appearances offensively—to attack people who have not actually done anything wrong, by accusing them of bad appearances. But there have also been broader, institutional costs.

The Investigation of Edwin Gray

One of the most significant is that the appearance standards themselves serve to distract focus from truly bad things that may be going on. This point is dramatically illustrated by the 1986 ethics investigation into the expense practices of then–Federal Home Loan Bank Board Chairman Edwin J. Gray. In 1986, shortly after Mr. Gray began trying to slow down the deregulation of federally insured savings and loans, the *Wall Street Journal* and the *Washington Post* ran several front page stories criticizing Mr. Gray for apparent improprieties in his and the Board's expense practices. Though Gray had been following past Bank Board practices (as well as the advice of Bank Board counsel), the press accused him of appearing to be too close to the savings and loans he was regulating. The detailed expense information upon which the stories were based, however, was supplied to the newspapers by savings and loan [S&L] officials, among them Charles Keating, who wanted to drive Gray out of office. They believed, correctly, that Gray was an obstacle in the path of unrestrained deregulation. By discrediting Gray, Keating hoped to force the appointment of someone more willing to push for deregulation, allowing his bank to invest its federally insured funds any way it chose.

At the end of Mr. Gray's term in June 1987, Gray left office with his reputation muddied by sensational press accounts and ensuing government ethics investigations (none of which recommended any remedial action against him). Today, the most comprehensive books on the S&L disaster portray Gray, whatever his lapses, as a well-intentioned public servant who warned about the impending disaster while jousting with S&L speculators; their lawyers, accountants, and hired experts; the thrift lobby; White House Chief of Staff (and Keating ally) Donald Regan; and such prominent members of Congress as House Speaker Jim Wright and the Keating Five [five U.S. senators investigated for accepting more than $1 million in contributions from Keating, who was convicted of securities fraud in 1991]. In the end, questions about the appearance of Gray's expenses have been supplanted by questions about exactly how many hundreds of billions of dollars the American taxpayer lost in what has been called the "worst public scandal in American history." Our preoccupation with appearances allowed those guilty of real misconduct to neutralize Gray when it mattered most—when there should have been a vigorous national debate on the wisdom of allowing high-rolling S&L operators to speculate, virtually without control, with taxpayer-guaranteed money.

Substantive Issues and Problems

Other post-Watergate ethics and criminal investigations have also diverted public attention from underlying substantive problems. There appears to be general agreement, for example, that the congressional investigations into the Iran-Contra matter [a secret U.S. arms-for-hostages deal] focused far too much on individual wrongdoing and far too little on some of the fundamental institutional problems the scandal typified. Similarly, while the "Keating Five" hearing did dramatize rather vividly the unseemly way in which influence is often exerted on Capitol Hill, the opportunity for serious discussion about campaign finance reform or the permissible limits of "special interest" lobbying was often lost in the "whodunit" atmosphere of a quasi-criminal public ethics trial. More broadly, of course, even the casual reader of today's best newspapers cannot help but notice how many articles on serious national problems are pushed off the front pages by the latest scandal series.

> *"Many articles on serious national problems are pushed off the front pages by the latest scandal series."*

A second cost of the new prosecutorial ethics is that it heightens what is already an excessive fear of criticism among government officials. One of the principal themes of James Q. Wilson's brilliant analysis of government bureaucracies, *Bureaucracy: What Government Agencies Do and Why They Do It*, is that agency officials dedicate far too much of their time and resources to making certain that their activities appear good and worthwhile even if they are not, particularly when an agency's objectives are broad or ill-defined. The new prosecutorial climate substantially aggravates this problem.

Lacking Substance

Success in Washington more and more is gauged not by how many substantive accomplishments one can point to, but rather whether and how well one has avoided any charges of misconduct or ill-chosen words. It should not surprise that some of the most "successful" executive-branch officials in the last decades have been assiduous about maintaining proper appearances and cordial relations with the press, even if their substantive accomplishments have been minimal. Truly substantive reforms typically require officials to take stands antagonistic to one or more organized special interests. In so doing the official risks inciting those interests to search for ways to charge him with some form of improper conduct.

A third—and related—cost has been the deleterious effect the new ethics has had on the manner in

> *"These ethics investigations often are merely political battles wrapped in the garb of ethics."*

which substantive issues are actually debated within departments and agencies. Controversial ideas are not written down in Washington any more, or at least not permanently. Instead, we have what [author and scholar] Suzanne Garment has called "government by post-it-note." In the process we have less accountability, not more, and we lose the benefits from the discipline of written communications.

Finally, perhaps the most paradoxical cost of the new prosecutorial ethics has been its singular lack of success in achieving its principal objective: a bolstering of public trust in government in the wake of Watergate. We have seen the greatest regulation of ethics in our nation's history since Watergate. Yet, over the same period the recorded level of public trust in government officials has steadily declined to an all-time low.

The Case of Julius Caesar

Perhaps the public knows all too well that these ethics investigations often are merely political battles wrapped in the garb of ethics. It is worth recalling in this connection that one of the earliest government ethics "inquiries"—that which resulted in Julius Caesar's oft-repeated pronouncement that an emperor's wife must be above any suspicion of wrongdoing—was itself politically motivated and unrelated to ethical concerns. Indeed, the mythology that has developed around Caesar's "mere suspicion" standard for high officials illustrates, in microcosm, how we have deceived ourselves into believing that rules forbidding such things as the "appearance of impropriety" somehow separate ethics from politics.

Caesar's remark was made in response to the scandal created by Publius Clodius Pulcher's slipping into Caesar's palace during the women's festival of Bona Dea; Clodius's ostensible intention was, in today's euphemism, to "lunch" with Caesar's wife, Pompeia. When Caesar heard of the incident, he immediately sent a messenger to Pompeia declaring their divorce. The incident allowed Caesar to rid himself of a wife whose aristocratic connections were more embarrassing than useful now that he was in open war with the aristocratic party. Caesar invoked the "appearance of impropriety" principle in response to an inquiry as to how he could simultaneously divorce Pompeia and proclaim that he had no evidence with which criminally to charge Clodius. Caesar's response—that he was forced to divorce his wife because she had to remain above the appearance of wrongdoing—allowed Caesar to abandon Pompeia while retaining the unscrupulous, but popular, Clodius as a valuable political ally.

When we weigh the costs of excessive partisan influences on ethics investigations, and consider the need for possible counterreforms, we would do well to remind ourselves of this history and to ask whether substantive legal reforms—such as in the areas of campaign finance or lobbying—would far better promote public confidence than complicated ethical rules and highly malleable "appearance" standards, which too often are designed to preserve appearances but not to improve the way government actually works.

The Special Prosecutor System Should Be Curtailed

by Carl M. Cannon

About the author: *Carl M. Cannon is the White House correspondent for the* Baltimore Sun *daily newspaper.*

No equestrian statue of James H. Lake will ever adorn a city square. He is a Washington lobbyist, not a war hero. Still, now that Lake has fallen into the hellish clutches of a special prosecutor, here's an idea for how his fellow Republicans could honor his long service to Ronald Reagan and their party: They could end or at least sharply curtail the special prosecutor system.

This monument to Lake will be controversial. Some will object that a Special Prosecutor Repeal Act should be dedicated to those who really inspired it: the independent counsels themselves, with their messianic complexes, their multi-million-dollar spending jags, and their years-long vendettas. Men like Iran-Contra counsel Lawrence Walsh. Or the latest nominee, Jim Lake's buddy, Donald C. Smaltz. Others will favor the victims but ask, why Lake? Why not Mike Deaver? Or Ted Olson? Or Webb Hubbell? Or Margaret Tutwiler? Or Jim Guy Tucker? Or Elliott Abrams? A strong contender will be Elliott's wife, Rachel Abrams, who voiced the bitterness that all those caught up in the special prosecutor system seem to share.

About the Clintons

"I know something about Bill and Hillary Clinton right now," she wrote, after a passel of special prosecutors were sicced on the Clintonites.

> I know how their stomachs churn, their anxiety mounts, how their worry over the defenseless child increases. I know their inability to sleep at night and their reluctance to rise in the morning. I know every new incursion of doubt, every heartbreak over bailing out friends . . . every jaw-clenching look at front pages. I know all this, and the thought of it makes me happy.

Carl M. Cannon, "The Vendetta Machine," *Weekly Standard*, November 6, 1995. Reprinted with permission.

Rachel's husband could be arrogant and unbending, but those are not crimes. His real sin was that he helped run a policy in Central America [funding Nicaraguan rebels with proceeds from arms sales to Iran] that the Democrats hated. Not content to tangle with Elliott Abrams solely in the political arena, the Democrats followed a strategy all too common in the 1980s: They agitated for the Iran-Contra prosecutor to investigate him. Ultimately, Abrams was adjudged to have given less than complete answers to a hostile congressional committee. A liberal Democratic lawyer in the special prosecutor's office admitted to a grudge against Abrams; in any case, Walsh ended up with Abrams's scalp, in the form of two misdemeanor pleas. The process took five years and cost Abrams hundreds of thousands in legal fees, so his wife's outburst is understandable.

> *"The rap against the law has always been that there seem to be no limitations on a special prosecutor."*

Others actually suffered ordeals even more Kafkaesque, as it became the fashion to try to criminalize policy differences between the parties. Theodore B. Olson incurred the wrath of Capitol Hill Democrats by formulating the Reagan administration's policy regarding release of Environmental Protection Agency documents to congressional committees. When Judiciary Committee Chairman Peter Rodino didn't like the regulations, he called for a perjury investigation of Olson. After a six-year inquiry, the special counsel announced almost reluctantly that she couldn't charge Olson with a crime because he'd told the truth.

An Unrestrained Prosecutor

The special prosecutor law was enacted in 1978 as a belated response to Richard Nixon's firing of an independent counsel looking into Watergate. The law was amended in 1983 and 1987; it expired but was passed again in 1993, and President Clinton signed it back into law.

Its laudable aim was to shield investigations of high officials from potential political interference. The rap against the law has always been that there seem to be no limitations on a special prosecutor. He reports to no one, has an unlimited budget, doesn't have to stand for re-election. Conservative scholars such as Terry Eastland have questioned its constitutionality. The Supreme Court has been unwilling to throw it out, however. So special prosecutors remain free to engage in virtually unrestrained fishing expeditions, and no one answers the haunting question asked by acquitted former Labor secretary Raymond Donovan, "Which office do I go to to get my reputation back?"

In practice, what is strangest about the law is the capriciousness with which investigations expand to net particular individuals. Clinton confidant Webb Hubbell overbilled clients down in Arkansas and didn't report all his taxes. Not great conduct, to be sure, but what exactly does it have to do with the alleged misuse of federally insured funds that Whitewater is supposedly about? And even if the [loan conspiracy and fraud] allegations against Arkansas governor Jim Guy Tucker are true, they came to light only because his predecessor was elected president and an independent counsel was dispatched to dredge the swamp of home-state graft.

For his part, counsel Donald Smaltz was supposed to be looking into the relationship between Clinton's first agriculture secretary, Mike Espy, and Tyson Foods, Inc., the poultry behemoth based in Springdale, Ark. So how did he come to nab Beltway [Washington, D.C.] Reaganite Jim Lake? It appears that one of Lake's California agribusiness clients wanted to curry favor with the Department of Agriculture by funneling $5,000 to retire the campaign debt of Mike Espy's brother, and Lake was willing to fudge the paperwork. Smaltz pumped up this misdemeanor into a felony using a dubious device increasingly favored by federal prosecutors (they tried it on Al D'Amato's brother): the all-purpose wire-fraud statute. Another nagging question about Lake's case is why, after he himself pointed out the transgression to Smaltz and received immunity for it, he was forced to plead guilty when Smaltz announced, 10 months later, that he was going after Lake's firm. Was this fair? The question was put to Smaltz; himself immune to oversight, he felt free to decline any comment.

Partisan Politics

The larger question remains why an unfettered special prosecutor system still exists. The Republicans took over Congress in 1994, and they've wanted to put a leash on these guys for a long time. What they will tell you is that their determination to rid the Republic of this scourge was lost somewhere between Newt Gingrich's book deal, [Michigan representative] David Bonior's braying about GOPAC [a Republican political action committee suspected of federal campaign violations], and Ross Perot's contrived crusade to clean up politics. The truth is that they were enjoying entirely too much seeing the Clintonites squirm as a result of the appointment of a record number of special prosecutors.

> *"Political corruption could be probed by an independent counsel who reported to the attorney general and who had some constraints on his mandate."*

Margaret Tutwiler, who was put through the wringer on the apparently bogus charge that she rummaged into Clinton's passport file while serving the Bush administration, found this attitude shortsighted. She recounted running into then–White House communications director Mark Gearan at Logan Airport one day and buying him a drink at a time when Gearan was depressed over his own grand jury appearance and mounting legal bills courtesy of the Whitewater special prosecutor.

"Mark's 'crime' was showing up for 10 minutes at a meeting," she said scornfully. "For the future of our country, we have to find a way to keep these partisan fights out of the criminal justice system."

Chapter 4

Time for a New Law

Well, Republicans, the occupant of the White House feels your pain on this one. He may have signed the updated special prosecutor law, but he has all but said he regrets it. He particularly dislikes the fact that the new bill makes the threshold so low for appointment of a prosecutor. Maybe this is the time to call a truce and pass a new scaled-down law under which political corruption could be probed by an independent counsel who reported to the attorney general and who had some constraints on his mandate. While they're at it, congressional leaders may want to consider narrowing the legal definition of wire fraud and perhaps tighten the much-abused RICO [Racketeering Influenced and Corrupt Organization] racketeering statute as well.

In 1994, before Donald Smaltz was even sworn in as a special prosecutor, I interviewed a well-connected Republican on this subject. He thought it unseemly and ultimately self-defeating for Republicans to rejoice in Clinton's agony.

"It's an outrage," he told me. "The Republicans are stupid for caving in on this. They saw a chance for it to tie up Clinton, and they wink at the abuses."

This Republican never worked in the White House, though he was asked to. I asked him why. One factor, he said, was that he'd seen friends ruined and tormented by special prosecutors. "The reason I turned down Reagan and George Bush four times was that I like my business," he told me. "I like my freedom." But that was then. His name is Jim Lake.

Bibliography

Books

Robert Biersack, Paul S. Herrnson, and Clyde Wilcox, eds.	*Risky Business? PAC Decisionmaking in Congressional Elections*. Armonk, NY: M.E. Sharpe, 1994.
Jeffrey H. Birnbaum	*The Lobbyists: How Influence Peddlers Get Their Way in Washington*. New York: Times Books, 1992.
Anthony Corrado	*Creative Campaigning: PACs and the Presidential Selection Process*. Boulder, CO: Westview, 1992.
Anthony Corrado	*Paying for Presidents: Public Financing in National Elections*. New York: Twentieth Century Fund, 1993.
Peter deLeon	*Thinking About Political Corruption*. Armonk, NY: M.E. Sharpe, 1993.
Suzanne Garment	*Scandal: The Crisis of Mistrust in American Politics*. New York: Times Books, 1991.
William P. Hoar	*Our Corrupt Congress*. Dunwoody, GA: Soundview, 1992.
Brooks Jackson	*Honest Graft: Big Money and the American Political Process*. Washington, DC: Farragut, 1990.
Kathleen Hall Jamieson	*Dirty Politics: Deception, Distortion, and Democracy*. New York: Oxford University Press, 1992.
Greg D. Kubiak	*The Gilded Dome: The U.S. Senate and Campaign Finance Reform*. Norman: University of Oklahoma Press, 1994.
Dwight Morris and Murielle E. Gamache	*Gold-Plated Politics: The 1992 Congressional Races*. Washington, DC: Congressional Quarterly, 1994.
James L. Regens and Ronald Keith Gaddie	*The Economic Realities of Political Reform: Elections and the U.S. Senate*. New York: Cambridge University Press, 1995.
Robert N. Roberts	*White House Ethics: The History of the Politics of Conflict of Interest Regulation*. New York: Greenwood, 1988.
Shelley Ross	*Fall from Grace: Sex, Scandal, and Corruption in American Politics from 1702 to the Present*. New York: Ballantine, 1988.
Larry J. Sabato	*Feeding Frenzy: How Attack Journalism Has Transformed American Politics*. New York: Free Press, 1991.
Larry J. Sabato and S. Robert Lichter	*When Should the Watchdogs Bark? Media Coverage of the Clinton Scandals*. Lanham, MD: University Press of America; Washington, DC: Center for Media and Public Affairs, 1994.
Philip M. Stern	Still *the Best Congress Money Can Buy*. Washington, DC: Regnery Gateway, 1992.

Politicians and Ethics

Dennis F. Thompson *Ethics in Congress: From Individual to Institutional Corruption.* Washington, DC: Brookings, 1995.

Periodicals

Peter J. Boyer "The Ogre's Tale," *New Yorker*, April 4, 1994.

Richard Brookhiser "Whitewater Runs Deep," *National Review*, March 21, 1994.

John P. Canham-Clyne "Iran-Contra Revisionism," *Lies of Our Times*, June 1994.

Adam Clymer "Ethics Committees Stumble in Era of Partisanship," *New York Times*, August 14, 1995.

Jeff Cohen and Norman Solomon "White Water Under the Bridge: How the Press Missed the Story," *Extra!* vol. 7, no. 3, May/June 1994.

Thomas M. DeFrank "Travelgate Redux," *Weekly Standard*, September 25, 1995.

Maureen Dowd "Doing the Packwood," *New York Times*, August 6, 1995.

Howard Fineman "The Virtuecrats," *Newsweek*, June 13, 1994.

Stephen Gillers "The Packwood Case: The Senate Is Also on Trial," *Nation,* March 29, 1993.

Albert R. Hunt "The Best Congress Money Can Buy," *Wall Street Journal*, September 7, 1995.

Albert R. Hunt "The Gingrich Ethics Noose Tightens," *Wall Street Journal,* December 14, 1995.

Doug Ireland "Don't Ask, Don't Tell—Whitewater Watch," *Nation*, September 5, 1994.

Gregory Jaynes "Bubba-ocracy in America," *Esquire*, June 1994.

Kenneth Jost "Political Scandals," *CQ Researcher*, May 27, 1994.

Journal of Law and Politics Symposium on partisan influences on ethics investigations. Summer 1995.

David Kamp "The Triumph of Evil," *GQ*, January 1995.

Howard Kurtz "Yesterday's 'Sleaze,' Today's 'Character Issue,'" *Washington Post National Weekly Edition*, April 3–9, 1995.

Toni Locy "Gingrich's Paper Trail," *Washington Post National Weekly Edition*, October 9–15, 1995.

Eugene H. Methvin "Understanding Whitewater," *Reader's Digest*, June 1994.

C. Wright Mills "The Higher Immorality," *Kettering Review*, Winter 1994.

Viveca Novak "Arkansas Governor, Clintons' Partners in Whitewater Are Charged with Fraud," *Wall Street Journal*, August 18, 1995.

Peter Nye "Corporate Lobbyists' Heavy Hand in Writing 'Contract' Legislation," *Public Citizen*, May/June 1995. Available from 2000 P St. NW, Suite 600, Washington, DC 20036.

Robert Parry "The Hunters," *Mother Jones*, July/August 1994.

Jonathan Rauch "Suckers!" *Reason*, May 1994.

Michael Rust "Congress Shows a PAC Mentality," *Insight*, August 14, 1995. Available from 3600 New York Ave. NE, Washington, DC 20002.

Robert J. Samuelson "The Price of Politics," *Newsweek*, August 28, 1995.

Daniel Seligman "Varieties of the Payoff Experience," *Fortune*, June 13, 1994.

Bibliography

Rochelle Sharpe	"Capital Hill's Worst Kept Secret: Sexual Harassment," *Ms.*, January/February 1992.
Alicia C. Shepard	"A No-Win Situation," *American Journalism Review*, July/August 1994.
Robert Sherrill	"Phil Gramm's Trail of Sleaze," *Nation*, March 6, 1995.
Glenn R. Simpson	"Senator Dole's Greatest Harvest," *American Prospect*, Summer 1995.
Social Policy	Special issue on campaign finance reform, vol. 26, no. 1, Fall 1995.
Evan Thomas and Thomas Rosenstiel	"Decline and Fall," *Newsweek*, September 18, 1995.
Jenifer Warren	"Promises, Promises," *Los Angeles Times*, August 2, 1995. Available from Reprints, Times Mirror Square, Los Angeles, CA 90012-3816.
Nancy Watzman	"So You Want to Be a Lobbyist? Ten Steps to Guilt-Free Influence Peddling," *Public Citizen*, July/August 1993.
Mark Weinberg	"Public Officials Soliciting Campaign Contributions Beware," *Whittier Law Review*, vol. 15, no. 1, 1994.

Organizations to Contact

The editors have compiled the following list of organizations concerned with the issues debated in this book. The descriptions are derived from materials provided by the organizations themselves. All have publications or information available for interested readers. The list was compiled on the date of publication of the present volume; names, addresses, phone numbers, and fax numbers may change. Be aware that many organizations take several weeks or longer to respond to inquiries, so allow as much time as possible.

Americans Back in Charge (ABIC)
1560 Broadway, Suite 1900
Denver, CO 80202
(303) 863-3503
fax: (303) 863-1932

Americans Back in Charge is a nonprofit, nonpartisan organization that developed one of the first national term-limit models and helped pass the first term-limit law. It believes that the only way to accomplish structural reform is to limit congressmembers' terms of office and to limit the role of money in politics. ABIC publishes *Setting Limits: The Truth About Why Congress Defeated the Term Limits and Balanced Budget Amendment in 1995.*

American League of Lobbyists (ALL)
PO Box 30005
Alexandria, VA 22310
(703) 960-3011

ALL is an organization of registered lobbyists and others interested in the lobbying profession. It conducts professional development programs and seminars and programs to improve public understanding and recognition of the role of lobbyists in the legislative process. ALL publishes the monthly *ALL News.*

Center for Media and Public Affairs (CMPA)
2100 L St. NW, Suite 300
Washington, DC 20037
(202) 223-2942
fax: (202) 872-4014

The center scientifically analyzes how the media treat social and political issues as well as the media's impact on public opinion. CMPA's publications include the bimonthly newsletter *Media Monitor*, which reports on press behavior, and the book *When Should the Watchdogs Bark? Media Coverage of the Clinton Scandals.*

Center for a New Democracy (CND)
410 Seventh St. SE
Washington, DC 20003
(202) 543-0773
fax: (202) 543-2591

CND is a nonprofit organization that was established to promote fairness and democracy in America's electoral system. It works with citizen groups to reform campaign finance laws and to enhance democratic participation. The center publishes *Is the Love of Money the Root of All Evil? American Attitudes Toward Money in Politics*, *The World of Campaign Finance: A Reader's Guide to the Funding of International Elections*, *The Citizen Movement for $100 Contribution Limits*, and *Q & A: $100 Contribution Limits*. It also distributes the monthly *Update* newsletter.

Center for Public Integrity
1634 I St. NW, Suite 902
Washington, DC 20006
fax: (202) 783-3906
e-mail: ctrforpi@essential.org
Web site: http://www.essential.org/cpi

The center is a nonprofit research organization that strives to promote a higher standard of integrity in the American political process and in government. Its efforts focus on government and ethics, public service, and public policy. Among its numerous publications are *Short-Changed: How Congress and Special Interests Benefit at the Expense of the American People*, *Under the Influence: Presidential Candidates and Their Campaign Advisers*, and *Saving for a Rainy Day: How Congress Turns Leftover Campaign Cash into "Golden Parachutes."*

Center for Responsive Politics (CRP)
1320 19th St. NW, Suite 700
Washington, DC 20036
(202) 857-0044
fax: (202) 857-7809
e-mail: info@crp.org

The center conducts research on congressional and political trends. Its project areas include campaign finance, ethics in government, political foundations and public policy, the "inner workings of Congress," and Congress and the media. CRP's publications include *PACs in Profile*, *Speaking Freely: Former Members of Congress Talk About Money in Politics*, *Capital Eye*, and *Cashing in from A to Z— an Index of Lobbying, Lawmaking, and Campaign Money in 1995*.

Citizen Action
1730 Rhode Island Ave. NW, Suite 403
Washington, DC 20036
(202) 775-1580
fax: (202) 296-4054

Citizen Action works to establish public financing of elections at the national, state, and local levels. The organization publishes research on the connections between campaign contributions and public policy; its reports have covered contributions by the health and insurance, oil and gas, and chemical industries, as well as by wealthy individuals. Citizen Action's publications include the reports *Buying Control: The Special Interests Take Congress* and *Business as Usual: 1995 Campaign Contributions to House Members Continue to Grow*.

Common Cause
2030 M St. NW
Washington, DC 20036
(202) 833-1200
fax: (202) 659-3716

Common Cause is devoted to making government at the national and state levels more open and accountable to citizens and to improving government performance. It organizes lobbying to promote reform, which the group considers necessary to reduce the influence of political action committees on Congress. It publishes *Common Cause Magazine*, which covers topics regarding government performance and political ethics.

Council for Excellence in Government
1620 L St. NW, Suite 850
Washington, DC 20036
(202) 728-0418
fax: (202) 728-0422

The council seeks to strengthen public service and to improve the effectiveness of U.S. government. It works in strategic partnerships with other organizations to improve all levels of government. Its publications include *A Survivor's Guide for Government Executives* and *The Prune Book: The 45 Toughest Financial Management Jobs in Washington.*

Institute for Philosophy and Public Policy (IPPP)
University of Maryland
Van Munching Hall, Rm. 3111
College Park, MD 20742
(301) 405-4753
fax: (301) 314-9346

IPPP investigates the conceptual and ethical aspects of public policy formulation and debate. It seeks to develop curricula that will bring philosophical issues before future policymakers and citizens. The institute publishes the quarterlies *Philosophy and Public Policy* and *Report from the Institute for Philosophy and Public Policy.*

Investigative Reporters and Editors (IRE)
138 Neff Annex
University of Missouri School of Journalism
Columbia, MO 65211
(573) 882-2042
fax: (573) 882-5431

IRE is an organization of editors, educators, reporters, and students that provides educational services such as computer-assisted reporting. Its publications include *Reporter's Handbook: A Guide to Documents and Techniques*, *Computer Assisted Reporting: A Practical Guide*, the monthly newsletter *Uplink*, and the bimonthly *IRE Journal.*

National Association of Business Political Action Committees (NABPAC)
801 N. Fairfax St., Suite 215
Alexandria, VA 22314
(703) 836-4422
fax: (703) 836-4424

NABPAC is a network of corporations and associations that maintain political action committees (PACs). It promotes effective management of member PACs and lobbies for matters related to the continued operation of business PACs. It publishes the monthly *NABPAC Newsmemo on Campaign Finance and Election Law* and the quarterly newsletter *NABPAC Notes*, which provides information on campaign finance law revisions and other matters of concern to PACs.

Public Citizen
1600 20th St. NW
Washington, DC 20009-1001
(202) 588-1000

fax: (202) 588-7799
e-mail: publiccitizen@citizen.org
Web site: http://www.essential.org/public_citizen

Public Citizen is a nonpartisan organization that promotes government and corporate accountability, consumer rights in the marketplace, and safe products through lobbying, research, public outreach, and litigation. It publishes the bimonthly magazine *Public Citizen* and numerous other publications and reports.

U.S. Term Limits
1511 K St. NW, Suite 540
Washington, DC 20005
(202) 393-6440
fax: (202) 393-6434

U.S. Term Limits is a nonprofit, nonpartisan organization chartered to restore citizen control of government by rallying Americans to limit legislators' congressional and state and local government terms of office. It publishes a number of papers as part of its Term Limit Outlook Series and the monthly newsletter *No Uncertain Terms*.

Index

200

Index

Index

Index